PIERCE BROSNAN

CONTENTS

LIST OF ILLUSTRATIONS

ACKNOWLEDGEMENTS

My thanks to Rebecca McKenzie, Donal Reilly, Phil Kent, Kerr Reilly, Liam Bennett, Pierce Wallace, Mary Daly, Carol Drinkwater, Stuart Turner, Adam Ant, Garry Cooper, Saeed Jaffrey, Christopher Fettes, Yat Malmgren and the staff and students at the Drama Centre, Alfie Pritchard, Benita Harvey Brebach, Rebecca Edson, Chris Dunham, Marjorie Sommerville, Gill Button, Keith Richmond, Louise Johncox, Gary Oxley, Eileen Anson, Joe Bangay, Charles Collier-Wright, Chris Morgan, John Kierans, Sandra Parsons, Colin Curwood, Julie Turner, Colleen Kay at Thames Television, Katharine Sanders, Henry Fitzherbert, Roger Kasper, Giles Havergal, Christine Roberts, Lee Beaumont, Colin Johnston, Jean Kirton, Douglas James, Lorna Ferguson, John Skinner, Pablo LaBritain, Graham Brough, Kevin Monahan, Louise Annan at Glasgow University Library, Sandro Monetti, Kathryn Pogson, Jonathan Margolis, Cedric Porter, Leslie Dunkling, Kathryn McCord, Helen Myers, Nadene Hansen, and to all those people who spoke to me but wished to remain anonymous. Last, but by no means least, my thanks to Ben Dunn, Hannah MacDonald and Kirstie Addis, my editors at Virgin.

I am also indebted to the library staff at Mirror Group Newspapers, Associated Newspapers, News International, *Irish Independent* and *The Irish Times*. Finally, I'd like to thank InterCity East Coast, Ryanair, Abbey Gate Hotel, Tralee, Westcourt Hotel, Drogheda and Castle Hotel, Dublin, for help with travel and accommodation during the research of the book.

In addition, the following publications proved a rich source of information and I am grateful to them: *Cosmopolitan, Daily Express, Daily Mail, Daily Mirror, Daily Telegraph, Daily Star, Evening Standard, Glasgow Herald, GQ, Hollywood Reporter, The Kerryman, Mail on Sunday, Meath Chronicle, Melbourne Herald Sun, My Weekly, National Enquirer, Namaskaar, Observer, People Magazine, Punch, Putney & Roehampton Herald, OK!, Screen International, The Stage, Star, Sun, Sunday Independent, South London Press, Southend Standard, Sunday Express, Sunday Mirror, Sunday Mirror Magazine, Sunday Times Magazine, Thurrock Gazette, Time Out, Titbits, Variety, Wandsworth Borough News, The Washington Post, Woman, Woman's Own, Preview*, and *Yorkshire Evening Press*.

PREFACE

Whatever it is – the glamour, the crowds, the bright lights or the stars – there's something magical about a West End movie première. And something in the air that cold, November 1995 night in London's Leicester Square told you it was going to be an extra special evening for anyone foolhardy enough to brave the cold wind blowing in from the North Sea.

The famous square emerged as the capital's entertainment heartland in the Victorian age. And it's been playing host to big budget movie premières ever since the cinema became *the* mass entertainment medium between the wars. Wherever you look – be it at the four giant cinemas that dominate the square or the handsome bronze statue of the Little Tramp, erected in the gardens in memory of Charlie Chaplin – you're reminded of the silver screen.

However, one cinema in particular, the Odeon Leicester Square, instantly conjures up the glamour, history and magic peculiar to the area. With its sleek black lines, this art deco-style monument to the movies is undeniably the best known – and best loved – picture palace in London. Seating almost 2,000, it has played host to countless star-studded opening nights down the years, but none more glamorous than the *GoldenEye* première that night.

Superspy James Bond has always had a special place in British hearts. Perhaps because, in this multi-media age where entertainment is king and just about every movie hero – be it Schwarzenegger, Stallone or Willis – is American, 007 is the cinema's one enduring character who is British through and through, yet can still pull in the punters from Boston to Berlin, Bombay to Bangkok. So perhaps it shouldn't have been any surprise that the metal barriers hastily erected in Leicester Square held back the biggest crowd seen in London's showbiz hot spot for many years. Police estimated the size of the good-natured horde – some of whom were hanging precariously from branches to get a better view – to be at least 1,000. There seemed to be almost as many reporters huddled outside, notebooks at the ready. Every newspaper had someone on the scene; there were photographers by the dozen, not to mention camera crews from television stations around the world. A dozen police officers were standing in front of the barriers to prevent the crowd from surging forward while beefy security men in black suits and bow-ties clustered around the cinema entrance, whispering into their walkie-talkies and doing their best to look mean.

As the première drew nearer, fans young and old glanced at their watches ever more frequently, and looked up excitedly every time a gleaming limousine turned the corner from Charing Cross Road and glided to a halt outside the Odeon to disgorge its precious human cargo. So hyped up were the crowd that sometimes a cheer would go up before they disappointingly realised the VIP was just another faceless movie business executive with an attractive wife.

The first 'stars' – if stars they really be – to arrive were a couple of former Page Three girls, dressed in the obligatory mini-skirt and tight-fitting top, sporting manes of peroxide blonde hair and looking as if they'd spent the entire day stuck under a sunlamp, working on their fake tans. Soon afterwards the big names began to arrive. First, Live Aid 'hero' Bob Geldof turned up with his new girlfriend, French actress Jeanne Marine. Then U2 star Bono, escorting blonde actress Patsy Kensit, appeared to a cheer from the crowd. Racing ace Damon Hill smiled for the cameras and told newsmen: 'It's every man's dream to be Bond.' The crowd was growing more excited by the minute. You could almost feel the collective adrenaline rush. Next to arrive was Tina Turner – singer of the film's theme song – in one of her trademark blonde wigs, wearing a man's-style black tuxedo.

The appearance of the new Bond girl, blonde Izabella Scorupco, in a stunning bright red designer gown, predictably sent the pulses of both press and public racing. 'Give us a smile, darling!' yelled one of Fleet Street's photographers, for once on their best behaviour. 'This way, love!' called another. Other VIPs who turned up included Dame Judi Dench, who plays a steely M in the movie, producer Cubby Broccoli and director Martin Campbell.

Yet everyone was waiting for the real star of the evening – Pierce Brosnan – to arrive. Suddenly, there he was, stepping out of a limousine, looking every bit as suave as Ian Fleming's famous secret agent. This was the man who one lovestruck female journalist had gushingly described as 'more handsome than a man has any right to be'. Up close, you could see what she meant. Immaculately dressed in a dinner suit and bow-tie, he boasted a golden, movie star suntan, sparkling white teeth and a head that didn't have a hair out of place. He really could have stepped from the pages of a Mills & Boon novel.

On his arm was his latest girlfriend, beautiful American journalist Keely Shaye-Smith, who could herself have passed for a Bond girl. 'He's definitely my favourite Bond,' she giggled. Joining the couple were his mother, May, twelve-year-old son Sean – instantly dubbed double-O-three-and-a-half (get it?) by the tabloids – and grown-up stepchildren Christopher and Charlotte.

It's hard to think of a single critic who would have stuck out their neck at the time and predicted that *GoldenEye* – the seventeenth Bond film – was going to be the most successful 007 film ever. By the early nineties, Bond was regarded by many in the chattering classes as a tired, worn-out figure, long past his sell-by date, with about as much to do with the modern world as another 'boys' own' hero of the past, Biggles. The secret agent's cause hadn't been helped by Tim Dalton's lacklustre performance in *The Living Daylights* and *Licence To Kill*, neither of which had exactly set the box office alight. Both were arguably most memorable for their theme songs, respectively sung by A-Ha and Gladys Knight. As for Dalton, he was handsome enough, but lacked the necessary charm and cheek, and failed to display even the hint of a sense of humour. But in Brosnan, the producers had found a man who could make Bond hip once again. A dashing, heart-throb actor who appealed to both young and old, male and female. Tough but tender, with a ready wit, he gave 007 a relevance for the nineties that a year earlier would have seemed impossible. And *GoldenEye* proved to be the blockbuster that Bond fans everywhere had been praying for. In total, it's grossed some $350 million and its runaway success has given a whole new lease of life to the Bond movie series.

However, who exactly was this desperately handsome man – credited with virtually single-handedly saving Bond – seen sharing a joke with Prince Charles at the Leicester Square première and, if anything, looking more like a future king than the balding, controversial heir to the throne himself? (The *GoldenEye* première took place less than 24 hours after Diana's 'bombshell' *Panorama* television interview, in which she questioned whether her estranged husband had what it took to follow in the Queen's footsteps.)

Somewhat confusingly, the new Bond was born in Ireland and grew up in London, but first found fame in America. Consequently, some people assume he's Irish, others that he's English, and most that he's American. Stranger still, several people think he's Canadian. There was certainly little in his manner that night to suggest he'd spent many years – perhaps his most formative years – in London. But at the première he revealed: 'When I was eleven years old I saw my first-ever film – *Goldfinger* with Sean Connery – just a few miles away.' The youngster was enraptured and dreamed ever after of one day being Bond himself. 'Here we are, just a few miles from that cinema, and I am James Bond. It really is a dream come true.'

It's one of many dreams that have come true for Pierce Brosnan in a life that, in some ways, is every bit as fantastic as a Hollywood movie itself. 'I feel I've had three lives,' he says. 'As a lad in Ireland, as a young man in England and as an adult in America.' In reality, it's much more complex, as is the man himself. On one level, he's led a charmed life. On another, he's had a tough life. He's had more luck than most, and more bad luck than most. He's scaled the heights and plumbed the depths. And what fate has given with one hand, it's snatched back with another. For all his wealth, talent, good looks and undoubted charm, it's been a life of surprises, of unexpected twists and turns, touched by triumph and tragedy, every bit as dramatic as the flicks playing in Leicester Square's famous picture palaces.

1. SMALLTOWN BOY

Pierce Brosnan likes to boast of how he hails from 'the bogs of Ireland'. The phrase, which rolls neatly enough off the tongue, highlights the self-deprecatory streak in his nature and shows just how far he's come. But it isn't entirely accurate. It conjures up a mental picture of a damp, misty, marshy, godforsaken place in the middle of nowhere. In fact, the little town of Navan, County Meath, once famous for its furniture and carpets, actually lies less than 30 miles north of Dublin, where the River Blackwater meets the Boyne – a gentle, slow-moving river that even today reflects the place's pace of life. Off the tourist track, the 'only sight worth seeing', according to most guides, is Athlumney Castle, the ruins of which look down on the town. The last occupier, Sir Lancelot Dowdall, on hearing of the Catholic defeat at the nearby Battle of the Boyne in 1690, set it alight rather than see it fall into the hands of the advancing Protestant army.

Nowadays, with its indoor shopping centre and smart high street, Navan looks a relatively prosperous place. Of course, a lot has changed over the years. 'In the fifties, it was comparatively backward, like the rest of Ireland,' says Ken Davis, editor of the Navan-based *Meath Chronicle*, the county's century-old weekly newspaper. 'Children still went to school in bare feet. Poverty was widespread. Light bulbs were still unheard of in some areas and rural electrification wasn't completed until the sixties. Telephones were equally unusual. The only people to have had them in Navan would have been a few businessmen in the centre of town. Everyone else had to rely on letters or telegrams.'

The *Meath Chronicle*, with its dense columns of print, provides an interesting pointer to life in fifties Navan. Crime was virtually non-existent. The 'disappearance of a butcher's knife' was deemed a big enough story to make the front page, as were tales about 'schoolboys winning medals' and 'dust in the high street'. The local cinemas were showing Westerns such as *Geronimo* ('the Redskins versus the White Man in a fight to the death') and *Fort Worth* ('the story of one man's fight against lawlessness'). While most of the adverts seemed to be plugging farm products like 'Porkatine', which claimed to provide a cure for 'worms, cramps and rheumatism' while 'fattening pigs faster'. Photographs of Navan, which then had a population of 4,000, show horses and carts in the high street. Pubs still had stables. And tinkers used to bring turf (peat) into town on wagons to sell as fuel to townsfolk. 'The changes over the last 40 years have been unreal,' says local history librarian Andy Bennett. But the situation in Navan was typical of fifties Ireland – an era known for its 'depressed economy, high unemployment and low living standards'. Nevertheless, thanks to its then flourishing furniture industry and proximity to Dublin, conditions in Navan were considerably better than in many parts of the country.

In 1950, Tom Brosnan arrived in town. The son of a stationmaster (called Pierce), he grew up in Tralee, County Kerry, on Ireland's west coast. It's a hilly, mountainous and remote region that even today is a good four-hour train ride from Dublin. Nowadays the area is a popular tourist spot, famous for its breathtaking scenery. But the county, and Tralee in particular, had long been a place to leave, not visit. The town was hit hard by the Great Famine of the nineteenth century, and during the Depression of the 1930s 'many townsfolk depended on money sent by relatives in America', according to a local guide. So it wouldn't have been unnatural for the then 35-year-old Tom to head east in search of a steady job.

He found work in the John Hogg & Co. furniture factory, on the old Dublin Road, Navan, as a machinist. Operating a bandsaw, his job involved cutting shaped panels out of sheets of wood that would then be used to make chairs, tables and cabinets. 'It was dangerous work,' says Paddy Brennan, manager of the factory, now owned by the Crannac Co-operative Society. 'There were no guards of any sort and he could have easily lost a finger.' Employees started work at 8 a.m. and finished at 5 p.m. They also had to work on Saturday mornings. But in 1950, according to the ledger, Tom Brosnan was earning £7 9s 4d a week, good money for the time. In contrast, a mechanic would have earned £4–£5 a week and a labourer £3 a week. Nearly 50 years on, Tommy Flanagan still works at the factory. 'When I joined as an apprentice sand paperer in 1950, I took home just £1 5s 1d a week,' he says.

Men and women met at old-fashioned dances, usually organised by a variety of bodies such as farmers' associations and churches. Tom was tall, shy and a little lonely, and his family feared that marriage had passed him by until he met May Smith at a Catholic Young Man's Society (CYMS) dance in 1951. The couple were soon in love. 'He was a good-looking man and she was a very pretty girl,' recalls one old friend. 'They made a handsome couple.'

Christened Mary, following her birth on 3 April 1932, May (as she was always known) was the second of Phil and Catherine Smith's three children. (A brother, also called Phil, was born in 1930, and a sister, Rosie, was born in 1936.) Newspaper articles about Pierce Brosnan have invariably played up the 'rags to riches' aspect of his life, but in fact his mother came from a solid, well-respected Navan family. Her father had joined Esso as a tanker driver on leaving school, but worked his way up to become boss of the company's County Meath depot (in Navan). By the time she was born, he was in charge of a dozen men – six tanker drivers and a similar number of yard men. He was doing so well that by the mid-thirties he was able to buy a two-acre plot of land in Convent Road, overlooking the River Boyne, and employ a local company to build a three-bedroom house, with a kitchen and bathroom, to his own specifications. The family called the house Boyne Crest. Mr Smith later sold off one acre, and two more houses were subsequently erected on the site. His daughter, Rosie Farrell, says: 'It was a lovely house and Phil, May and I had a very happy childhood there.' As for her father, she says: 'He spent his entire working life – 40 years – with Esso, eventually rising to have the top job in the county. He was cautious with money and a good businessman.'

Many people were surprised when May, who was then working at Navan Carpets factory, announced she was marrying a man nearly twice her age. Tom's parents were naturally delighted that their son was finally going to be married. And whatever reservations May's parents may have privately harboured, they gave the match their blessing and the wedding took place at St Mary's Catholic Church, Navan, on 16 August 1952. The marriage certificate lists Tom's address as 24 Academy Street, and May's as Boyne Crest. He was two months short of his 37th birthday, while May, who was under 21, was classified 'a minor'. However, the document mistakenly records her name as Mary Smyth. About 50 people attended the wedding, and the reception afterwards was held at the Cunningham Arms Hotel in nearby Slane.

The newly-weds spent their honeymoon in Tralee – staying with Tom's sister, also called May – before returning to Navan. May moved into his little whitewashed cottage in Academy Road, a row of single-storey cottages which then backed on to the River Boyne. (A new road now separates them.) Conditions were primitive. One of the current residents still had to fetch water from a mains tap in the street when she moved in during the 1980s. Each home consisted of just two small bedrooms and a lounge/eating area. There was no bathroom and residents had to use 'dry toilets' at the bottom of the back garden which drained into the river. Another elderly resident, who has lived in the street for nearly 50 years, says: 'We had a tub behind the terrace and had to wait for it to fill with rainwater before we could take a bath.'

The marriage was a disaster from day one. Despite their shared good looks, all too soon they found they had little else in common. Then May discovered she was pregnant. The dates suggest that Pierce was almost certainly conceived during the honeymoon in Tralee – during the first few days of the marriage. Family and friends hoped the warring couple would put their troubles behind them and pull together for the sake of the child.

Little Pierce was born on 16 May 1953 – exactly nine months to the day after his parents tied the knot – at Lourdes Maternity Hospital, Drogheda. Although the birth wasn't formally registered until April, 1957, nearly four years later. He was christened Pierce (after his grandfather, great-grandfather and great-great-grandfather on his father's side) Brendan (a County Kerry patron saint) Brosnan. There has been some talk since about him being born with a tailor-made celebrity name. But the name Brosnan – which derives from Brosne, a local town and river – is popular in County Kerry. And Brosnans fill an entire page of today's Tralee area telephone directory. As for Pierce (which derives from Piers, itself a derivative of Peter), it's more common now as a surname but was a popular first name in the nineteenth century.

After the birth, May returned to the little Academy Street cottage that was to be Pierce's first home – a house that would, of course, be worlds away from the fabulous LA mansion he would one day own. But by the time Pierce was two, his parents' shaky agreement to stay together for the sake of their son – and their families – had fallen apart. And he would spend the next ten years being shunted around the family.

Looking back, relatives wonder if the pregnancy came too soon, on the back of a quick and intense romance. The newly-weds had little time to get to know one another before preparing for the arrival of their child. The rows began almost immediately and neither Tom nor May was prepared to compromise. May had a quick tongue, but there was even greater concern about Tom, who seemed to enjoy arguing merely for the sake of arguing. And the more they argued, the more frequent became Tom's drinking bouts, which in turn led to more rows.

'My father was the first person to notice that something was wrong,' says Rosie Farrell. 'Part of the trouble was the age gap. May was so young when she married Tom and they just weren't suited.' But that wasn't the only problem. She adds: 'Tom was a jealous person and didn't want her to have a life outside the marriage.' Pierce himself told a girlfriend that Tom 'wouldn't let his mother wear lipstick when she left the house'. His future stepfather, Bill Carmichael, went even further, claiming Tom behaved violently towards May, at one point even threatening her with a shotgun.

A former neighbour recalls: 'As things deteriorated, May would spend more time at her parents' house, and when Tom got home from work the house would be empty even though it was practically unthinkable at the time for a wife not to have her husband's meal on the table when he got home at the end of the day. He used to send a youngster from the factory around to his house with blocks of chipwood for the fire. But one day, the lad turned up and May wasn't home so he pushed the blocks through the letterbox. When Tom got home later, he found the front door wedged shut and had to go around to his neighbour's and get in through the back door. Afterwards he and May had a furious row.'

Following the break-up, Tom quit his job in Navan and left for England (while May moved back in with her parents). Little could he have known that he would only see his son a couple of times ever again.

Today, Tom Brosnan's relatives readily admit the man was no saint, but refuse to believe he turned a gun on his wife. 'He upset me a few times and we had our rows,' says niece Mary Daly (Pierce's cousin), who lives in Tralee. 'He was contrary and would say things out of turn, but was his own worst enemy.' While her brother, Pierce Wallace, knows from first-hand experience just how difficult he could be to live with. 'I shared digs with Tom in London and we had a lot of fights,' he says. 'If I didn't go to Mass on a Sunday he'd give me a hard time.' Wallace moved out after just a year. Both he and his sister were too young to be fully aware of what was happening at the time of the split, but Mary, a tall, slim woman with the Brosnan good looks, says: 'We all sensed something wasn't quite right.'

A single mother living apart from her husband in the rural, smalltown Ireland of the 1950s was considered a scandal. 'The influence of the Catholic Church then was unbelievable,' says one of Pierce's childhood friends. 'Things such as separation and sex before marriage were regarded as beyond the pale. In those days you didn't separate, you just struggled on – Ireland was full of couples whose marriages were little more than a sham. But anyone who dared breach the Church's morals was shown no mercy.' You only have to look at a list of books that were banned for being 'indecent or obscene' – such as George Orwell's *Nineteen Eighty-Four* and John Steinbeck's *The Grapes of Wrath*, not to mention novels by George Bernard Shaw, H. G. Wells and Graham Greene – to realise just how painfully conservative a society Ireland was in the 1950s.

'It was terrible for May,' says Rose – Pierce's Aunt Rosie – who lives in Kells, just a few miles from Navan. 'All nudge, nudge, wink, wink, with people gossiping about her and pointing her out in the street.' It was a life of misery and humiliation, and relatives still recall May's face 'burning red' when she drew stares, taking Pierce to Mass at St Mary's

Church. And try as she might to ignore the women who clustered together and talked conspiratorially about her, Rosie says: 'Eventually we all agreed it would be better if she went to England to start a new life.' Bill Carmichael adds: 'When Tom left her, the people of Navan blamed May. Even her sister and sister-in-law didn't want anything to do with her. It was very shaming and that's why she decided to go to England to train to be a nurse.'

However, those who knew the family well feel there was more to May's decision. 'She got the chance to go and she did,' says one source. 'It wasn't so much a case of being forced to go as of wanting to go. She wanted to have a second chance in life.' There were other factors, too. May had set her heart on being a nurse, but while the training was free in England, she'd have had to pay in Eire – if she was accepted in the first place. 'Nursing was a pretty snooty profession in Ireland at the time,' adds the source. 'You had to be of "good character" to even be offered a place as a trainee nurse – and having separated from her husband, it's unlikely May would have been accepted.'

Making the move was one of the most difficult decisions of May's life. But as Carmichael points out: 'As a student she knew she would not have enough money to look after Pierce.' So, after landing a trainee's post at Paddington General Hospital, she left him with her parents. However, it's debatable whether Pierce has ever totally forgiven either parent. Even today, he makes a point of saying: 'I was abandoned by both my parents.'

The Boyne Crest cottage commands a fine view across the River Boyne towards the town centre which is still dominated by two churches, both called St Mary's, one Protestant and the other Catholic. The house has been modernised since Pierce's day. Its present owner, architect David Duignan, values the property at around £150,000, and is particularly proud of the fine orchard, planted long ago by Pierce's grandmother.

Young Pierce, with his shock of black hair, adored his maternal grandparents, Catherine and Philip, who doted on him. But they were not to provide the stable, secure upbringing he craved. By the time he was six, both were dead. 'Grandfather died first and Grandmother lasted only a few months after that,' says Pierce. 'I loved them both very much and was devastated by their loss.' Following their deaths, Pierce went to live with his Auntie Rosie. But she found it difficult to cope with yet another child, so Pierce was sent to stay with May's great-aunt, Eileen Reilly (who had two children), at her little two-up, two-down home – 2 St Finian's Terrace.

At first glance, the cul-de-sac, dating back to 1911, is little changed, consisting of two rows of terraced houses, one of which backs on to the other. With their slate roofs, they are typical of countless other terraces in the South Wales valleys or Lancashire mill towns. The house adjoining number 2 is run-down. The paint on the front door is peeling and the windows look as if they haven't been washed since Pierce lived in the street. Families of ten weren't unusual in the 1950s, and as many as five children slept to a room. But it would be wrong to brand the street a slum. 'People were poor but there was no real deprivation,' says Liam Bennett, probably Pierce's closest childhood friend. 'No one went short of food or clothing. And you could always make a penny or two by doing an errand for someone in the terrace.'

For the next five years Pierce would share a bedroom – divided by newspapers hanging from a washing line – with Eileen's son, Donal (who was nine years older), the nearest thing he would ever have to a brother. 'My mother brought him up as her own,' says Donal, who now works in a timber yard in Drogheda, about ten miles east of Navan. 'But she was a big woman and when it was time to go to bed, even James Bond wouldn't have argued! She worshipped the ground he walked on, she fought his battles and loved him as a son, but knew that his living with us was always a temporary arrangement.'

Money was tight. Nobody could afford to have a telephone or central heating installed. Families huddled around the open fire in the living room in the winter, and only one household in the street had a television. 'All most people had was a radio,' says neighbour Una Hosie, who still lives in St Finian's Terrace. But Eileen, whom Pierce would later describe as 'a wonderful woman', always seemed to cope, as did everyone in the street. One way of cutting bills was by growing vegetables in the back garden.

Mother-of-five Mrs Hosie recalls: 'I'm glad he's done so well. Poor Pierce – he was a lonely little boy . . . we're all so proud of him. He often played with my son, Andy, and the rest of my boys – and I'll always see him there standing at the front door with his little polished shoes.'

In those days youngsters were more easily pleased than today. 'We used to play cowboys and Indians,' says Tony 'Toto' McGoona, who was a couple of years younger than Pierce, and won notoriety as a boy when he accidentally set fire to his family's house. 'We'd play all sorts of games like kick the can, spin the bottle, rounders and football.' Now a carpenter, ironically living in the very house in St Finian's Terrace where Brosnan grew up, he adds: 'Pierce wasn't much of a footballer, though, so we used to stick him in goal. He wasn't as robust as the other boys in the street. I always thought he seemed a bit withdrawn.' Robust or not, Pierce had a constant companion in Chip, a black and white mongrel belonging to his 'aunt'. 'That dog really adored him,' says Donal. 'It followed him absolutely everywhere and if he was ever missing for tea, Mum would tell me with a smile, "If you want to find Pierce, just look for Chip!" '

Meanwhile, despite trying to forge a new life for herself in London, May did her best to stay in touch. 'Every couple of weeks there would be a letter waiting for him,' says Donal. 'She'd send the *Reveille* for Mum and the *Beezer* for Pierce. Sometimes she'd send little toys, too.' The point is echoed by Bill Carmichael: 'May never abandoned Pierce. He always had a home, and every week she'd send pocket money for him and his upkeep. That girl was so poor; she always had ladders in her black nurse's stockings. But she always sent money for Pierce.' However, Liam recalls that her absence depressed him, saying: 'Sometimes you wouldn't see him playing out for days at a time.'

Brosnan, who admittedly is somewhat inclined to romanticise his early life, says: 'I felt the lack of a family and I yearned for a family. I had such dreams and aspirations. I suppose I felt anger that my father had just ditched me and run out of the back door. I think my mother was very brave in gambling that, in leaving me, she could go and create a better life. In doing that, though, I felt a certain amount of anger. You know, "How could you leave me?" My life in Ireland was very solitary and there was a lot of loneliness. I felt like an outsider. I felt different. Maybe I came to use that feeling as a way to protect myself.'

The people of Navan have mixed memories of the boy. One neighbour recalls him wearing 'short corduroy trousers and hobnail boots'. While old friend Andy Hosie, now an electrical contractor, says that even then he showed the charm that would become his hallmark in later life, 'offering to teach the little girls in the street how to ride a bike'. While a cousin, Kerr Reilly, now a bus hire boss, recalls 'the daredevil Pierce' who went on all the rides at a funfair. However, a lot of people simply don't remember today's Hollywood star. 'Pierce was a pretty quiet kid by all accounts,' says Ken Davis of the *Meath Chronicle*. 'He doesn't seem to have stood out.' Except in one respect – his height. He was six feet tall by the age of eleven which was exceptional at the time – and was soon dubbed the 'Long Fella'.

He was a good kid, by all accounts, and was an altar boy at St Mary's – but like the other lads in the terrace, he wasn't averse to taking the odd apple from a nearby doctor's orchard. 'I was stopped by a policeman once with a jersey full of apples,' recalls Pierce. 'I was terrified

I was going to end up in jail.' But the undoubted highlight of the week for Pierce was going to the cinema. It provided a brief escape from reality. 'We'd play football with the rest of the lads but nothing could beat going to the pictures,' says Liam, who is one month younger than Pierce, and now works as a carpenter. 'We'd look through the *Meath Chronicle* and see what was on at the Lyric and Palace. Our favourites were cowboy films starring Randolph Scott and James Stewart, or comedies with Laurel and Hardy or Norman Wisdom.' At the time, nobody remembers Pierce saying he wanted to be a film star – but years later he claimed: 'I was weaned on Saturday-morning pictures and always dreamed of being in the movies.' He and his pals were also fascinated by guns, according to Liam, who adds: 'We lived in a fantasy world. We'd climb trees and gallop home from the picture house after seeing a cowboy film.'

Some people in St Finian's Terrace will tell how Pierce was 'spoilt rotten' by Mrs Reilly and the other women in the street because he was a near-orphan. But such claims should be put in perspective. Ireland was ravaged by tuberculosis in the immediate postwar years; four thousand people died of it in 1948 alone. And his 'Auntie Eileen' lost her husband Val and four of her six children to the disease. Nothing frightened her more than the thought of losing little Pierce, too.

'She'd never have forgiven herself if he'd caught TB, especially as he wasn't her child,' says Donal. 'It was the nearest thing to the plague in Ireland at the time – children taunted kids from infected families – so she made sure Pierce had regular check-ups and X-rays.' Similar, perhaps exaggerated, fears explained her insistence that Pierce wear shorts until he left Ireland, even though it made him look a bit daft, according to pals. 'My mum thought that if you didn't get sunlight on your legs you'd get rickets,' says Donal with a smile. 'She was an old-timer.' Judging by Pierce's strong, healthy adult physique, her concern obviously paid off.

Having been 'abandoned' by his parents, though, Brosnan presented an easy target for bullies, and was teased and taunted by other children. One old friend, Andy Hosie, remembers: 'He was a bit introverted and was knocked around a bit. He wasn't a fighter.' And the softly spoken Donal says: 'Children can be cruel and there's no doubt Pierce suffered. One kid in particular, Ken McGoona (Toto's brother), gave everyone a hard time, and his jibes were always below the belt. He taunted Pierce by telling him: "You'd have nowhere to go if the Reillys hadn't taken you in. You'd be homeless and living on the street." That sort of ribbing would have upset anyone and Pierce was a sensitive lad. Luckily for

Pierce, my mum, who was nearly six feet tall and weighed fifteen stone, feared nobody. When she found out what Ken had been saying, she went around to his house and gave him and his family a piece of her mind. She was that kind of woman.'

In one interview, Pierce recalled 'having a punch-up' with Ken McGoona, who went on to boast in a newspaper about beating up the future Bond all those years ago. 'I remember Pierce's mum sending him a proper cap gun and the rest of us kids being really jealous of him,' Ken told a tabloid. 'One day he wouldn't let me play with the gun, so I just gave him a thump and ran off. He was the sort of kid who would rather read than get into mischief. His auntie made sure he was in bed by 7 or 8 p.m. while the rest of us were out until 10 p.m. He was a big lad but he used to cry.'

A friend says: 'Nobody should underestimate how big an effect Pierce's childhood had on him. It could have crushed many children. That he survived relatively unscathed is a testament to his internal strength.' But any bullying he suffered would pale beside the treatment he and his pals received at the Scoil Mhuire Catholic Boys' School. 'Corporal punishment was a part and parcel of school life at the time,' says Ken Davis of the *Meath Chronicle*. Nothing, though, can excuse the behaviour of the sadistic De La Salle Brothers – a religious order who were Christian by name, but not by nature – under the stern headmastership of Brother Damian. Pierce was sent there at the age of eight. It may have been just a few streets away from the St Anne's Loretta Convent School where he'd been taught by nuns as an infant, but it could have been on a different planet. Several old pals reckon the young Brosnan may have been singled out for humiliation due to his domestic situation.

'On the way into the classroom you'd run to your desk as fast as you could so you didn't get slapped much,' says Liam. 'It was a brutal place and none of us liked it one bit. You simply couldn't avoid being hit. The Brothers didn't think twice about using the leather strap – and the Brother who taught us was particularly hard. We'd hear the swish of the strap all day long as he lashed out at one pupil after another. You'd be slapped for the simplest spelling mistakes. And we went to school in absolute dread. Sometimes you'd break out in a cold sweat at night just thinking about the school. There were over 40 boys in a class and the Brothers were under pressure – but they shouldn't have treated us as punchbags. If you got 30 words wrong in a spelling test, they'd hit you with the strap 30 times. It was that inhuman. I don't think anyone who was there has happy memories of the place.'

Pierce, like all the boys, lived in fear of the 'devil's kiss', as they called the strap. 'I remember being taught by the Brothers only too well,' he says. 'I remember being beaten by these perverted, mangled human beings if I got my sums wrong. I know there are some people who will say the Brothers gave them a fine education. But I'm afraid that wasn't true for me. I remember nothing but grief at the hands of these men. Religion was rammed down my throat. It was pretty brutal but somehow I came through it; I was a survivor.'

The school curriculum was straightforward enough, and there were lessons in English, Irish, Arithmetic, History and Geography. But the brutal, authoritarian nature of the regime, coupled with his awkward personal situation, help explain why Pierce didn't shine in the classroom, on the sports field or on stage. 'He wasn't at all interested in acting or sport,' says one childhood friend. 'There were photos of school plays, and football and hurling teams hanging up in the school hall, but he wasn't in any of them. The only running he ever did was on errands for his great-aunt. Every morning he would dash into town to buy cigarettes from the supermarket because they were tuppence cheaper than anywhere else.'

The only consolation for Brosnan and his classmates must have been the fact that life at the school was even tougher just a few years earlier. 'I'm left-handed, so they used to tie my left hand behind my back so I couldn't use it,' says Donal. In his day, the Brothers used to beat pupils with an eighteen-inch long stick – not unlike a truncheon – again and again. 'I don't know how they didn't break your fingers,' he says. 'Every day you'd be beaten, but it was accepted at the time. I remember one day I was looking out of the window at a dead sheep being carried from the adjoining field. The Brother screwed up his leather belt into a ball and threw it at me, giving me a black eye. He could have blinded me. We all despised them. They tried to beat religion into you, but they just ended up beating it out of you. A lot of them deserved to go to Hell.' Unsurprisingly, few former pupils expressed regret when the school, a victim of changing attitudes towards corporal punishment and a fall in vocations to the De La Salle Order, was transferred to state control in the seventies.

At the time, though, Eileen – and May – were even more worried about the threat posed by Tom Brosnan, going to extraordinary lengths to keep him away from the boy. Recalls Donal: 'I always found Tom all right, but Mum was terrified he might come and take Pierce away. After all, she wasn't his legal guardian and if he'd taken him away there was nothing she could have done, as she didn't have any power of possession.

'If Tom was ever in town it was panic stations. Everyone in the street knew about Mum's fears and we had this early warning system. As soon as anyone saw Tom they'd pass on the news. Word would get back to Mum in no time at all, and she'd get me and my sister Anne to take Pierce and hide him in a hole in a field at the back of our house. So when Tom came, he never saw him.' But while Eileen's intentions were good, the lasting legacy for young Pierce was a bitter childhood memory of a father who abandoned him.

'I must have been very small,' says Pierce, relating one pathetic childhood memory of his father, 'but I remember once looking out of the window when I was staying with one of my aunts and seeing a man walking away from the house with a camera in his hand and his head down, and a cousin saying to me: "That was your daddy". It didn't mean anything to me at the time, of course, because I couldn't remember him. But he had obviously come to see me and take a photograph, but somebody in the family turned him away.'

Eventually, nearly ten years after leaving Pierce in Ireland, May decided the time was right for him to join her in England. She broke the news as gently as she could to Eileen, without whom he would have been homeless. But it was still a blow. 'It was hard on my mum,' says Donal. 'She looked upon him as a son and she took it bad. But she knew he belonged with his mother and knew his leaving was inevitable.' Eileen also wondered how he'd adapt to life 'across the water'. 'She'd never been outside Ireland, and going to England then was like going to the other side of the world,' says Donal. 'We heard all sorts of stories about the place.'

As for Pierce, he was understandably 'somewhat confused' by the situation, according to friends. Of course, he wanted to be with his mother. But at the same time he faced a leap into the unknown, a leap that would involve turning his back on his adopted family and friends, and his beloved Chip.

The big day finally came. His uncle Phil turned up at St Finian's Terrace, drove him to Dublin Airport and put him on the plane – but the exact date is disputed. 'The day I departed – 12 August 1964 – was the very same day Bond's creator, Ian Fleming, died,' says Brosnan, who took to the skies, clutching some holy water in an aspirin bottle in one hand and rosary beads in the other. 'Call it fate, I don't know . . .' But Donal's sister, Anne, insists it was 23 August 1964, saying the date will be etched on her mind forever.

'I'll never forget that day,' she says. 'There were so many tears. Pierce was crying too, but he was also excited. After all, he was going on a plane for the first time. He looked so forlorn, wearing little grey trousers and a green overcoat which barely covered his knees. My mum gave him a big squeeze and a kiss.' Then he was gone. 'It was terrible, we thought we'd never see his little face again.'

The rest of Navan may have soon forgotten about the 'Long Fella' but not the Reillys – he'd always have a special place in their hearts. He used to sing an old country and western song, ' "A Jack To A King", for Mum,' says Anne. 'Whenever I hear it on the radio, I think of little Pierce and it still brings tears to my eyes.' While Donal reveals: 'Sometimes I would hear Mum crying at night – over Pierce. Even Chip pined for him and would jump up excitedly whenever the doorbell rang.'

A chapter in Brosnan's life was coming to a close – a chapter that would hold many unhappy memories. 'I don't think I'll ever be able to exorcise those memories from my mind,' he once said. 'I was brought up on guilt and pressure.' But as his old friend Liam thoughtfully observes: 'Making the move was a big wrench for him at the time, but to be honest, he'd had a sad and lonely life in Navan – and few of the opportunities open to him in London would have been open to him had he stayed. I'd say the biggest break in Pierce's life was getting out of the place.'

2. THE BIG CITY

It's hard to convey the shock Pierce must have felt on arriving in London, which could then still lay claim to being the hub of a great, if fast-shrinking, empire. Everything about the metropolis – its roads, buildings and sheer size – was on a different scale to Dublin, let alone Navan. Come boom or bust, the big city's streets were always crowded with commuters and clogged with traffic. More than twice as many people lived in the sprawling city than in the whole of Eire, and the mighty River Thames made Dublin's River Liffey look like a stream.

But change was in the air in 1964. The Labour Party, led by Harold Wilson, scored a famous election victory, ending the 'thirteen wasted years' of Conservative government. The young generation was turning its back on society's stale conventions. A new era – the era of the Swinging Sixties, Carnaby Street, pop glory, long hair, love and peace – was dawning. Suddenly London was the youth capital of the world. The Beatles topped the charts and spearheaded a British invasion of America. And a stylish new television show, *The Avengers* – that was soon to win a cult following – had just gone on air.

Admittedly, life wasn't quite so exciting in Putney, the well-heeled suburb in south-west London on the banks of the Thames – now popular with people like Duran Duran's Simon le Bon, and the BBC's Sue Lawley – that was to be Pierce's first home in England. 'Record Heat Brings Holiday Rush' cried the front page splash in the *Putney and Roehampton Herald* that August bank holiday. (Some things don't change.) Locals had to make do with the latest *Carry On* yarn – naturally starring Kenneth Williams and Barbara Windsor – at Putney's ABC cinema. And the paper's entertainment editor, who was oblivious to the pop music revolution that was underway, stubbornly predicted that the Beatles would be 'as dead as mutton in twelve months' time'.

The Putney of the sixties was as prosperous as the Putney of today. But some things, such as prices, have changed dramatically. Back then, tea was 1s 6d a pound, you could buy a five-bedroom semi-detached house for £10,000 or rent a bedsit for £5 a week, while a new Vauxhall Viva – which apparently offered passengers 'a millionaire's ride' – could be yours for less than £600. On the other hand, a postman took home just £13 a week.

Besides the culture shock, Pierce also had to get used not just to living with his mother, May, for the first time in living memory but with the new man in her life, panel-beater Bill Carmichael, Pierce's new stepfather. Those first few weeks must have been difficult and tense, particularly for mother and son as they got to know one another again.

Thankfully, the new arrangement worked. 'Pierce had an affectionate relationship with his mother that wasn't visibly scarred by the years spent apart,' reveals a close friend. And Pierce himself describes his stepfather as 'a kind, gentle Scot'. But he soon discovered that his real mother was a very different sort of woman to Eileen Reilly, the only 'mother' he'd known until then. 'His "Auntie Eileen" was a big, warm, cuddly, emotional, loving woman,' adds the source. 'But May wasn't the huggy sort. That wasn't her way.'

It must have also soon become apparent to the youngster that his mother was very much the dominant character in her relationship with Carmichael, a passive, softly-spoken character – quite unlike Tom Brosnan. 'He was a gentle, sweet man, who rarely raised his voice,' adds the source. 'Bill was the sort of guy it was hard to dislike and he and Pierce always got along. His hobby was breeding budgies.'

The new family's first home was a flat in Chelverton Road. At one end was Putney High Street, at the other a modern, nondescript-looking pub, The Quill. It's a pleasant street, lined by big, solid, comfortable three-storey homes with bay windows. But in the sixties a lot of the houses were subdivided into flats. Now things have gone full circle and the houses have been turned back into single residences. It's Volvo estate territory and the cost of an average home is £500,000. In any event, it was a long way from St Finian's Terrace.

Young Pierce sensed that the move to England would change his destiny forever. 'When I arrived I somehow knew I was going to be different from the other boys back home in County Meath,' he says. 'If I look at my life as a play, Ireland was the first act – my spirit and soul are Irish – and London was the second. In Ireland, I was brought up in the country, but I always wanted to go to America and, in my innocence, I mistook England for America! So when I arrived in London, I was looking for the big cars with the wings. No wonder I was the odd kid out!'

In fact, the move worked overwhelmingly to his advantage. Just take health treatment. In England it was free. If you so desired, you could see a doctor or dentist every day of the week, every week of the year – and not have to pay a penny. This wasn't the case in Ireland. 'I remember Pierce saying he'd never been to a dentist before coming to England,' recalls Rebecca McKenzie, a future girlfriend. 'Maybe that was a slight exaggeration – but whichever way you look at it, it's still an awful lot of cavities. He needed extensive work on his teeth and he told me that he pretty much had to visit the dentist every week during his first year in England.'

The local cinema in Putney High Street was also where he first caught sight – in glorious Technicolour, no less – of the cinema icon who was going to play such a central part in his life. 'All the films I had ever seen in Ireland were black and white Norman Wisdom movies or westerns,' he says, recalling the time he went to see *Goldfinger*. 'And suddenly I looked up at the big screen for the first time and saw a naked lady painted in gold and a cool man who could get out of any situation. I was captivated, magicked, blown away. It stirred things in my loins I had never known before! "Wow," I thought. "I wish I was James Bond!" '

Life in the big city could have been very lonely for the lad from Navan. He knew no one of his own age, and neighbours admit that at that time Chelverton Road wasn't the sort of street where people put down roots. There must have been days when Pierce pined for his pals Liam and Andy, and little Chip, and for the familiar sights and smells of the Irish town where he grew up, while at the same time doing his best to block out the hellish memories of the De La Salle Brothers.

Within weeks of arriving, he started at Elliott Secondary School, Putney. The first day of term was 8 September 1964. Opened seven years earlier at a cost of nearly £700,000, the five-storey, large glass building, set in landscaped grounds, was a planner's dream, reflecting the hopes of forward-looking, postwar Britain. Thirty years on, the school – like many quickly erected postwar buildings – is showing its age. It lies at a crossroads of prosperity and poverty. Large, detached houses overlook its north boundary, and around the corner you'll find mock-Tudor mansions with alarms on the wall and the obligatory BMW parked in the drive. But it also borders the Ashburton Council Estate, which in the sixties was home to a number of problem families.

Nowadays, Pierce readily admits he didn't know what to think when he arrived at the mixed, 1,500-pupil comprehensive that first autumn morning in his new school uniform – grey trousers, red, black and yellow tie, and a blazer with an elephant's head crest on the pocket. (Apparently, if you look down on the school from the sky, the layout of the buildings and playgrounds resembles an elephant's head!) 'I was so naïve,' he says. 'I knew nothing – certainly not the facts of life. I went from a school with seven classrooms to a large comprehensive. I couldn't believe the size and the freedom. Talk about culture shock!'

The school was divided into four 'houses' – Norman, Saxon, Dane and Celt; he was in Norman House. The apprehensive youngster joined the

2nd year class with all the other new arrivals from south-west London. 'Most of the kids were from Ashburton or other council estates in the area,' says one of Pierce's classmates. 'No one had much money and it was a rough-and-tumble sort of school.'

Right from the start, though, the lanky Irish lad stood out – at least, as far as the rest of the pupils were concerned. 'I was an outsider and that made me different,' says Pierce. 'I got ribbed a lot because of my very strong accent and was nicknamed "Irish". I think the way the English make fun of the Irish is unfortunate. But I was also painfully shy.' And as in Navan, his family's insistence that he wear shorts for his first couple of years at Elliott made life that much more unpleasant. 'Being so tall for his age made it doubly embarrassing for him and he hated having to wear them,' says classmate Dennis Tritton.

A future girlfriend, Rebecca McKenzie, remembers Pierce telling her how he hated those first weeks at Elliott almost as much as he'd hated his earlier school. 'He was number 33 in his class, but whenever he was asked to call out the number it came out as "thoirty-tree",' she reveals. 'He was teased constantly by the other boys and girls. So he vowed to get rid of his Irish accent – and it only really came out when I knew him if he was tired or drunk.'

However, his worst beating had nothing to do with his Irish accent. He was simply picked on by the class bully, Kevin Saxby, who was looking for a fight. 'One playtime, he started punching Pierce,' recalls classmate Phil Kent. 'And Saxby was hitting him where it would hurt – he had on a big pair of boots and was kicking Pierce in the crotch and whacking him around the head. It looked horrific but the reason I remember it so clearly is because Pierce didn't do a thing. Saxby was laying into him – left, right and centre – and he just tried to protect himself the best he could. Not once did he did try to hit back.

'Some people thought he was a bit of a wally because he just stood there, soaking up the blows. But in a way, Pierce's strategy worked. The other kid eventually got bored and walked away. Word of the incident soon got around because it was so unusual and none of the bullies ever really bothered him again. I suppose they thought if he didn't lose his temper then, what was he going to be like when he really lost his temper? Afterwards, though, Pierce looked a mess – he was pretty badly bruised.

'The irony was that Pierce was a lot bigger than his opponent. Looking back, Saxby must have thought it would make him look good if he beat up this big, quiet kid – but if Pierce had fought back, he'd have probably flattened the bloke. That wasn't his way, though. In all the years I knew Pierce, he never threw his weight around or hurt anyone.'

Brosnan wasn't the only pupil in the class – which reflected London's cosmopolitan mix and included black, Chinese, Hungarian and Polish children – to be preyed on by bullies. 'He got a bit of stick because of his accent,' says Kent. 'But there were other kids there with far worse accents. One Hungarian lad's English was terrible and he got a really rough ride. The black kids got called "nigger" or "wog" and the Chinese guy was nicknamed "Chinky". But a fat white kid got it worst – he had a terrible time.'

Nowadays Brosnan likes to claim he hung around with a crowd he refers to as 'the toughies' but usually adds: 'Deep down, though, I always knew I didn't belong with them' – a claim which surprises some of his old classmates.

'In my recollection, he always kept himself to himself,' says Phil Kent. 'He didn't really get involved with the other lads, lark around in class or join any of the gangs. He just used to get on with his work. It wasn't that people didn't like him – there was nothing to really dislike about him. He made some acquaintances but I don't think he made any real friends. Most kids just assumed he wanted to be on his own but, looking back, he probably was lonely. He certainly wasn't the type to jump from a bridge or swing from a rope like James Bond. I was surprised when I discovered he was a film star, because I always thought people like that were lifelong show-offs. But Pierce was never like that at school. He wasn't the least theatrical and he certainly wasn't a leader.'

Businessman Tritton, who lives in Lancing, says: 'Me and Pierce used to hang around together sometimes but he was very quiet. We saw Tottenham together a few times and once he got arrested at the ground because there was crowd trouble. He was picked out of the crowd because he was so tall.The police decided to take him home but changed their mind when they realised they would have to take him all the way to Fulham. So instead they let him rejoin the crowd – after a ticking off!'

Every day pupils at Elliott had to be at their old-fashioned desks, with built-in inkwells, by nine o'clock in the morning. Electronic pips would signal the end of each 40-minute lesson and youngsters would head off – usually at a distinctly leisurely pace – to the next lesson. For the first three years they had to study the usual subjects – English, Maths, History, Geography, Biology, Art and Religious Instruction. But they were able to specialise during their last two years, in the run-up to their O-level or CSE exams. School finished at 4 p.m.

Classmates agree that Pierce didn't particularly shine in the classroom, and his two solitary O-levels in English and Art (even though they were A-grades) seem to bear this out. 'He wasn't an outstanding pupil,' recalls one ex-pupil. 'I don't think he'd have ever become a brain surgeon or got on to *Mastermind*. He was very average.' While a former female classmate says: 'Most of the teachers liked him because he did as he was told but some of the lads thought of him as a bit of a "goody-goody".' The one exception to the rule was in art, according to Kent, now a Wandsworth-based builder. 'He was very good at drawing and used to create these wonderful cartoon strips. I'd say he was naturally artistic.'

Unlike Bond, Pierce did not excel on the games field. Boys had to play soccer and rugby in the winter, and cricket in the summer. They also had regular PE lessons in the school's well-equipped gym. But Kent says: 'He wasn't the least bit sporty.'

At school, Brosnan got his first real exposure to drama. 'We used to go down to a little theatre in the Upper Richmond Road called Group 64,' says another former pal. 'We all thought it was a soft option – a good way of getting out of certain lessons and having a laugh – but it obviously influenced Pierce. Although I don't remember him ever talking about wanting to be an actor.'

The quality about Brosnan that Kent recalls most clearly is his neatness. 'Pierce was absolutely spotless,' he says. 'Every morning he'd turn up in a clean white shirt – and it would still be clean when he went home at the end of the day. Some people thought he had money because he was always so smart. Everything about Pierce was tidy, from his polished black shoes to his neat, tidy desk top with all the pens and pencils neatly laid out. Most kids scribbled all over their exercise and text books but Pierce's always looked new. Being tidy must have been instilled into him by his mum at an early age.'

It was perhaps a case, repeated the world over, of a proud woman from a respectable family background struggling to keep up appearances. 'Money might be tight,' you can almost hear May saying, 'but that's no excuse to let standards slip.'

Unlike his old classmates, teachers at the school have virtually no recollection at all of the one pupil who's since become a household name. And if you ask any staff member at Elliott today about Brosnan, they're almost certain to reply: 'He wasn't here long anyway. It was a year or two at most.' In fact, Pierce was at Elliott School for five long years. And it's a measure of how little impact he made that so few teachers at the school can remember a single thing about the boy. Even the drama staff, who you'd expect to have something to say about him, are invariably stumped for words.

The school has a sizeable drama department – which has grown over the years, thanks in part to the presence of a purpose-built theatre, seating 200. Now part of a new performing arts faculty, it has played host in recent years to works by Tennessee Williams, Brendan Behan and William Shakespeare. But the young Brosnan showed little or no interest in treading the boards or even in getting involved behind the scenes. Former head of drama, Robert Sabine, who joined Elliott School 30 years ago and is now semi-retired, says: 'I'll be quite frank – I don't have any memories of the boy. If he'd shown any interest in drama, I'd have remembered him. But as far as I can recall, he didn't take part in a single production. He certainly didn't come forward – nor was he recommended to me.' Dr Diana Devlin, now a teacher at the Guildhall School of Music and Drama, who taught English and Drama at Elliott from 1964–67, also finds it hard to place the young Brosnan. She says: 'I helped stage a school pageant in 1965, "The Feast of the Christmas Rose", involving some 200 pupils and I'm sure I'd have remembered him if he'd taken part.'

Part of the reason for Pierce's lack of interest may have been peer pressure. Most of the bovver-boot-wearing toughs wouldn't have approved of anyone in the class getting involved in 'poncy school plays', according to one classmate. 'We were more interested in drinking, going to the pictures, bunking off school and getting off with girls.' And Pierce admits he – perhaps unconsciously – adopted their reactionary stance towards the arts while at Elliott. 'I jeered at people who played the piano or took part in school plays,' recalls Pierce. 'That was cissy.'

However, Rebecca McKenzie has an interesting theory. She believes his acting career began at Elliott School but suggests that it was the classroom and the playground, not the stage, where he gave his first – real-life – performances. 'As a child, he had to adopt a totally new persona when he arrived at the school, pick up a new accent and try and blend in with the other kids,' she says. 'It was a very traumatic period for him and changed his character for good. So I think, in a weird kind of way, he started acting as soon as he arrived in England.'

Still, how does one explain how Brosnan – who's since achieved so much, and so much more than the 'toughies' – left so slight a mark at Elliott? Part of the explanation lies in the fact that by the time he left, the school was in crisis.

A damning exposé – provocatively titled 'Chaos in the Comprehensives' – which appeared in the Daily Mail in March 1972, less than three years after Pierce left in 1969, paints a vivid, frightening portrait of what life at the school was really like. And while the investigation no doubt provided ammunition for the newspaper's right-wing, conservative agenda, former classmates of Brosnan's say the reality was nowhere near as sensational as the authorities subsequently claimed. Even Dr Devlin admits: 'It was a tough school and things were a bit chaotic.'

Newspaper reporter Gloria Stewart, who went undercover as a teacher for the assignment, kicked off her three-day investigative feature thus: 'As I pushed through the heavy glass doors of Elliott School on that first day, I was confronted by a typical sight. A gangling teenager was beating up a ginger-haired youth. They had on the uniform of the toughies: heavy bovver boots, blue jeans and knee-length overcoats.'

It's sometimes forgotten that there was more to the sixties than a bunch of hippies indulging in drugs and free sex, simultaneously calling for peace, love and understanding. For while a lot of middle-class kids embraced the era's liberal ethos, a lot of working-class kids went to the opposite extreme, adopting a military-style uniform – Ben Sherman shirts, No. 1 (skinhead) haircuts, turned-up jeans etc. – that was in stark contrast to the colourful hippy fashion style. And by 1969, this was the look that had been adopted by the toughies, the bullies, the thugs – whatever you want to call them – in Pierce's class.

Discipline became increasingly difficult to enforce as the 1960s wore on. And after living with the De La Salle Brothers' strict, authoritarian regime – where a simple spelling mistake was sure to earn you a taste of the strap – Pierce suddenly found himself in a place where you could get away with almost anything. It must have been unsettling, to say the least.

The *Daily Mail* claimed one Maths teacher had virtually given up with his class. 'They're completely out of hand,' he was reported as saying. 'The last teacher gave up altogether after a couple of weeks and retreated to the staffroom.' And Stewart painted a grim picture of the typical class. 'Most of the boys were slouched over their desks or had their feet up,' she says. 'My simple request, "Please sit at a desk of your own", elicited obscenities and when I attempted to call the attendance register I soon realised my mistake. The girls tittered and the boys answered each name in chorus. The row in the room was ear-splitting. Several times I shouted "All right now, shut up", with no result.

'Every lesson was like a battle with a hostile army. A boy would sit through an entire lesson, doing nothing but twitching his bovver boots in my direction. Some children would sing, some would hum. One thirteen-year-old boy, who had some kind of nervous trouble, sat imitating a cuckoo, with several of his friends joining in the chorus from time to time.'

Most of the staff seemed to accept they commanded no respect and would be defied, jostled and even knocked to the ground, said the *Daily*

Mail. One elderly woman teacher was thrown to the ground while breaking up a fight between two boys and spent weeks hobbling around in pain. A physics teacher was attacked by a pupil who threw a heavy microscope at him. 'I had a split lip and a tooth was loosened,' he was quoted as saying. 'I was on tranquillizers every day for a week, my nerves were so shattered.' While another teacher 'had a desk thrown at her, left the school with a broken arm and was never seen again'. And it wasn't just teachers who were on the receiving end of violence – one boy was stabbed with a penknife.

Vandalism was also a major problem at the school. One day, a pupil filed through the pipes and flooded the place with scalding water. Stone throwing was a regular occurrence. A room on the top floor 'looked like a bomb had hit it', lockers were smashed to pieces and the fire alarm was set off as often as five times a day. Locking teachers in classrooms was also a common occurrence. High levels of truancy and absenteeism were other major causes for concern. But many teachers seemed to turn a blind eye to truancy. 'I'm just glad when the troublemakers don't show up,' one teacher was reported as saying. 'Then I can get on teaching the others.' And absenteeism for causes other than truancy ran pretty high. The average attendance was about 80 per cent but this dropped to about 65 per cent in the week before and after Christmas, the newspaper revealed.

Things weren't much better in Pierce's day, according to ex-pupil Phil Kent. 'The school went downhill dramatically in the late sixties,' he says. 'Vandalism was rife, kids would smoke in the classroom, there was a lot of trouble after school and you couldn't leave anything in your desk or locker without it being stolen.' He pins much of the blame for the fall in standards on the arrival of new, young teachers who embraced the era's liberal ideals. 'We all respected the "old school"-type masters,' he says. 'One of them made us line up our desk legs with lines he'd drawn in felt tip on the floor and Heaven help anyone whose desk was an inch to one side. The maths teacher would hit you over the knuckles with a ruler if you misbehaved and another would throw the blackboard rubber at disruptive pupils.'

But too many of the new staff members were unable to control the half dozen troublemakers in Brosnan's class. 'One woman teacher would tell kids to be quiet and they'd ignore her and just carry on screaming. I remember one kid in our class thumping another teacher on the arm and spitting in her face. Some of the girls were just as bad as the boys and they'd swear at the women teachers and give them a hard time.

'It undoubtedly affected our studies and it got to the stage where it wasn't worth going to some lessons because you knew it was a waste of time – the teacher would be too busy trying to control the troublemakers to have any time for the rest of us.'

What chance did pupils such as Pierce and his classmates stand in this sort of environment? The *Daily Mail* investigation concluded that high staff turnover was one of the main reasons behind Elliott's chronic lack of discipline. Only about 30 of the 120 teachers had been at the school for more than 3 years – although considering their daily ordeal, you can hardly blame them for not wanting to stay.

Thankfully, the situation is much improved today. Of course, the school has its troubles. (A local policeman says: 'We get the usual problems with youths there and on the estate – drink, drugs, petty crime.') But Elliott has gained over £400,000 in additional funding since winning grant-maintained status, its examination results have improved dramatically, A-level results are above average and more people now want to send their children there than there are places. 'It's one of London's big successes when it comes to education,' concludes a local magazine.

Ironically, Tom Brosnan had been living in London for much of the time Pierce had been at Elliott School, working as a carpenter. Like his son, Tom loved going to see films, especially cowboy films. He would often go down to the West End to catch the latest release – particularly if it starred John Wayne. ('But if he didn't like a film,' says a relative, 'he was the type to walk out in the middle.') Who knows, perhaps he and Pierce even ended up in the same cinema, just rows apart, watching the same film?

Whatever Pierce and his mother May say, Tom never forgot about his son, according to sister-in-law, Joan, who insists that he sent Pierce both money and gifts. 'Tom was just glad to know his son was growing up to be a fine boy.' She recalls him watching teenagers lark around in his home town of Tralee and remarking wistfully: 'Pierce would be the same age as them – only taller. I wonder what he's up to now?' And despite claims to the contrary, Tom made at least two visits to Pierce's Putney home. His nephew, Pierce Wallace – who would soon join him in London – says: 'I remember on one trip home Tommy telling us that he went to see Pierce and May, but he wasn't allowed to take pictures of Pierce. Nor was Pierce allowed to answer any of his questions.'

But Brosnan's stepfather recalls things differently: 'Tom came here to see Pierce when he was about eleven,' says Carmichael. 'He had a small box of chocolates for his ex-wife, but what do you think he brought for the son he hadn't seen all those years? Well, I'll tell you – nothing. Nothing at all. I was upstairs and May let Tom in and then told Pierce he could come downstairs to meet his father. When he came back upstairs he cried his eyes out and said, "Bill, I don't want to see him again." I don't really know why. But I do know that if I was seeing my son for the first time in years I would have bought him the biggest present I could afford.'

This, too, is something that Tom's side of the family find hard to believe. 'We grew up with Tommy,' says his niece, Mary. 'My first memory is of him giving us money. He was always so generous – he was the sort of person to give you the shirt off his back.'

Several years later, Wallace recalls visiting Chelverton Road with Tom one evening in the hope of seeing Pierce. 'Tommy took me to London in 1969 on my nineteeth birthday. It was the first time I'd ever seen a black man. He was always saying, "We'll go down to see Pierce one of these days" – and the day eventually came. We caught the bus to Putney and I told Tom to wait in the pub down the road. I knocked on the door, only to find out he and May had moved to a new address. Needless to say, Tom was disappointed.'

Pierce and his parents had moved to 5e Vera Road, Fulham, about a mile away. The little L-shaped street, off Munster Road, consists of three-storey, terrace-style blocks of flats. It's now in the process of being gentrified and flats there can sell for up to £100,000 – but in the late sixties they cost just £1 a week to rent. Says Aaron Valenti of estate agents Ludlow Thompson: 'It's not one of the better roads in the area. Hence property has always been that bit cheaper.'

Pierce soon became pals with a lad in the street, Stuart Turner, who would be his closest teenage friend. 'I hung around with him more than anyone,' Turner says. The two were both very much children of the sixties and were caught up in that great flowering of British rock music that began with the Beatles. 'We used to see a lot of bands,' says Turner, who is one year older than Brosnan. 'We got in free to see Pink Floyd at Imperial College, caught the Doors at the Round House and saw Santana, Frank Zappa and The Who at the Bath Festival. We also saw the Grateful Dead.'

It's an era which Pierce himself recalls affectionately, saying: 'I have great memories of being a teenager in London, of being a mod, hanging out at clubs, of going through the whole sixties thing, becoming a hippy, discovering acting, going off to rock festivals, the Isle of Wight, long hair, freezing my balls off in some bloody tent with a bunch of people taking bad LSD.'

The friends would hang around with other kids in the area, or play each other their latest records. 'He slept in a box room measuring about six feet by six feet,' says Stuart. 'I remember May couldn't wait to get out of Vera Road – she was a real tough cookie.' As well as playing his records, Pierce also wrote poetry. 'It dealt with love, happiness and mysticism,' adds Stuart. 'I suppose he was influenced by some of the songs we were listening to at the time.'

Turner, who went to school in Fulham, paints a picture of Brosnan that couldn't be more different from that painted by former Elliott pupils. 'Pierce struck me as quite a confident person,' he says. ' I certainly wouldn't have called him shy – he seemed to know where he was headed. The only time I ever remember him being lost for words was when we went back to some girls' flat once and he told a joke and it didn't go down too well.' And Turner disputes claims made by their old friend Dennis Tritton that 'Pierce was never a hit with the ladies'. The ex-skinhead even boasted of how he beat the future 007 'hands down' when they were both love rivals, vying for the attention of Tritton's future wife Janice.

'I remember Pierce asked me to dance and I told him to go away,' she told a tabloid. 'He was scruffy with long, greasy hair, three days' growth of beard and this dirty old RAF coat which he never seemed to take off in all the time I knew him. He was a real hippy-type and looked horrible. None of the girls would give him a second glance. He wasn't at all good-looking and none of us girls would sit next to him on the bus home. He was never that successful with the girls. He never seemed to chase them. I don't recall any of the girls in the class particularly fancying him. They used to hang around with the toughies.'

That's simply not true, insists Turner, saying: 'Pierce always took great pride in his appearance but had a style all of his own. He used to wear a long old coat, and a cravat or a neckscarf. Looking back, I suppose he dressed a bit eccentrically. He was also a bit of a ladies' man, even then. Girls would notice him – he had the looks, the character and the mannerisms. But he wasn't the least bit big-headed.'

The young Irishman was also something of a joker. 'I remember going to see a film in the West End with Pierce,' says Stuart, now a gilder. 'The queue straddled the pavement and an usher told us to line up against the wall. Pierce made a really dramatic thing out of it, putting his arms up against the wall as if he was about to be arrested. It was hilarious. I remember him putting a red nose on at the bus stop a few times as well. He was always clowning around and doing daft things.'

How does one explain this apparent contradiction between the shy schoolboy and the cheeky Vera Road teenager? It's possible that while he felt at home in his immediate circle of friends, he was considerably less at ease in the corridors and classes of his rowdy comprehensive. After all, those who seem shy in a large gathering can become different people in the company of trusted friends.

Just a few streets to the west of Vera Road is Bishops Park, an oasis of greenery which follows the curving River Thames from Craven Cottage (Fulham Football Club's home) to Putney Bridge, looking out across the broad expanse of water to Putney's famous rowing clubs and riverside pubs, surely one of the most enchanting views in the capital.

It was here in the summer of 1968 that the fifteen-year-old Pierce met Carole Bevans, also fifteen, who was to be his first girlfriend. She was strolling down a path with a friend when she bumped into the gangly, good-looking Brosnan, who was playing guitar in the sunshine with a group of boys, including Turner. 'I introduced him to her,' he says. 'She was very pretty with long, black hair.'

The two went out together for a couple of years. 'He was a really nice boy, funny and good to be with,' says Carole. 'Although he could never laugh at himself. He was always quite proud and a bit vain. I thought he was very good-looking and he had lovely eyes.'

Sometimes the couple would go out as a foursome with the girl who had been with Carole at the park that day, Jane England, and her boyfriend Roy Finan. 'I remember Pierce once saying, "I'm going to be an actor",' he recalls. 'And I said, "You're never going to be an actor as long as you have a hole in your head." I guess I was wrong.'

But this was one teenage love story without a happy ending. 'We went to a party in Wallington and stayed the night,' says Turner. 'The next morning Pierce rang her up to see if she wanted to meet, and she ended their relationship over the phone. He put a blanket over his head, then walked down to the end of the garden and just stood there looking glumly at the ground.' Another friend says: 'He was very sweet on her and was absolutely gutted when she gave him the elbow.'

However, Carole, now a medical practice manager living in south London, has no regrets. 'I packed him in,' she says. 'I know it might sound a bit strange to other women, especially now he's 007. And I suppose it was very upsetting for him, but I had made my decision that it was time to go our separate ways. I just wasn't interested in the sort of acting life he wanted and he wasn't interested in what I wanted to do. It never would have worked.' The mother-of-two continues: 'I'm not really surprised he has been as successful as he has been because he was always so ambitious. I think he was driven because of the way he'd been abandoned when he was young. As long as I knew him he never had anything nice to say about his father and I think he was trying to prove something by being someone.'

3. WHAT NOW?

After leaving Elliott School in the summer of 1969, Pierce found work as a trainee commercial artist at a photographic studio off Lacy Road, near Putney High Street – just a few minutes' walk from his old Chelverton Road flat. A quarter of a century later, the studio can still be found in the big ivy-clad Victorian house, virtually hidden from view by a high wall, next to The Coat & Badge public house. However, Ravenna Studios, as he knew it, has gone. In its place is Gate Studios, home to a number of small photographic companies.

The then boss, Len Burnham, who retired from the business a few years after Pierce left, says: 'The school would let us know if they had anyone they thought was suitable and that's how Pierce ended up with us. I don't think the job was advertised. He was a good kid, but of course nobody expected he'd end up where he is today.' The studio, which employed about a dozen people, carried out commercial photographic work for a wide range of companies, including Harrods, Selfridges and Kay's mail order catalogue. At sixteen, Pierce would have been the youngest, most junior member of staff, earning just £10 a week.

'His job involved cutting up board, putting down electrostat and generally helping to prepare for photo-shoots,' says Len's son Tim, who was just a couple of years older than Pierce when they worked together at the studio. 'His job title might have been trainee commercial artist but most of his work really involved draughtsman-type work.' Adds Tim, who now runs a small advertising agency: 'None of us believed his name when he joined – we thought he'd made it up – but he showed real promise as an artist.'

Most of the staff at Ravenna Studios remember Pierce as 'quiet' or 'shy' but he was only sixteen and it was his first job. But even then 'he wasn't a bad-looking bloke', according to his colleagues – so he was occasionally roped into appearing in an advert. Sadly, none of the pictures survive. Despite his good looks, though, he was no Romeo. 'I can't ever remembering him having much of an eye for ladies,' says Tim. 'He certainly never chased the local girls like some of the other lads.'

While his artistic streak meant he was more suited to the Ravenna Studios job than many of his classmates, Pierce still thought there had to be more to life. 'I didn't know where I was going,' he admits. 'I just knew I didn't want to end up being a plumber or electrician. The guys

I hung out with at school were traditional guys from solid homes. But they were English. I was Irish. I was different.'

The chief significance of the studio in Pierce's life was that it introduced him to the world of drama. 'One morning, the fellow who worked in the dark room was talking about this theatre club, the Oval House,' says Brosnan. 'He'd heard my enthusiasm for movies and invited me along.' Despite his initial reluctance, he was eventually persuaded to try it out. 'I was eighteen, went into a back room with about twenty-five other young people and took part in a workshop,' says Brosnan. 'I found I could act out all the stuff from my childhood; I could let it all out and just go mad. It was brilliant.'

He started going to acting workshops twice a week and then every night. And within a couple of years, Pierce had made the momentous decision that was to change his life forever. Roy Eubank, who ran the photographic studio when Pierce worked as an assistant downstairs, says: 'I distinctly remember bumping into him in Putney High Street one lunchtime. He excitedly told me he was leaving to become an actor. I told him, "Don't be silly. Acting's a difficult business. You're much better off staying here with us and learning to be an artist." Thankfully for him, he ignored my advice! But the chances of him "making it" just seemed so remote.'

The Oval House theatre lies across the street from the famous cricket ground (home to Surrey Cricket Club), and a five-storey block of council flats. Around the corner is Kennington Park Road, a busy six-lane thoroughfare, and the Oval underground station. A few hundred yards to the north is Vauxhall main line station. Traffic clogs the streets, fumes fill the air and rubbish clutters the streets. The area is typical of many inner-city London areas. And somewhat fittingly, bearing in mind Pierce's Irish roots, it's an ethnically diverse area with immigrants from all over the world. A former youth club, by the late sixties the Oval House had evolved into an arts centre, largely thanks to the drive of the visionary alternative drama guru, Peter Oliver. Nowadays, graffiti scars the walls of the two-storey building and stage props lie discarded at the side of the car park. All that was visible through the foyer windows in the summer of 1996 was a blackboard with the depressing message: 'The Oval House is quiet just now – alas, this is what cuts do to the arts! All our classes and workshops have finished – our café is closed until the autumn. There will be no summer children's work/carnival activities.'

It's an unlikely spot for a theatre to flourish, and an even less likely starting point for a career that would take one of its 'graduates' to

Hollywood, where he'd land the part of 007, the public school-educated spy created by old Etonian, Ian Fleming – but this was the birthplace of Pierce Brosnan the actor.

Over the years, the Oval House has proved a fertile breeding ground for the acting profession, throwing up such diverse talents as Steven Berkoff, (the flamboyant, shaven-headed actor who is probably best known for playing the arch-villain in 1984's *Beverly Hills Cop*), Gary Olsen (of the popular ITV sitcom, *2point4 Children*), and Tim Roth (star of a string of Hollywood movies including *Reservoir Dogs*, *Pulp Fiction* and *Rob Roy*). Another Oval House regular in the early 1970s, performing there with an experimental theatre group, was Mike Figgis (who went on to direct the hit movie *Leaving Las Vegas*, which won actor Nicolas Cage the 1996 Oscar for Best Actor).

When Pierce arrived at the Oval House as a wide-eyed teenager in late 1969, it reflected all that was best or worst about the time, depending on your point of view. It was the year John Lennon married Yoko Ono and the two of them staged their joint bed-in for peace at an Amsterdam hotel. More than 150,000 people paid £2 10s to indulge in three days of sex, drugs and rock'n'roll at the Isle of Wight rock festival – and catch the likes of Bob Dylan in action. It was the year the Rolling Stones scored a smash with 'Honky Tonk Women' and the cult movie *Easy Rider* was released. It was the permissive sixties at their most permissive, the last hurrah of the hippy movement before cold reality began to bite.

Despite relying on traditionally conservative bodies like the Arts Council and Lambeth Borough Council for much of its funding, the Oval House was among the most radical theatres of the era, winning notoriety for staging way-out, controversial plays. 'It was a real hothouse of talent and a time of tremendous creativity, becoming the model for many of today's fringe theatres,' says Alfie Pritchard, who helped co-ordinate many of the events.

However, others viewed if differently. 'Lambeth Youth Office kept trying to close us down,' says Pritchard. 'They thought we were fornicating all day. Of course, we weren't!' Newspapers also viewed the Oval House's activities with great suspicion. For instance, Cedric Porter, entertainments editor of the *South London Press*, scathingly says: 'They were too far-out for us. They were living on another planet most of the time.' Nor were the centre's drama productions of much interest to the acting profession's own newspaper, *The Stage*, where one correspondent dismisses their work at the time as 'lesbian, feminist or otherwise controversial theatre with strictly limited appeal'.

Radical gay and feminist groups used to hold meetings there every week as did the extreme black power group, the Black Panthers, who were responsible for the theatre hitting the headlines, for all the wrong reasons, in August 1970, when it was the centre of a race riot – some indication of how 'alternative' a venue it was at the time.

Trouble flared when a schoolboy was robbed at the Oval under-ground station by two youngsters who then took refuge in the centre, where a dance was being held. Two plain clothes officers were refused entry and when uniformed officers arrived, they were met with chants of 'Fascist pigs'. The bobbies were told: 'Our people are one. We've got no time for the police. We have our own law.' A crowd of men dressed in black then held up their fists in the Black Power salute and started chanting 'Kill the pigs', the signal for an attack on the police.

'The two detectives were showered with bottles and cans and one was spat on,' reported the *South London Press*. 'A man swung a chair off the stage and cracked it across a constable's arm. He was kicked to the floor and suffered a head injury which needed five stitches. Two other constables were knocked unconscious, a police inspector was struck over the head and taken to hospital with a suspected hairline skull fracture and several other officers were injured before fleeing into the street.'

Of course, young Pierce wasn't involved – but it does show how the Oval House contrasted with the typical English theatre, professional or amateur. Three men were later found guilty at the Old Bailey of 'riotous assembly and assaulting police officers' and the trial judge condemned the riot as 'a disgraceful incident'. However, you can't help feeling that James Bond would have had the situation under control within minutes.

The occasional riot notwithstanding, the Oval House must have been quite an eye-opener for the youngster with the slight Irish accent. 'We wanted to break down barriers and push performance theatre to the limits,' says Pritchard. And there's no doubt the club and its members achieved their objective, whether it involved actors 'fondling members of the audience' or staging spoof shows involving groups like the Theatre of Atrocity. Drugs were also on hand to help the creative juices flow. 'Dope was freely available and most of us would indulge from time to time,' admits Alfie. 'But it wasn't a religion as it became at some radical fringe theatres.'

The Oval House became much more than a mere theatre to the young Brosnan. When he arrived that first night he still didn't know where he fitted into the grand scheme of things in the outside world. It wasn't surprising – London's a vast city and can be a lonely place for those who have lived there all their lives, let alone someone from another country. However, unlikely as it sounds, it was there he at last found somewhere he 'belonged'.

'I went there on a rainy Tuesday night and this veil of inhibition lifted from me and I had a wonderful time,' he says. 'It was basically a kind of group grope. It was all about sensing and feeling things but it was magnificent because I feared it was going to involve getting up and reading Shakespeare! God, it was a rich feeling to find refuge – a sanctuary, as it were. It was suddenly like being part of a family. I immediately felt I had come home. I loved telling people I was an actor but I think I was really just an exhibitionist!'

He was accompanied a few times by Stuart Turner, who says: 'I went along to these encounter groups with Pierce where you would sit around in a circle and stick your tongue out at people and things like that. It was pretty far-out stuff.' Another time he recalls Pierce 'eating a bag of cream buns and gradually smacking them all over his face'.

The theatre became a 'second home' to a lot of people, not just Pierce. 'Some would be there all day, every day, seven days a week,' says Alfie. 'Just hanging out in the canteen, Perdoni's café around the corner, or one of the local pubs, The Hanover Arms or The Surrey Tavern. There was a sense of family and, while there were rows as there are in all families, it gave us a sense of identity, a sense of community and a sense of belonging.'

Occasionally, if they'd been working late and were planning a performance the following day, Pierce and some pals would spend the night at the Oval House. That was how he ended up seeing the Rolling Stones in Hyde Park. 'I was doing street theatre,' he recalls. 'We were supposed to be doing something or other with puppets, that sort of thing, and roaming around with them, but we all ended up just watching the gig, which was pure magic.

'I remember Jagger in his little frock, letting off the butterflies. The imagery was unique, and for me as a kid, thinking the world revolved around me, it was astonishing. But I wasn't particularly shocked by Brian Jones's death. When Jimi Hendrix went, though, it really blew me away.'

As if to celebrate his rejection of the 'straight world' – as his new friends dubbed the rest of society – he got his ear pierced. 'I was young, frivolous and full of abandon – a hippy with long hair down to my shoulders and a little goatee beard,' he says. 'Why? Because I thought I was gay, but no, I'm not gay. It was fashionable to have a pierced ear then.' However, the revelation that he thought he may have been gay comes as a surprise to all those who knew him at the Oval House. 'If he did question his sexual orientation, he never let on,' says one old friend. 'He never struck me as anything other than rigidly heterosexual.'

Much of the theatre group's 'work' – if that's the right word – involved taking the Oval House's radical version of performance theatre to the streets, to ordinary folk in the area, many of whom had never been to the theatre in their lives. 'Street theatre, in the modern sense, was relatively new then,' says Alfie. 'And we used to go out to council estates and adventure playgrounds and put on shows. It required a lot of improvisation – and was the sort of thing that could either make you or break you. A lot of kids used to come in and tell me, 'I wanna be an actor', but after being sent out to perform they just didn't come back. I remember Pierce getting mud thrown at him and kids running up to us and shouting, "Piss off, you bastard", but he never batted an eyelid.

'A lot of us would just sit around drinking ourselves into oblivion a lot of the time, but the great thing about Pierce was he just got on with it. He was very focused on becoming an actor. He had a real intensity and passion for the theatre.'

His first professional performance was in *The Little Prince* at Southwark Cathedral, a show that ran for all of two nights. There followed two and a half years of various forms of theatre, taking any theatre work he could get, whether it was working with the Theatre of Education, performing at the Edinburgh Fringe Festival, staging street shows in Amsterdam or putting on 'socially conscious' shows outside the gates of Ford factories with the left-wing Red Ladder Company. He even enjoyed a two-week stint as a fire-eater at a circus. Nevertheless, he still had to support himself, and took whatever part-time work he could find, be it labouring or mini-cabbing.

One person who remembers the young Brosnan at the Oval House is Catharine Sanders, now a freelance writer and mother of two. 'It was full of eager youngsters like Pierce and myself who were ready to do absolutely anything,' she says. 'There were people coming and going all the time and Peter Oliver tried to steer all these young people in the direction they wanted to go. Of course, in a way it was a pure fluke Pierce was there – if he hadn't been dragged along by a workmate he might never have been an actor. I don't think he stood out more than anyone else there, but the Oval House obviously fired up his enthusiasm for acting. And he was certainly no lady-killer. I think he's one of those men who's got better looking with age.'

Another eager youngster at the drama club was Colin Curwood. 'It was a pretty anarchic and right-on place,' he says. 'Little theatrical groups would spring up one week and be gone a few weeks later. But the important thing to us kids was that it was doing something different. It was a great place to go after school or work and hang out. It was a bit like going to a psychedelic church hall.'

He got to know Pierce when they and a handful of other regulars teamed up to form their own group, Theatre Spiel. He took a number of pictures, some of which still survive, of the 'wannabe actor' performing various routines. 'He was pretty shy to begin with and I gathered he had a disturbed family background, but he soon came out of his shell,' says Colin, who was a couple of years his senior. 'We used to spend a lot of time riding around on the Tube. The idea was to take performance to the public, and we even tried to get London Transport to sponsor us but they didn't take the bait.

'Pierce developed this amazing act where he'd don a wig and a fake nose ring and then pretend to play a stringless violin while a full orchestra was blaring out of a cassette recorder. Most people who came across us were dumbfounded and thought we were a bunch of lunatics. But the British public are pretty reserved. And if someone didn't like what we were doing they'd usually just get off at the next station and change carriages. One day, an old busker with a violin got into our carriage. He greeted Pierce like a long-lost friend, put his arm around him and started playing away while Pierce mimed along to the music on his stringless violin. It was hilarious.'

Now a Cambridge-based photographer, Curwood also took photographs of Brosnan dressed like a chicken during a festival of street theatre in Bradford, Yorkshire, and wearing a tutu in Brighton during a carnival. 'He didn't half get some funny looks that day!' says Colin, adding: 'I still find it hard to equate Pierce as he is now with the chubby Irish boy I knew all those years ago. Of course, if I'd known I was photographing the future James Bond, I'd have taken a lot more pictures.'

In hindsight, Alfie Pritchard thinks Brosnan was 'quietly ambitious', adding: 'He always had a quiet confidence about him.' At that time, though, when a lot of people at the Oval House saw themselves as 'artists' rather than 'actors', and were openly contemptuous of mainstream theatre, television and cinema, 'ambition' was a dirty word.

'There's no escaping the fact that Pierce was good-looking and that caused some antagonism,' says Alfie. 'People were jealous of him. Not so much for his good looks and the fact that he was attractive to women – he certainly wasn't a rampant Romeo – but because his looks made it more likely that he would succeed in what we called "the straight world". I think there was also a feeling among certain members that he was a bit "straight". He used to go drinking with the rest of us and we'd often end up blind drunk somewhere in the West End. But he never did anything really outrageous; he never wanted to stare into the abyss.'

As well as appearing in street theatre, Brosnan also appeared in productions at the Oval House. He played 'One-man' in *Pucka Ri* – a Celtic rock opera, complete with chickens, a large pregnant goat and the Balloon and Banana Band – performed at the centre's little upstairs theatre (formerly the youth club chapel), seating just 50 people, in April 1973. Set in a post-nuclear world where everyone except one man (Pierce) has become a mutant, it tells how the Earth's forces decide to regenerate this Everyman, who is eventually coupled with the Midwinter Child. Reviewing it, the *Evening Standard* commented: 'The show abounds with splendid ceremonial images and the music is stirring, but there are too many loose ends for *Pucka Ri* to be totally successful.' (Pop fans might be interested to learn that the Balloon and Banana Band's lead guitarist, Brian Willoughby, went on to join The Strawbs.)

Three months later, in July, Pierce appeared in *Feast Of Fools*, which evolved out of *Pucka Ri* but was staged in the main auditorium (formerly the youth club gym), seating 250 people. Originally planned as a one-off, the show proved so popular with the public – who were asked if they were serfs or gentry on arrival and had to pay accordingly (respectively 25p or 40p) – that it eventually ran for two weeks.

'The hall was decked out as a medieval banquet room and the show was sexist, racist and jingoistic but great fun,' recalls Alfie Pritchard. 'If I remember correctly, Pierce played a randy crusader who ended up in the stocks having food thrown at him.' The theatre group was very much in favour of audience participation but one night things got out of hand – even for them. 'A member of the audience attacked me on stage,' he adds. 'I remember seeing Pierce grinning out of the corner of my eye. Luckily I wasn't badly hurt.'

Under the circumstances, the *Evening Standard* gave the production a pretty good review, worth quoting in full:

> Strange goings-on in a barn-like structure opposite The Oval cricket ground. The place is called Oval House, the standard of hygiene is nothing to tell mother about, but there is a good deal of boisterous fun to be had.
>
>   The show, called *Feast Of Fools*, is based on a loose and rather sketchy impression of medieval times. 'Are you gentry?' inquired the bosomy creatures in charge. If you are, you get to sit at a table

and drink some sweet-tasting muck which is all the authorities will allow, eat a lump of chicken and watch acrobats, jugglers, fire-eaters and a lot of antique horsing around.

There is a band called the Balloon and Banana Band which belts out competent rock. A pretty girl does a reasonable strip. (She dropped a distinctly grubby bra in the dregs of my drink, but I am inclined to be tolerant about these things.)

She was straightaway raped by a randy crusader (Pierce) who was put in the stocks for his trouble. The humour is bawdy. ('Put her down, she's a nun. My God, anything in uniform.') One of the actresses let me kiss her. A worthwhile evening.

All in all, it was a fairly typical Oval House production – provocative, challenging and way, way out.

Soon afterwards, Pierce left the Oval House to enrol as a full-time student at the Drama Centre, having applied earlier that year. However, he would never forget the place which set him on the road to stardom.

More than twenty years later, by which time Pierce was a celebrity known around the world, he popped in unannounced one day – and bumped into Alfie, who's now training to be a psychotherapist, but lives in a flat above the theatre. 'He had a walk round, reminisced about the past and laughed when he got to the toilets because he used to have to clean them when he was here all those years ago,' says Alfie. 'It was like he'd never left. Okay, he might wear an expensive suit these days. But he had none of that "I've made it – I'm a star" attitude and didn't need to put on any airs and graces. He really hadn't changed.'

4. THE DRAMA STUDENT

It's hard to imagine a less likely launch pad for movie stardom than the former Methodist church with its crumbling front wall and rusting railings in the Prince of Wales Road, north London. 'When I first saw it I thought "What a dump",' recalls one student. But this is the site of the Drama Centre, one of the foremost theatrical schools in the country. And it's here that Pierce Brosnan arrived in the autumn of 1973 to embark on a new chapter in his life, a chapter that would open up a wonderful world of possibilities undreamt of by most of his old Elliott classmates.

Somewhat fittingly, the Drama Centre – which has always prided itself on its students' broad range of backgrounds – lies in Camden, known for its large Irish community. The area was less trendy then than it is today. Although even now, Prince of Wales Road, which runs from the bottom of Haverstock Hill to Kentish Town and is made up of council flats and shabby Victorian terraced homes, is a world away from the trendy wine bars and restaurants clustered around Camden Town underground station.

The radical, controversial school was set up by Swedish-born Yat Malmgren and Christopher Fettes in 1963 to bring the European-style 'method' approach of acting – which drew on the work of Stanislavsky and Rudolph Lavan and was popularised by American screen legend Marlon Brando – to Britain. 'At the time a lot of people were rather suspicious of the Drama Centre,' says Carol Drinkwater, who studied there in the early seventies. And even today, according to Malmgren, 'the school is regarded as something peculiar and strange'.

However, it has proved a fertile breeding ground for a succession of stars, including Simon Callow, who starred in *Four Weddings and a Funeral*, Frances de la Tour, best known for her *Rising Damp* role, *Jewel In The Crown* heroine Geraldine James, and Carol Drinkwater, who played James Herriot's wife, Helen, in *All Creatures Great and Small*. Since Pierce's departure, it has nurtured further talent in the shape of Tara Fitzgerald – who starred opposite Hugh Grant in *The Englishman Who Went Up a Hill But Came Down a Mountain* – as well as Bond girl Maryam D'Abo, who starred opposite Timothy Dalton in 1987's *The Living Daylights*.

Every year hundreds of young hopefuls apply for the thirty-odd places on the school's three-year course. They all have their own private reasons for so doing – often surprisingly similar reasons. In words that could have come from Pierce's lips, one recent student says: 'As a child I always felt uncomfortable, out of place.' And while it's hard to imagine the flamboyant Callow ever being bashful, he says: 'I terribly wanted to be released from myself as I then was and I looked to the Drama Centre to break down my shell. I thought it would change my life one way or another forever. I knew it might break me but I hoped it might make me.' He adds perceptively: 'I think that's partly the motive of anyone wanting to become an actor.'

Before being accepted, Pierce, like other applicants, faced a grilling from an interviewing panel that Callow describes as a collection of people looking 'more like hanging judges than drama school tutors'. Prospective students had to present two pieces for audition, one from a classic selected by the school and the other a modern speech of the student's choice. They also had to answer loaded questions like: 'Do you have a talent for acting or simply a craving for attention?' or 'What on earth makes you think you can act?' which could have easily thrown a twenty-year-old. But Pierce passed with flying colours.

'A lot of people with a profound craving for attention mistake this for a talent for acting,' says Fettes, now the school's principal. 'One of the qualities I look for in an applicant is charisma. You either have it or you don't and Pierce obviously had it – in abundance. You can spot a certain disposition to this craft straight away.' As for Brosnan's lack of formal qualifications, he adds: 'Many highly intelligent people just don't fit in at school. I do not believe that having two O-levels says anything about a person's intelligence. Pierce is much brighter than most of those who've gone on to higher education, collecting worthless pieces of paper.'

But if Brosnan imagined the hard part was over, he was in for a surprise. For the Drama Centre ran some of the toughest acting courses in the country. 'You're thrown in at the deep end and you either sink or swim,' reveals a source. Students were expected to work twelve-hour days, six days a week. The first part of the day was spent in the deceptively titled 'movement class'. In a rigorous routine that might well have been devised by Bond creator Ian Fleming – who had his hero performing 'slow press-ups and straight leg lifts' – both male and female students had to limber up in leotards and go through 'ninety minutes of pure hell,' recalls Aaron Harris.

Not that the female members of the class objected to seeing Brosnan in a tight-fitting body stocking which left little to the imagination. Another old classmate, Cliona Nunan, who played Titania to Pierce's Oberon in a Drama Centre production of Shakespeare's *A Midsummer*

Night's Dream, and is now carver and gilder for the Royal Painting Collection, says: 'Certain men should never be seen in leotards. But Pierce and another guy, Paul Geoffrey, were quite gorgeous and in our first term they were chased by some of the girls.'

However, a number of graduates have spoken out against the school's controversial attempts to get students to 'abandon their inhibitions and release emotions that can be used on the stage'. One former student says: 'I remember Christopher (Fettes) asking a girl, "Have you ever felt like killing a child who wouldn't stop crying?" At other times, he'd force you to relive an emotionally shocking experience. It was very traumatic, both for the individual concerned and the rest of the students. Sometimes people would storm out, yelling, "This isn't acting, this is sick".'

A BBC documentary about the Drama Centre, called *Theatre School*, lifted the lid on the sort of treatment students could expect. In one memorable scene, a staff member scathingly tells a student: 'You look like a dead fish.' Another student, recalling his time at the school, says: 'It was a universe of terror. At times, Christopher could be an absolute monster. He was merciless with students and would rip them apart.'

Another aspect of the Drama Centre, highly unusual among British drama schools, was the emphasis on identifying a character with a particular animal. 'For instance, you might think of yourself as a chicken if you were playing an old spinster,' says one ex-student. 'Or a tiger if you were sleek and sexy.' Actress Carol Drinkwater reveals: 'I got into the habit of pretending I was an animal before going on stage – and when I left I discovered a lot of actors and directors didn't like that sort of thing.' Today, as in Pierce's time, students often visit nearby London Zoo to get inspiration as to what animal is most like a role they are expected to play.

But God help anyone who was tempted to skip classes. That was unforgivable. And if students missed 'eighteen or more' classes a term they would be thrown out, according to a college spokesman. Classmate Kathryn Pogson, who has since worked for the Royal Shakespeare Company and appeared in the hit TV series *We'll Meet Again*, says: 'In my recollection, if you were five minutes late you weren't allowed to attend the rest of the day's classes – and if that happened three times, you were out!' Fettes is quick to defend the centre's high standards: 'Discipline is essential in an actor, and if people didn't show up they had to go because it affected the group's cohesion.' Unlike some of his classmates, Pierce quickly adapted to the tough regime. 'He was a remarkable student,' says the now elderly Malmgren, who gave private acting lessons to Sean Connery before he found fame. And even though the Year of '73 was by all accounts exceptional, Pierce still became its natural leading man. 'He had an innate confidence in himself, worked terribly hard and showed a maturity beyond his years in so many ways,' says Fettes, 'particularly in his relationship to girls.' This is echoed by Brosnan's classmate, Harris, who says: 'He seemed very worldly and mature to me, a green eighteen-year-old from Limerick.'

From the very first day, Pierce wholeheartedly embraced the 'actor's lifestyle', even down to his dress – though he was short of cash and was known to his classmates as 'Boracic' (from Boracic Lint – 'skint' in Cockney rhyming slang). 'He never made any secret of the fact that he didn't have any money,' says actor Garry Cooper, who arrived from Hull to join Pierce's class and remains a friend. 'But he had this knack of trawling thrift shops and picking up elegant clothes for next to nothing.' In fact, so stylishly dressed was the young, bohemian-looking Irishman – be it in a beret or cravat, frilly shirt and well-cut trousers – that Kathryn Pogson recalls: 'I remember Christopher telling us, "If you want to look like an actor be sure to dress like Pierce Brosnan!"'

Not that he was the group's undisputed sex symbol and star turn. 'He was obviously good-looking,' says Kathryn. 'But there were a lot of other good-looking guys on the course besides him. He was just one of the gang, sometimes he was good, sometimes he wasn't, but like the rest of us, he was learning all the time. We didn't all go around in awe of him, thinking, "Wow, this guy's so amazingly talented", wondering if he was going to be the next James Bond!'

Many of the students were desperate to lose their regional accents, but Pierce's Irish brogue had already had the edges taken off it by living in London for nearly ten years and was 'hardly noticeable', according to Cooper. 'The only time I was really aware of it was when he was angry or drunk. Then the Irish would slip out.'

The first year of the course is designed to give students a thorough grounding in the basics of acting, teaching them how to use their bodies as instruments and to develop the vocal skills associated with their craft. They also build the stage sets and provide the technical support for Third Year public performances.

Between classes and during the lunch break, they can relax in the canteen – a long, narrow, shabby-looking room with tables and chairs, and a worn-out sofa in a corner. The sound of students doing singing exercises usually echoes down the corridors. On a sunny day, students congregate on the steps outside the centre and chat and smoke cigarettes while others practise their lines in the background. That's pretty much how it was in Pierce's day, and how it is today.

But with the sixties such a recent memory, everyone knew how to let their hair down and have a good time in Pierce's day. After classes the students would head for the nearest pub, The Crown. 'None of us had much money, so we used to try to make a drink last all night,' says Kathryn. Pierce was a member of The Fat Boys, the name adopted by the poker-playing members of the drama group. 'The stakes didn't go much higher than 10p because we had no money, but we always had a lot of fun,' says Aaron, who plays Detective Sergeant Harris in the hit television series *Wycliffe*.

It was a pretty wild year, according to Christopher Fettes. 'There were massive punch-ups between students fighting for the girls' affections, and I was always having to go and bail them out of the police station at two o'clock in the morning.' Former convent schoolgirl Cliona can still remember her shock at some of the goings-on. 'The whole thing was a real eye-opener for me,' she says. 'Everyone was jumping into bed or living with someone else. Drugs were very much in fashion, too.' One student recalls: 'It was that post-hippy, LSD time where anything went – and we'd occasionally go up to Hampstead Heath and drop some acid.' Staff at the Drama Centre were only too aware of the situation but felt powerless to act.

'We used to go to the Round House for lunch,' recalls Fettes. 'There was so much dope being smoked that clouds of the stuff would hit you as soon as you opened the door – and by the time you'd got a sausage roll you were usually smashed out of your head. There were loads of drugs around – you name it, they did it, and the amount of stuff they got through on some of these marches is nobody's business – but a lot of people didn't know how to handle them and consequently got into trouble.

'I know there were a couple of students who were having problems paying their fees and started selling dope. Of course, we banned drugs from the school – because, contrary to what some people think, they don't do anything to enhance an actor's performance – but I know that certain illegal substances changed hands in the canteen. However, it was also a very creative period. There was a lot more optimism among young people than there is today. In Pierce's time, students felt more passionate about things – they thought they could change the world – and in some ways I think he and the others were very lucky to have been students at that time.'

Within weeks of enrolling at the Drama Centre, Pierce met a striking Canadian brunette, Rebecca McKenzie, who had come to England in the summer of 1973 to study cookery. A Canadian friend, Francesca Mallin, was a classmate of Pierce's and told Rebecca that she just had to meet 'this handsome guy' on her course.

'I first saw him at a party,' says Rebecca. 'I remember going to put my coat in a bedroom. The room was dark and I could just make out a man and woman lying together on the bed. I thought it was a bit strange and went downstairs to try to find this special guy and he was nowhere to be seen. That's when I realised it was Pierce on the bed!' When they were introduced, Rebecca's first impression of him was, 'Wow, he is a good-looking guy', and they spent much of the night dancing in the lounge. 'He wasn't a bad dancer,' she says. 'Although I think he may have been a little intimidated by me that first night because I'm five feet eleven inches tall and I was wearing these green platform shoes, so I was looking right into his eyes.'

A couple of weeks later Pierce asked her out. 'He was very eager,' she recalls. 'We met up on a Sunday and he spent the whole day showing me the sights of London. He bought me lunch and he bought me this and he bought me that and I was beginning to feel a bit guilty, so eventually I said, "Why don't you let me buy you something?" Later on, he told me he was glad I'd offered because he was down to his last few pence!' He ended the date by planting a long, lingering kiss on her lips.

They were soon an item. Brosnan smuggled her into the Drama Centre to see him play a butler in his class's Christmas play, and he began sleeping over at the house McKenzie shared with two girlfriends, 'usually ending up on the couch in the living room'.

That Christmas, Rebecca returned to see her parents in Canada, and when she got back in January 1974, Pierce was waiting at the airport to meet her. 'His hair was permed in a wave effect,' she recalls with a chuckle. 'I couldn't believe it. He asked me what I thought of it and I was as diplomatic as possible.' By then, she and Pierce had started talking about moving in with each other – even with his naff soccer-style hairdo – but she admits: 'Back then it was a big step. Neither of us had ever lived with anyone else.'

Years later, Pierce would say he enrolled at drama school in the hope of 'meeting lots of lovely young ladies' and that a romantic liaison was the last thing on his mind. 'That wasn't at all the way I'd planned it,' he said, referring to the relationship. Rebecca, now a mother of two who lives in Toronto, Canada, and works in local government, recalls: 'For both of us, it was our first serious relationship – and we were smitten with each other after a few weeks. There was something exotic about the affair. He was Irish and looked it, with his black hair and blue eyes, while I was from such a different land and background.'

In February they moved into a bedsit at 38 Narcissus Road, West Hampstead. 'There was a rather strict landlady there called Mrs Butler,' says Rebecca, whom Brosnan had by now affectionately dubbed 'Becca'. 'So we both wore rings and pretended to be married. We didn't know if the landlady would let us the room if she thought we were "living in sin".'

It was very basic, consisting of a bedroom and kitchenette. There was no fridge, phone or even television and they had to share the bathroom with the other couples in the house. 'The rent was £5 a week, but the thing I remember was how cold it was that winter,' says Rebecca. 'We had to put another £5 in coins into the gas and electricity meters to keep warm that first week.' Money was tight and to save bills the couple would do their laundry in the tub and then take a bath, or vice versa. 'But it didn't matter,' she adds. 'It was exciting just to be living together on our own.'

A few weeks after moving in, Pierce helped Rebecca make some marmalade from a box of Seville oranges she'd been given. 'There were bowls of the stuff all over the place,' she says. 'But Pierce never complained and we sold the jars to a health food store and made a bit of money.' She also threw a surprise 21st birthday party for him at their little flat in May. 'When Pierce opened the door and everyone jumped out, he practically had a heart attack,' she says.

Students weren't supposed to work during the college year but Pierce appeared in a kids' show during the Easter holiday. 'He played a nutty professor and really looked the part,' she says. 'He loved dressing up.' Meanwhile, his studies were going well and he sailed through his end of year exams, leaving him more time to be with his girlfriend.

'It was very easy living with him,' says Rebecca. 'It was a pretty rosy time. We were family to each other as well as lovers. I don't think he was "a man of the world" when I met him. I got the impression he hadn't had many girlfriends. He was certainly no Don Juan. We were just kids – but we certainly had the will! We were buddies. We never really had any rows. It was a very balanced relationship.

'We were both real bargain hunters and loved the flea market at Portobello Road. I'd always cycled around London and when I bought Pierce a bike for his birthday, we began to cycle everywhere together.' One of their favourite haunts was nearby Highgate Cemetery, where Karl Marx is buried. 'We spent a lot of time just walking around looking at the gravestones,' says Rebecca. 'It might sound a bit morbid but it's a fascinating place, and living in a bedsit, we liked to get out as often as possible.'

But the couple also just spent time at home together. 'I did most of the cooking, but on Sunday mornings he would do really great fry-ups. That was his speciality.' Being a cookery student, McKenzie also used to experiment in the kitchen. 'Pierce usually ate whatever I made, but he wasn't very keen when I gave him caramel glazed apples with scrambled egg one night. I can't say I blame him. It wasn't one of my better recipes!' He was also surprisingly domesticated. 'I was amazed to discover he could sew and mend his own clothes. It was pretty rare to find a man that domesticated at the time. But I suppose with his mother working full-time he'd had to fend for himself and I think it did him a lot of good.'

The happy domestic arrangement was completed by the addition of a tabby cat called Woodstock – named after the bird in the Peanuts cartoon. All in all, it was a very loving relationship and Pierce would always be there for her. 'He was a very warm, caring person,' she says.

Just like everyone else, however, Pierce had his idiosyncrasies. Then, as now, he was fascinated by all things American – a by-product of his love for the movies. 'He smoked Camel cigarettes and stuck up the old packets on the walls of the flat,' says Rebecca. 'And I remember him saving up for weeks to buy a pair of Levi's jeans.' He also bit his fingernails and had a habit of playing with the ring he'd worn in his left ear since his Oval House days.

'I guess he was vain in certain ways,' says Rebecca. 'He always took care combing his hair in the morning and liked to look sharp. I remember him saying once that he thought he was better-looking than Clark Gable, and he was! But he was such a good-looking guy – he had beautiful skin, there wasn't a pimple to be seen – that he didn't really have to worry that much about his appearance. When friends saw us they used to joke, "Here come the beautiful couple".'

Once a month, the two of them would have Sunday lunch with Pierce's mother May and stepfather Bill, at the modest two-bedroom Edwardian house – now worth about £80,000 – in Edna Road, Raynes Park, south London, which they had saved so hard to buy.

'It was spotless inside and May fussed around him like a mother hen,' says Rebecca. 'She was very capable but obviously wore the trousers in the household. She also struck me as a very strong woman. I remember Pierce telling me how she'd failed her nursing exams two or three times, but just kept on persevering until she got them. His relationship with his mother hadn't been visibly scarred by the years spent apart. But while he was very close to her, he was also very independent.'

In the summer of 1974 the couple moved to Tufnell Park. They shared a flat with another girl, but things didn't work out. Their flatmate wasn't the only problem. 'The place was full of mice,' says Rebecca. 'You'd open a packet of cereal in the morning and you'd see these little eyes looking back at you. I was terrified of them and would scream my head off.' And did Pierce go to the rescue, showing Bond-like bravery against the four-legged fiends? Apparently not. While Brosnan wasn't exactly afraid of the furry little creatures, says Rebecca, 'he was a bit dithery'.

That summer, the lovebirds enjoyed a six-week holiday together in Canada, which Rebecca's mother had financed. 'Pierce was very excited about the trip,' she says. They flew out to Toronto (it was only Pierce's second time in a plane), visited her family's weekend home in the 'cottage country' north of the city, which is dotted with pretty lakes, and took a trip to the capital, Ottawa.

With the start of his second year at the Drama Centre, Brosnan once again threw himself into his studies. Unlike many of today's students, he didn't have to worry about the school fees, now more than £5,000 a year. He received a full grant, and looking back sentimentally says: 'I remember those years with great tenderness. There were no problems. We all had a grant and lived in similar circumstances. It was marvellous.'

However, managing money wasn't his strong suit, according to Rebecca, who says: 'When he got his grant at the beginning of term he'd be very generous – he was an impulsive spender – but by the end of term he'd be scraping around for pennies.' Though the couple always got by – even if it did sometimes mean 'eating potatoes every day of the week'.

Despite his easy-going nature, he had a growing determination to make it to the top – perhaps influenced by a growing awareness that he had what it took to make it. 'He was very centred, very observant and a fast learner,' observes one ex-student. 'Some people would talk, half-jokingly, about him being a film star, which certainly stiffened his resolve.' And his pillow-talk, says Rebecca, would sometimes revolve around his impatience with his classmates. It was a pivotal time in his life – for at long last he'd discovered he had a God-given talent that others didn't possess.

'I'll always remember one day chatting to Pierce in the canteen and asking him what his ambition was,' says Kathryn Pogson. ' "I want to be a Hollywood star," he replied without hesitation. He knew where he was going.' But Garry Cooper, who has appeared in television shows like *Emmerdale*, *Casualty* and *Heartbeat* since graduating, points out: 'He was obviously ambitious – but the ambition didn't form an overbearing part of his character.'

The second year was spent fine-tuning the students' acting skills and getting the members of the group 'to bond'. Outside directors were brought in, but any performances staged were usually for the sole benefit of the class. However, the third and final year was geared far more to public performances – and it was here, on stage, where it counted, that Brosnan really showed his mettle.

'His height and good looks, together with his inner strength, usually won him the powerful, charismatic, leading man roles,' says Cooper. And Pierce subsequently gave a series of 'extremely authoritative performances', according to Fettes. He played everything from a 'tigerish warrior' to a middle-aged actor-manager down on his luck – in plays such as Chekhov's *The Three Sisters*, John Ford's *'Tis Pity She's A Whore* (about the guilty passion of a brother and sister for each other) and Lope de Vega's *Fuente Ovejuna* (a masterpiece from Spain's golden age of drama about a cruel rebel leader). In the ultimate test of nerves for a young actor, all were staged in front of a paying public.

'Being Irish, he possessed an exceptional imagination and feel for language,' says Fettes. 'I think his unusual background also gave him a greater sensitivity into the working of other people's minds – and helped him bring a lively sense of reality to all his roles. Whatever he tackled – German naturalism, French farce or Jacobean tragedy – he did it with such style.'

For his final year presentation, attended by a handful of agents, Brosnan gave a dazzling showcase of the skills he'd acquired during his years as a drama student. The course tutors had drummed into students that there were eight basic personality types – and students now had to attempt to play all eight at the presentation.

Among the characters Pierce chose to portray was an IRA terrorist on the run, a timid Indian shopkeeper, a psychiatric patient and a flasher. 'He was the only one who could play all eight personality types,' recalls a fellow student. 'A lot of the students could only get beneath the skin of two or three personality types, but he had an amazing facility to understand the motivation of any character. It taught him a lot about his potential.' This tour de force also mesmerised the hard-to-impress Malmgren, who says: 'He proved himself as a classical actor, a character actor and a romantic actor. Above all, by delving into a character's psyche, he showed he knew his craft inside out.'

At the end of the year, just 16 of the original 32 students graduated. ('You don't survive the course unless you've got a hard core,' observes Tara Fitzgerald.) They proudly collected their acting diplomas, even though 'it wasn't worth the paper it was written on', according to one student. Now came the biggest challenge of all – finding work. For in a profession notorious for its high level of unemployment (usually between 25 and 50 per cent), finding that all-important first job has never been easy.

'We embarked on an endless round of summer auditions,' recalls Cooper. But before you can get a job you need an agent. 'Without one, you've had it,' says Fettes. And knowing the odds are stacked against an unknown drama student landing a job, agents are naturally cautious about adding them to their books. 'Out of a class of twenty-five drama students, maybe five will have a career in the business,' says one agent. 'Others will have work for a bit, then it will drop off.' In fact, about half the graduates of the Year of '73 were destined for a career in the business. But only one was destined to achieve stardom.

The end of the 1976 summer term heralded just as dramatic a change in Pierce's personal life. For at the start of his final year, he and Rebecca had moved into a flat in Leighton Road, Kentish Town. 'It was luxurious, compared to the other places we'd lived in,' she says. 'It even had central heating.' They spent a romantic weekend in Paris – where Rebecca discovered to her amusement that Brosnan couldn't speak a word of French – and enjoyed a brief winter break in Brighton, 'staying in a B&B and browsing in antique shops'.

After spending Pierce's second year working in the canteen at the Oval House, and then working as a freelance cook for a while, Rebecca took over the running of the Drama Centre canteen in January 1976. But while the arrangement allowed her and Pierce to see more of each other, she says: 'It also changed our relationship in a way. I remember he wouldn't want to pay for things. He'd come to the counter and say, "Give me this and give me that, I'll pay you later," and I had to tell him, "I can't give you free food in front of everyone else." It caused a bit of friction.'

At the end of the course, she and Pierce threw an end-of-year party – and all his classmates and tutors came along. 'I remember the floor was covered in wine at the end of the night,' she says.

However, by then Rebecca, who'd been going out with Pierce for two-and-a-half years, had decided cooking wasn't for her. 'I eventually got bored with it and began looking for something more challenging,' she says. 'I decided to go back to college to study English literature.' But while she could do the course at no expense in her native Canada, she'd have had to pay to study at a British university.

'Our paths seemed to be diverging anyway,' says Rebecca, adding that both had ruled out marriage because they were too young. 'Pierce was going to be on the move – which put a question mark over our relationship, because I couldn't face a life of following him around the provinces from rep to rep. And while he was a good actor and I had a lot of faith in him, I suppose part of me wondered how long it was going to take for him to "make it". It's a very competitive profession.

'In our hearts, we both understood that an era had ended and that, perhaps inevitably, we were going our separate ways. However, we didn't see it as a permanent parting. We were such good friends that we more or less assumed we'd get together again at a later date, although neither of us really knew what the future held in store.'

On the day of Rebecca's departure, Pierce travelled with her to Waterloo Station, where she would catch a train to Southampton and then travel back to Canada by boat – with Woodstock. 'It was a very emotional parting because we'd come to rely on each other so much,' says Rebecca. 'But it was also very amicable. I'll never forget the train pulling out of the station and Pierce waving me off.'

The couple kept in touch for a couple of years. 'I know Pierce had other girlfriends but he wrote regularly and I've still got stacks and stacks of his letters,' she says. 'He always kept me up to date with what he was doing. I remember one whole letter was about meeting Laurence Olivier who was one of his heroes.' But in 1978 Rebecca, by now living in Toronto, got involved with a new boyfriend – an artist – who didn't want her to have anything to do with her old boyfriends, least of all Pierce.

'That summer Pierce started calling me from England,' says Rebecca. 'It must have cost him a fortune because he'd be on the phone for up to twenty minutes a time.' The calls infuriated her possessive new lover. 'He hated Pierce ringing up, it caused rows between us, and he told me I had to end it. So the next time Pierce called I asked him not to phone me again.' It must have been a cruel blow to be rejected in such a way by the woman who, until then, had been his greatest love.

Ironically, Rebecca later split up with her artist boyfriend when he tried to attack her with a knife. And the following year (1979) she visited England – perhaps in the hope of rekindling her romance with Brosnan. She called him, not knowing that his circumstances had changed. 'He said "Don't call me anymore" and simply hung up,' says Rebecca. 'I guess it was tit for tat. I could understand that. I'd done the same thing to him.'

But that's not quite the end of the story. For in 1985 Rebecca happened to be in LA. By then, Pierce was starring in *Remington Steele*. She contacted the film production company and the pair hooked up. 'Pierce seemed pleased to hear from me, we made up and I spent a day at the studio with him,' says Rebecca. But her meeting with Pierce's wife, Cassie, was more frosty, perhaps understandably given the fact that she was an old flame. 'I remember her saying to me, "Oh, you look so slim now!" which struck me as a funny thing to say. "Miaow!" I thought.'

5. AN ACTOR'S LIFE

The summer of 1976 was one of the hottest of the century, and Britain basked in record sunshine. It was a time of endless queues for ice cream, bikinis in Hyde Park . . . and water shortages. Householders were told to put bricks in their cisterns, a Minister for Drought was appointed, and the crowd cheered when rain stopped play at Lord's cricket ground.

Of course, whatever the weather, the British always have a complaint. Either it's too hot or too cold, too sunny or too wet. But Pierce wasn't complaining that summer. For, unlike many of his drama school friends, he'd landed a job within weeks of leaving – at the Theatre Royal, York. It may have been as a lowly assistant stage manager, paying a meagre £36 a week, but it was a first tentative foot on the profession's ladder – and even more importantly, it was his passport to an Equity card.

Dating back more than 1,000 years, York has been dubbed the 'Bath of the North'. It's a city of ivy-clad and timber-beamed buildings, tea rooms and restaurants, museums, pretty pubs and historic churches. Famous for its Minster – seat of the Archbishop of York and home to countless treasures – it's a cultured, handsome and prosperous-looking place. Tourists flock to see its charms, and in the summer it's difficult to avoid the camera-clicking visitors pounding the ancient streets or craning their necks to get a better view from an open-deck tour bus.

A playhouse has existed on the site of the Theatre Royal since at least 1744. Some of the original architecture remains, but most of the building dates from the nineteenth century, and the four-tier auditorium is typically Victorian in appearance. A modern foyer, incorporating a stylish café-bar, was added in 1967. It's decorated with poster-size photographs of leading men and women going through their paces in some of the theatre's more memorable productions. But Brosnan is conspicuous by his absence.

On the other hand, perhaps we shouldn't be so surprised. After all, the job – which would involve a little acting as well as stage management – was his first. Arriving in mid-July, he found theatrical digs in St John's Street, and was almost immediately put to work – as assistant stage manager on his first production, Alan Drury's *Up And Away*.

The theatre's stage manager, Colin Johnston, reveals that Brosnan was less than excited about his new job, which involved making props (recalling his very first job), scouting for furniture, supervising rehearsals and making sure actors were in the right place at the right time.

'He obviously didn't really want to be a stage manager but you have to go wherever you can to get an Equity card,' says Johnston. 'Even then he was very focused and knew that he wanted to go into television and films.'

In the theatre's next production, Frederick Knott's *Wait Until Dark* (staged in August), Pierce got to appear on stage as well as help out behind the scenes. He played Sam Henderson, a photographer who is conned into smuggling a heroin-stuffed doll through customs. It was a small part and the action centred on the attempt by three crooks, led by the evil Roat, to get Sam's blind wife, Susy, to hand over the doll. The *Yorkshire Evening Press* singled out Brosnan's stage wife, played by Amy Nissen, for praise, but there was no mention of the young Irishman. However, he was at least mentioned in the programme, his two-line biography stating: 'Trained at the Drama Centre, London. This is his first appearance at York. Other theatrical experience – Oval House Theatre Company.'

Despite speaking no more than half a dozen lines, he still tried to bring his method acting skills to the part. 'Method acting and repertory theatre didn't really mix,' says Johnston. 'Pierce needed some time to himself before going on stage. In contrast, the old hands would turn up at the theatre a couple of minutes before going on stage and just recite their lines.' Even with such a small part, things could still go wrong. 'He had to fling open a door and invariably the lock jammed,' recalls Johnston, adding with a laugh: 'Pierce also borrowed a camera of mine for a prop and buggered up my lenses. He still owes me for that!'

But the play is also notable – in hindsight – for a rare, previously unpublished photograph of one of Brosnan's early stage performances. Sporting a moustache and polyester shirt (unbuttoned to the chest to reveal a silver medallion), flared trousers and a grandad-style cardigan, he looks every inch a seventies man – a huge contrast to his suave and sophisticated image in *Remington Steele* and *GoldenEye*.

Offstage, though, Pierce dressed somewhat more stylishly. 'He looked more rugged then than he does now,' according to one female admirer. 'He used to wear jeans, a denim jacket and a T-shirt, and he had a light stubble on his face – before it became fashionable! His teeth were slightly crooked then but, of course, he's since had them fixed.' He also wore his shirt collar up – like former Manchester United star Eric Cantona – and it became something of a trademark. 'Every actor has his own little idosyncracies,' says one old pal. 'It makes you stand out and you're taught to develop them at drama school.'

At the time, Johnston thinks Brosnan modelled himself on American movie stars like Marlon Brando and James Dean. 'I remember his party

piece was reciting the famous Robert De Niro line from *Taxi Driver* –
"Are you talkin' to me?" – in a New York accent.' (And Brosnan himself
later listed Robert De Niro and Robert Duvall as his favourite performers
– along with a certain Sean Connery.) Perhaps surprisingly, though, he
was then keen to play down his Irish roots. 'I distinctly remember him
telling me that his parents were Irish but he was born in London,' adds
Johnston.

He and Pierce shared digs for a while. The boarding house where they
lived was run by an eccentric old landlady, who was fascinated by the
theatrical world, particularly its camp side, and eventually married a
Spanish waiter so he could stay in England with his gay lover. 'She
pretty much gave us carte blanche to do what we wanted,' he says. 'The
house was disgusting, though. It was overrun with cats who would go
to the toilet all over the place and their droppings would just lie there
until someone cleaned them up. I remember we once found a mouldy
orange under a chair that looked as if it had been there for years.'

Meanwhile, Pierce and the rest of the cast and crew at the theatre
began preparing for their next play – a production of Arthur Miller's *A
View From The Bridge*, a modern-day tragedy written in 1960, which tells
the story of a Brooklyn longshoreman's possessive love for his beautiful
daughter.

Besides his usual behind-the-scenes duties, Brosnan also got to play
two minor characters – Mike and an immigration officer. His programme biography by now covered all of six lines and included
the information that Pierce had 'one of the most demanding jobs in
the theatre' and was 'involved not just in rehearsal and performance
but in assisting the Stage Manager as well!' The play opened to
favourable reviews and a local newspaper critic praised his 'enjoyable
cameo role'.

However, it wasn't all work. 'It was a long, hot summer and we had
a ball,' says Johnston. 'A whole gang of us would often go to The
Staircase Club or The 21 Club on a Friday night. Most of the company
weren't from York, and weren't planning to stay there long, so we
tended to socialise among ourselves. Pierce was the life and soul of the
party. He had a very dry sense of humour and could send people up
without them realising it.'

'There was a straight scene and a gay scene at the theatre but there
wasn't much mixing between the two – and there was never any doubt
which way Pierce swung! He had absolutely devastating charm. He was
very confident and sure of himself and had the women swooning left,
right and centre. The front-of-house ladies adored him and the canteen

staff had a real soft spot for him and used to give him extra helpings of beans on toast. He flirted with a lot of girls, but to my knowledge never took things any further.'

Not so, according to Lee Beaumont, who claims to have enjoyed 'a romantic liaison' – to use her words – with the young actor. 'I used to hang around in the café-bar and help out backstage,' says Lee, then aged twenty, who was taking a year out before going to drama school. (Somewhat confusingly, she was called Linda Davies in 1976, but changed her first name to Lee at drama school because she 'thought Linda was boring' and her surname to 'Beaumont' when she got married. 'If someone asked Pierce if he remembered Lee Beaumont, he wouldn't know who the hell they were talking about!' she jokes.)

'I still remember our first meeting. I was talking to a friend outside the theatre when he walked out. "He looks nice," I thought and our eyes met. It was a definite case of mutual attraction. Shortly afterwards, we bumped into each other at a party, chatted for hours, and started going out. He was a definite charmer. He was very much a gentleman and was the type to open doors for a woman. He was quietly spoken but had those smiling Irish eyes and the gift of the gab. Neither of us had much money and a night out to us meant going to the pub for a drink.'

The couple also whiled away many a happy sunny afternoon in the Museum Gardens – the landscaped parks a hundred or so yards from the theatre which lead down to the River Ouse. Peacocks strut around the park as if they own the place, cruise boats glide by, and young lovers kiss on the grass, as they've always done, oblivious to the rest of the world. 'It was a magical time,' recalls Lee. 'I remember Pierce spent a small fortune buying me ice creams that summer!'

In October, the Theatre Royal staged a new production of *Macbeth*. John Rhys-Davies played the lead role and Amy Nissen played one of the 'Weird Sisters'. But Brosnan had to make do with playing Macbeth's servant, which again gave him little or no chance to prove himself as an actor. He got to speak just two lines, not even appearing until Act Three, Scene Two, in this less than memorable scene:

Lady Macbeth: Is Banquo gone from court?
Servant: Ay, madam, but returns again tonight.
Lady Macbeth: Say to the king, I would attend his leisure. For a few words.
Servant: Madam, I will.
   (*Exit Macbeth's servant*)

All this must have come as something of a disappointment to the star student who'd played a string of lead roles in his years at drama school. And Johnston says: 'He made no secret of his frustration and he was keen to get on stage whenever he could – even if the role involved just a handful of lines.'

Over the next couple of months, Pierce helped put on a trio of productions. The first was an adaptation of *The Odd Couple*, the Neil Simon comedy that was turned into a hit television show starring Jack Klugman and Tony Randall. In a very different vein was November's staging of Dylan Thomas's *Under Milk Wood*, which poetically described a day in the life of the fictional Welsh fishing village, LLareggub (a reversal of 'buggerall'). In another about-turn, the popular farce, *Charley's Aunt*, then enjoyed a two-week run. In all three his involvement was frustratingly confined to behind the scenes work.

However, Brosnan finally got his chance to tread the boards again when he doubled up in that year's Christmas pantomime, *A Wizard Of Oz*, in which he played Fibula and a farm hand. 'Neither role exactly tested his method acting skills,' jokes a fellow actor in the production. 'But everyone involved had a lot of fun.' The witch was played by Marsha Fitzalan-Howard who shortened her name and went on to appear as Sarah B'Stard (opposite Rik Mayall) in television's *The New Statesman*. 'She invited all the cast to her parents' nearby stately home for afternoon tea one day,' adds the source. 'None of us had ever seen anything like it, Pierce included. It was palatial.'

After nearly 50 performances – ten a week – the pantomime ended in mid-January. Nearly 30,000 people had seen it, making it the theatre's most popular panto to date. And to Pierce's delight, a picture of him in the production ended up in the local newspaper, even though he was dressed as a farm hand.

The end of *A Wizard Of Oz*'s run coincided with the end of Pierce's six-month contract at the theatre. It was time to move on again, but that was an actor's life, as he was only too aware. Few of those at the Theatre Royal guessed he would go on to such heights. 'He didn't stand out as being destined for stardom,' says Johnston. 'Although you can never really predict who's going to make it – I've met so many good actors who've got nowhere and bad actors who've found fame. But he certainly got the breaks.'

His departure also marked the end of his short but sweet northern romance. 'He went his way and I went mine – there was no bitterness,' says Lee, who went on to land a small role in Derek Jarman's *Jubilee*, but has now returned as a production assistant to the Theatre Royal. 'Having gone out with him, though, I can legitimately say I used to be a Bond girl,' she adds with a laugh. 'You wouldn't believe how proud my fourteen-year-old daughter is that her mum once went out with 007!'

After his six months was up, Pierce found himself out of work, like so many struggling actors. 'I wrote letters,' he says. 'I wrote and I wrote. I worked as a taxi-driver and a dish-washer. I even worked in a greengrocer's. I could have gone back to commercial art, but somehow I felt if I did so I would be going back to square one. I felt I'd rather do some meaningless job instead.'

After enrolling at the Drama Centre, and then going to York, Brosnan had gradually lost touch with old friends like Stuart Turner. Once back in London, though, he re-established contact, albeit for a while. One of the last times Pierce hooked up with his adolescent friends was at Dennis Tritton's wedding in Shoreham. 'We stayed in a deserted house and walked along the beach,' recalls Turner. 'It was a great weekend.'

He and Pierce would also meet for the occasional drink in London – but the last time Turner saw him was at a party in 1977, when the actor was living in a basement flat in Bagleys Lane, Fulham. Among his flatmates was Pablo LaBritain, drummer with the punk rock group 999, which scored a string of minor hits with songs like 'Nasty, Nasty'.

'Everyone was trying to carve out careers in their particular field, so we didn't see a lot of each other,' recalls LaBritain, who still plays with the band. 'I was usually touring.' But despite no one having much money, they still managed to throw some wild parties, like the one Turner attended. 'It was a pretty chaotic night,' he recalls.

Another old friend at the party recalls retreating to the corner of a dimly lit bedroom in a bid to escape the pandemonium. 'All of a sudden Pierce walked in,' he recalls. 'He stood in front of a mirror, oblivious to my presence, and started striking poses with a cigarette,' he reveals. 'It was hilarious.'

Before long, though, Brosnan landed a role in Tennessee Williams's new play, *The Red Devil Battery Sign*. The American writer – best known for writing *A Streetcar Named Desire* – was involved in the production from day one. And to this day Brosnan treasures a telegram from Williams, now framed, that reads: 'Thank God for you, my dear boy.'

Set in a Dallas hotel, it's the story of a Mexican musician (played by Keith Baxter) and a senator's daughter married to a gang boss (played by Estelle Kohler) who act out a tempestuous affair. Strumming flamenco guitarists in the lobby provide uneasy reassurance while marauding gangs go on the rampage in city streets. After originally being lined up to play the part of Wolf – leader of the fearful-sounding Wasteland Boys – Pierce was offered the part of McCabe, the young male love interest, following a last-minute sacking. 'It was a poetical and lyrical play, but wasn't one of Tennessee's best,' the actor later admitted. 'But I was hungry – and it was a great break.'

Rehearsals began at the Round House, just around the corner from the Drama Centre, in May 1977. Estelle Kohler can still remember the first day the young Brosnan arrived on the set. 'He was a handsome young man,' she says. 'Although perhaps a little overweight.' And she, Pierce and the rest of the cast were thrilled to be working with Williams. 'We were all in awe of Tennessee,' recalls Ken Shorter, who in fact got to play the part of Wolf.

It transferred to the 1,000-seat Phoenix, in the heart of London's theatreland, at the beginning of July. Designed by Gilbert Scott, the Charing Cross Road venue opened in 1930 with Noel Coward's *Private Lives* starring Laurence Olivier, who later appeared there with Vivien Leigh. Others to tread its boards include Sir John Gielgud, Alec Guinness and Albert Finney. More recently, it has been associated with the hit musicals *Are You Lonesome Tonight?* and Willy Russell's *Blood Brothers*.

'Whenever you start in a play you always think it's going to be a great success, and we had high hopes for the production,' says Kohler, who has since appeared in many West End shows, including the long-running revival of J. B. Priestley's *An Inspector Calls*. However, the three-hour long *Red Devil Battery Sign* received decidedly mixed notices. The *Daily Telegraph* called it 'the work of a great talent in ruins'. While the *Evening Standard*'s Milton Shulman praised the performances but added, 'they cannot save a bad play'. The poor reviews didn't help box office business and takings never rose about 40 per cent of the gross.

Within two weeks, the American producer, Gene Persson, had put up a notice stating that he planned to pull the plug on the show after it had run up losses of £60,000. But the cast voted to defy the closing down notice and keep the production running, even though they would be working for nothing, hoping against hope that box office takings would rise and Persson would have a change of heart. Even Tennessee Williams dipped into his own pockets to help pay for press advertising. But by 23 July, the *Guardian* was reporting: 'The death throes of the *Red Devil Battery Sign* drag on painfully and anyone who's keen not to miss the play had better hurry along today.' Meanwhile, the finger-pointing had begun. 'Tennessee is not the most logical human being in the world,' said Persson. 'His life has been one of turmoil and most of his productions have been full of turmoil too.' But the owner of the Phoenix, Veronica Flint-Shipman, said: 'It's very depressing that someone like Mr Persson can get hold of a play like this and ruin it.'

Eventually the cast conceded defeat and the ill-fated play closed. 'So many people were owed money that it became impossible to carry on,' says Kohler. For Pierce and the rest of the actors it was a sobering reminder of the inherent instability of the acting profession. 'It was the first time a lot of us had been stung,' says Shorter. And Brosnan discovered that even when you landed a part there was no guarantee the play itself would be a success. 'Everyone was sad that it had come to such an ignominious end and we all went our separate ways,' adds Kohler. 'It was a really miserable time.'

Desperate to find work, that autumn Pierce fired off applications to a number of theatres, including the Palace Theatre in Westcliff, a sleepy seaside town adjoining Southend. 'He enclosed a photo and sounded interesting so I invited him along for an interview and offered him a part,' says theatre director Chris Dunham.

The role was in the gritty Northern drama, *The Changing Room*, penned by David Storey, which examined a day in the life of a rugby league team. (The writer had first looked at the sport in his novel *This Sporting Life*, which was turned into an award-winning film starring Richard Harris in 1963.) Even though the pay was just £45 a week, Pierce couldn't afford to be picky and jumped at the opportunity. It had an all-male cast and is perhaps most memorable for its nudity and coarse language. 'It wasn't the first time a naked man had appeared on stage at the theatre,' says Dunham with a grin. 'But it was the first time fifteen men had appeared naked on stage together!'

Pierce's character, Fielding, was something of a loner – not unlike Pierce, who once said: 'I don't have a lot of male buddies. I'm a fairly insular kind of person. I find it difficult to make friends. I worry that maybe people aren't going to like me.' He played the part with a convincing Northern accent. 'I pretty much left everyone to develop their own characters,' says Dunham. 'But even in such a large cast, it was obvious Pierce was going places. He was confident, knew where he was going and stood out.'

However, the play was a little too radical for the taste of Westcliff's elderly, conservative population. The local newspaper reviews focused on the play's 'bare buttocks and bodies' and the 'raucous, bawdy and uninhibited' nature of the entertainment. And even Dunham admits that it wasn't one of the Palace's more popular shows.

After a performance, cast and crew would adjourn to the neighbour-ing public house, The Plough, where 'Pierce could drink with the best of them', according to Dunham. But he probably needed to refresh the parts that other drinks didn't reach after prancing around on stage naked and having to change in a dressing room with a hole in the outside wall. (Builders were making alterations.)

In 1992, the Edwardian theatre – which, in truth, is more at home staging productions like Agatha Christie's *Murder On The Nile* than *The Changing Room* – celebrated its 80th birthday by publishing a souvenir booklet. It printed a list of 'great stars' who had appeared at the Palace. They included Una Stubbs, Roy Hudd and Terry Scott. But of Pierce, perhaps the biggest star to have trod its stage, there was inexplicably no mention.

His next stop – Glasgow's Gorbals, once notorious for its slums – couldn't have been more different from genteel Westcliff. Unlike the Palace, which was obliged to put on productions that would have local appeal, The Citizens' prided itself on being at the cutting edge of theatre, staging shows that were risqué, left-field and almost always controversial – prompting the *Observer* newspaper to call it 'the most cosmopolitan, idiosyncratic, mischievous and wilful theatre in Britain'.

Founded in 1945 by James Bridie, The Citz – as it's known throughout the acting profession – was the new name given to the Victorian jewel, the Royal Princess's Theatre, lying on the south of the River Clyde, fifteen minutes' walk from the city centre but worlds away. Bridie wanted to make Glasgow independent of London which now, as then, dominated British theatre. In its early years, The Citz had mixed success, but by the fifties had already established a name for controversy by putting on banned plays for theatre members only. It was the arrival of a new director, Giles Havergal, in 1969 – to be joined shortly by the flamboyant Robert David MacDonald and Philip Prowse – that really put The Citz on the international theatrical map, winning it fame and notoriety in roughly equal measure. Appointed at a time of crisis, Havergal sparked uproar by staging an all-male version of *Hamlet* in 1970 – and the theatre has never looked back.

'At one stroke, Havergal installed the most radically chic, and sexiest young theatre company in Britain,' enthused Michael Coveney in his book about the theatre, simply called *The Citz*. He went on to carve it a distinctive niche. 'There have been nods in the direction of the mainstream humanist European postwar theatre of Bertolt Brecht,' said Coveney. 'Eclectic flashbacks to the more Slavic extravagances of Meyerhold and Eisenstein . . . rare Coward revivals . . . British premières of Proust, Tolstoy, de Sade and Balzac . . . and daring assaults on the darker recesses of Jacobean and Restoration repertoire.' It soon became an 'actors' theatre' with stars like Glenda Jackson, Shirley Anne Field, Maria Aitken and Rupert Everett happy to work for a pittance to gain the prestige of having The Citz on their CV, which in turn helped to attract bigger audiences and generate a media buzz.

In 1977, when Brosnan arrived, The Citizens' Theatre looked like a building that had survived the Blitz. The surrounding slums had been bulldozed and it stood on a patch of razed Gorbals ground with only a bingo parlour and a huddle of shops for company. Along with the swimming pool opposite and bingo hall, it was the last public building standing in the area. With its shabby façade of Corinthian pillars supporting six battered Victorian statues it, too, looked ripe for demolition. The 'final vulgarian touch', wrote Coveney, was the notice plastered by the front entrance, declaring in huge block capitals: ALL SEATS 50p. After this the ornate nineteenth-century interior, with its horseshoe-shaped auditorium seating 750, came as something of a surprise.

The first production Pierce appeared in there was the world première of Noel Coward's play, *Semi Monde*. Written in 1926, it had never been performed publicly because of its homosexual overtones. Set in the lounge of the Ritz Hotel in Paris, it sought to capture the restless frivolity of the interwar social scene – a bitchy world long gone and little mourned. The stage was ringed by a wall of mirrors, while balloons and streamers hung from the ceiling, conjuring up a lavish party atmosphere.

Actress Ann Mitchell was among the 30-strong ensemble cast – and has fond memories of Pierce, who played a character called Harry Leftwich. 'He was witty and charming and looked a bit like Cary Grant in those days,' she says. 'His features weren't as chiselled as they later became, but possessed a certain embryonic beauty.'

By the seventies, though, *Semi Monde* was a rather dated period piece. There was too big a cast to involve the audience, and the cast of characters themselves – made up of the idle rich or hotel waiters and waitresses – didn't have a lot going for them.

In a review headlined 'Madly Gay Night with Coward Fails to Shock', the *Glasgow Herald* described the play as 'merely a parade of Coward characters going through the motions'; *Punch* admitted the play was 'peopled by caricatures rather than people' but recommended students of Coward check it out, and the *Daily Telegraph* suggested 'the real mystery is how this conversation piece ever came to be written'. But *The Times* thought it 'a memorable production' and the *Guardian* described it as a 'retina-ravishing spectacle'. Sadly for the actors, the sheer size of the cast made it difficult for critics to single out anyone for praise.

In February 1978, Pierce appeared in The Citz's adaptation of James Hadley Chase's *No Orchids For Miss Blandish* – the once-notorious 1939 gangster thriller which the author set in New York, despite never having been there himself. The biting black satire was about a Miss Blandish, a bored society girl who is kidnapped on her 21st birthday, locked in a tiny room above a sleazy bar, raped by a repulsive hoodlum, Slim Grisson, and finally degraded and demoralised by drugs. She is eventually rescued – but too late to avert her complete mental breakdown and subsequent suicide. Brosnan played the shady, camel-coated Eddie Schulz.

This, too, got mixed reviews. The *Guardian* praised the cast's 'convincing performances', the *Observer* commented on the cast's 'well-intentioned but bizarre accents', adding that it was the best Citz production for some time. And while *The Stage* found it hard 'to justify the play's resurrection', it did at least praise Brosnan for his 'good support'. Not for the first time, though, it was Scottish papers which were most dismissive – with the *Scotsman* saying 'both the play and production are lacklustre and tentative', and criticising the American accents for being 'sporadic and unconvincing'; and the *Glasgow Herald* describing it as 'tedious'.

The following month Pierce appeared in his third play at The Citz, *Painter's Palace Of Pleasure* – a new adaptation of William Painter's sixteenth-century compendium of Italian tales, which provided the inspiration for many a Jacobean tragedy. The new production featured a composite version of three plays – Ford's *'Tis Pity She's A Whore* and Webster's two revenge dramas, *The White Devil* and *The Duchess Of Malfi* – the common thread in all three being incest between a brother and a sister. The forty-odd roles in the three original plays were reduced to just fifteen, with Pierce playing Vittoria's lover Brachiano alongside his old Drama Centre pal Garry Cooper (a conspiratorial Friar) in the epic, nearly five-hour long performance of 'Jacobean sex, blood and thunder'.

Despite the set's superb funereal images – with candles and skulls enclosed by towering, windowless walls – reviews were, as usual, mixed. True to form, the left-of-centre *Guardian* gave it the thumbs-up, describing it as 'impressive', the *Daily Telegraph* found it a 'compellingly curious evening' and the local *Glasgow Herald* admired the 'deathly decor' but was disappointed by the production's lack of coherence.

Whatever the critics made of The Citz's various productions during his time there, Havergal has nothing but praise for Pierce. 'A number of actors had joined us from the Drama Centre and that's what interested us in him,' he says. 'He was a very striking-looking guy and went on to do some excellent work here.'

Glasgow was also the scene of another romance for Brosnan – this time with Patti Herley, a trainee nurse he met in 1978. Her marriage had just ended and she was holding a farewell party at the flat she was about to leave. 'My friend Trish worked at The Citizens' and brought some people along to the party,' she says. 'Pierce was one of them. As soon as he walked in I thought he was rather nice and our romance started then and there. That's what it was like in those days.

'He was delightful, very warm and affectionate and had a terrific sense of humour. Although in those days Pierce didn't have the drop-dead good looks he does today. He was fatter and had a chubby schoolboy face with crooked teeth. We had lots of fun.

'I remember one very funny occasion when I'd moved into another flat, a nurse's flat which I shared with my sister. Pierce had stayed the night and one morning Pierce and I were in bed when we heard this incredible banging at the door. Suddenly my sister rushed in and said that it was my husband. He said he had no hot water and needed to shave but I suspect it was just an excuse for coming around.

'Pierce panicked completely. He started wailing, "What if he finds me here?" The next thing I knew, he grabbed my blue silk dressing gown and dashed naked into my sister's bedroom. As my husband came in Pierce struggled into the robe and leapt out of the window. He hid in the bushes until the path was clear then scurried back to the flat and afterwards we had hysterics about it.' It's hard to imagine James Bond fleeing a girl's bedroom with such haste and so little style.

'He was a great guy,' says Patti. 'I wasn't even divorced and feeling rather hurt, and Pierce was wonderful, very loving and caring. He was very demonstrative; there was always lots of hugging and kissing. For a while we were both in love and it was extremely passionate while it lasted. I suppose we both knew it wouldn't last, though, because he was an actor going back to London and I was a nurse in Glasgow.'

His involvement in the *Red Devil Battery Sign* may not have been altogether happy, but it did help Pierce land a part in his second West End show, *Filumena*. Its flamboyant Italian director, Franco Zeffirelli, was known to cast beautiful young men in his plays and films. And rumour has it that after seeing Pierce's photograph in an actors' directory, he made a point of seeing him in the *Red Devil Battery Sign*. When he was preparing to stage *Filumena* in the West End, he therefore offered Brosnan a part.

The night they first met, Zeffirelli was with a group of handsome young male admirers. ('His sailor boyfriend was so handsome it wasn't true,' according to one member of the cast.) But despite Pierce's jokey claims of uncertainty about his sexual orientation, by now he knew that he was strictly a 'ladies' man'. And when quizzed as to what, if anything, happened that night, Brosnan says with a wry smile: 'I was never – ah – propositioned in any way. It was purely business.' Unfortunately, Pierce was under contract to The Citz for several more months – but Zeffirelli generously agreed to hold the part open for him until he was free.

It was an incredible opportunity for Pierce, who had now worked with Tennessee Williams *and* been chosen by Zeffirelli. His looks, presence and talent were already being spotted. He must have felt drunk with excitement and potential.

Eduardo de Filippo's sentimental comedy, *Filumena*, which had been adapted by Keith Waterhouse for British audiences, opened in November 1977 at the Lyric Theatre – one of Shaftesbury Avenue's oldest theatres. Having begun life by staging operettas, the 932-seat venue has subsequently specialised in light comedies. Hit productions include *The Winslow Boy*, *Habeas Corpus* and the long-running musical, *Five Guys Named Moe*. And Deborah Kerr, Antony Sher and Bob Hoskins have all graced the stage.

The Filippo play is the story of a fiery Italian couple, Filumena (played by Joan Plowright) and Domenico (played by Colin Blakely, then Frank Finlay). Rescued from a lifetime of prostitution by the wealthy Domenico, Filumena becomes first his mistress, then his housekeeper. After many years, though, Domenico decides to marry a younger woman. Filumena feigns a fatal illness and persuades Domenico to marry her in her dying moments. However, to his horror, she then rises from her bed, cured, and proceeds to explain various details about her three sons – one of whom, Michele, was played by Pierce – that shock him into silence.

The supporting cast included Trevor Eve, (star of the hit TV series *Shoestring* and *The Politican's Wife*) playing another son, Riccardo. During the production he met his future wife, Sharon Maugham (best known for her role in the long-running Gold Blend coffee adverts). Their courtship was punctuated by occasional flare-ups, say insiders, and one night Eve threw a chair out of a window in temper, hitting a passerby.

Unlike the *Red Devil Battery Sign*, the play proved an instant hit with the press and the public. The *Sunday Telegraph* declared Filumena 'perfect entertainment', the *Observer* called it 'a joyous event', the

Guardian thought it shone 'like a real gem' while the *Evening News* – which later merged with the *Evening Standard* – hailed the play as 'comedy of the highest class . . . a total triumph'.

Actress Marjorie Sommerville, who understudied the well-known actress, Patricia Hayes (playing the part of Rosalia) remembers the very first time Pierce joined the cast for rehearsals. 'This tall, rather shy man joined us one afternoon,' she says. 'The lighting was bad and everyone was rather blasé because they'd been through the scene so many times. But when he finished nobody moved because his performance was so magical.'

Working with the larger-than-life Latin maestro was 'exciting', recalls Brosnan, though it had its difficult moments. Disconcertingly, Zeffirelli had a habit of snatching a script out of an actor's hands and demonstrating how he wished each line to be delivered. 'He'd say, "Oh no, no, no! Itsa lika thees, you do thees . . . is no good, is no good!" ' recalls the actor.

One evening, after Blakely had left the cast and Frank Finlay was being rehearsed in, Pierce, for a reason inexplicable to him, fell foul of the temperamental Italian. 'He suddenly picked on me, tore me to shreds, went off, then came back and hit me a couple of times,' he says. The episode did little for his confidence and later that night he wandered down to Piccadilly Circus alone and contemplated his future. 'Confidence is a very fragile thing . . .' he says, trailing off in mid-sentence. 'My world was just torn asunder by that man and I wondered if it was worth the grief.' Shocked by the scene and knowing the distress it had caused Brosnan, Joan Plowright had a word with Zeffirelli and the following night he apologised for his behaviour. Try as he might, though, Pierce couldn't get the part to work Zeffirelli's way and says: 'As soon as Franco left town I went back to my way. I thought, "Bugger this!" '

Members of the cast recall Pierce well. Eileen Anson, who played a dressmaker, Teresina, says: 'When he joined I was still understudying the part. Some actors would treat you differently if you were an understudy. But he was always charming.' While Sommerville says: 'A lot of actors are always trying it on with the girls – or the boys. But Pierce didn't have the usual actor's flamboyance. He was somewhat reserved and deep-thinking which is unusual in the acting world. Most of all, though, I was struck by his immense personal charm.'

Despite Pierce returning to London, he and Patti kept in touch and she often drove down to London in her Citroen 2CV to stay at his scruffy basement flat in Fulham. 'Before I arrived he went out and bought a double bed in honour of my visit,' she says with a chuckle. 'I was quite touched.

'The Pierce I knew was usually penniless, though. His idea of a good night out when I visited him was to walk across Wimbledon Common to a pub called The Hand In Hand – a great place. The only time he wasn't broke was when he and a friend found a wallet stuffed with £10 notes. It came to £180 – a fortune back then. And like idiots they decided to blow the lot. They hit the clubs, ordering champagne all night before ending up at Claridge's for breakfast. I can still remember Pierce telling me: "Just imagine it, Patti, £60 for bacon, egg and sausage".'

He also wrote her several love letters, some of which she kept. In one, dated 21 May 1978, he asks Patti: 'Well, my love, how are you? You have been in my thoughts for most of the week and I look forward very much to seeing you again. I had a nice birthday. My parents gave me a snooker cue and a Marlboro lighter. So now I'm 25! Oh, guess who I met last week? The Fonz! Hey! He really was a nice guy. Very small little fella with a beard.' The letter ends: 'I miss you and look forward to seeing you. I love ya, Patti. You're in my thoughts. Love Pierce.'

Another begins: 'It was so good to hear you on the phone this morning. The time now is two in the morning and I'm propped up here in bed listening to a tape which reminds me of you, and us, when I was in Glasgow. Those nights then and the ones since I hold dear, and wish and want for many more.'

Patti, now a mother of three, married to a lawyer and living in Surrey, says: 'He was very much a one-woman man. He wasn't a philanderer at all – he was very loyal. In September 1978, he wrote to me to tell me he had fallen madly in love, but that if I ever needed a friend he hoped I could count on him. It was typical of Pierce. He was very much a gentleman.'

6. CASSIE

The woman whom Pierce had 'fallen madly in love' with was Cassandra Harris. His life is notable for the presence of three strong women. The first, his Auntie Eileen, a big woman who would physically fight his battles. The second, his mother, May, determined and somewhat domineering. But the third, Cassie – who was to be the great love of his life – was in many ways an even bigger influence on him. 'She was a unique woman,' he later said. 'She made me the man I am.'

The couple first met at a party in the summer of 1978. 'For me, at least, it was love at first sight,' says Pierce. 'I fell for her hook, line and sinker. She appeared like this vision before me: she was tall, she was blonde, she was bronzed, she was the most captivating woman I had ever met. I was absolutely bowled over by her beauty – and never dreamed she'd one day be my wife.'

However, that first meeting was hardly the stuff of romance. A friend of Brosnan's was staying at Cassie's house and had invited the actor – who was appearing in *Filumena* – around for a drink. 'My mate told me to help myself to the chicken in the fridge if I was hungry,' says Pierce, who admits he looked 'absolutely ridiculous' because his trousers were bunched at the ankles with bicycle clips, his hair was slicked back for the part he was playing and he was overweight from too much drinking. 'So Cassie arrived home to find a complete stranger eating her food and wasn't in the best of moods.

'Then she gave a party and, again, my friend asked me along. The evening wore on and the numbers dwindled until finally there were just a few of us left and the ice seemed to melt a bit.' Still nothing happened. 'My friend kept on telling me she liked me,' continues Pierce, 'so eventually I decided to do something about it and find out how she really felt. I bought a bottle of wine and some flowers, rang the doorbell and never looked back.'

As for Cassie, she soon changed her mind about 'the Irishman with the funny haircut'. She said: 'Once I got to know him I discovered we had so much in common – acting, books, music – and we never stopped talking.'

In the coming weeks, Pierce wined and dined his glamorous new girlfriend in traditional style, 'almost going broke' in the process. After all, he was still a struggling actor. 'She took some wooing,' he admits. 'There were a lot of candles and flowers and Van Morrison music, but you don't have to bedazzle a woman with wonderful gifts. It can be a simple thing like a quiet meal somewhere.' His determination paid off and within weeks he had won her heart.

Intriguingly, Brosnan once described Cassandra 'as a woman who had invented herself . . .' It's a telling comment. Everyone, to an extent, invents themselves. But what he meant was that Cassie had 'reinvented' herself (as he himself was to do). Anyone looking into her past is confronted by conflicting information, some of which is the result of her own 'story-telling'.

Born Sandra Colleen Waites, she often claimed she had an aristocratic Austrian mother. 'My noble origins didn't mean much in Australia because it's such an egalitarian society,' she once said. But like much of what she told people, that wasn't strictly true. Her father, Walter (or Wally), a builder born in 1919, and her mother, Roma, a hair stylist, were both of British descent. The couple married in 1939 and had two children, Sandra and Diane. Sandra was born in December 1941, the month of the Japanese attack on Pearl Harbor.

'Her parents were ordinary working folk,' says one old pal. 'And while Sandra was very fair, she never mentioned she was of Austrian or German descent, or had blue blood in her veins. Her mother certainly didn't talk with a German accent! She was a very down to earth woman.'

Sandra spent her early years in suburban Sydney before moving to Avalon, a seaside village on the Northern Beaches Peninsula several miles away. But when she was eleven years old, her parents split up. 'I think that made Pierce and I even closer,' said Sandra. One girlfriend from the time claims she had 'very bitter feelings towards her father following the break-up of the marriage' – something Walter Waites, a sprightly septuagenarian now married to his third wife, naturally disputes. Her mother, Roma, subsequently remarried, and Sandra took her stepfather's surname, Gleeson. (Tragically, though, Roma would be dead within a few years.)

Sandra attended Narrabeen High School in Avalon from 1955 to 1957 inclusive. The School Year Book for 1956 states that Sandra Gleeson was awarded the second-year history prize, and also received the prize for the 'most improved girl in second year'. The 1957 Year Book records that she passed the Intermediate Certificate examination. She left Narrabeen High at the end of 1957.

Every summer she and her family would visit a popular local holiday resort called Palm Beach. This was where she met Denice Reynolds who would become one of her closest teenage friends. She would even be bridesmaid at her wedding. 'We spent most of our time in the sea or on the beach,' recalls Denice, now a mother of four grown-up children, living in Gympie, Queensland. 'She was popular, full of life, loyal to her friends and adventurous. Nothing got her down. She got on well with her mother and stepfather, and if there was a party it would usually be at her house because her parents were very relaxed about that sort of thing.

'I remember Sandra always knew what she wanted to do. One day she told me how she wanted to go into acting or modelling. She certainly had the face and figure for it – she was tall and slender with long legs and a beautiful facial structure. Back then, though, neither of us ever wore make-up, and the Sandra I knew had little in common with the glamorous, sophisticated Cassandra of the future.'

After leaving school, Sandra worked at a local estate agent – but still dreamed of being an actress. She later claimed she began her acting career as a child at the Independent Theatre, Sydney, which has served as a training ground for many noted Australian actors. But Benita Harvey Brebach, who is writing a history of the theatre, says: 'There is no record of Sandra Gleeson at the Independent. She may have studied acting there and appeared in student or children's theatre productions, but certainly not in major productions.'

In 1960, Sandra enrolled at Australia's National Institute of Dramatic Art (NIDA) in Sydney. During that first year, she played minor roles in several student productions, and played the lead in Thornton Wilder's *The Skin Of Our Teeth*. However, she dropped out a few months before the end of the course.

While at NIDA she met Bill Firth, who was taking a building course at the University of New South Wales. 'We met through a friend,' says Firth, now a well-known Sydney architect. 'She wanted to borrow some tights so I lent her a pair of my sister's and then asked her out.' Love soon blossomed. 'She was a crazy, wonderful person and we were inseparable,' he recalls. The couple got married in 1964.

Sandra's first paid acting part was as a sexy air stewardess in a play called *Boeing Boeing* at the Palace Theatre, Sydney. The show subsequently toured Australia, visiting Melbourne, Brisbane, Adelaide and Perth. Actor Peter Jones, who also appeared in the play, but is best known for starring in the long-running TV series, *The Rag Trade*, recalls: 'She was a delightful girl.'

However, the long months on the road doomed her marriage to failure. 'It wasn't much fun being on my own in Sydney with Sandra hundreds of miles away,' says Firth. There were additional strains. 'I loved Sandra very dearly at first,' he adds. 'But she wasn't averse to stretching the truth and this landed her in all sorts of trouble. I found it difficult to cope with because you never quite knew what was for real.' A divorce followed, though Sandra and Bill, who has since remarried, remained friends. This fondness for 'stretching the truth' is also commented on by Denice Reynolds (now McDougall). 'The further Sandra went in life, the greater her imagination grew,' she says. 'In every interview I ever read, she knocked at least eight or nine years off her age. I learned to take a lot of what she said with a pinch of salt.'

Her private life might have been a mess following the breakdown of her marriage, but career-wise things seemed to be looking up. The ambitious blonde got a lucky break, landing a part on the Australian TV show, *Beauty and the Beast*, in which 'Beast' Stuart Wagstaff and an all-female panel discussed problems put to them by viewers. She also starred in an early Bruce Beresford film, *Five Days*, in which she and an actor playing an American GI on leave from Vietnam were shown nude in one scene, hand in hand on a moonlit beach. However, the nudity so shocked Australia's conservative television chiefs that Cassie was fired from the show. 'I received a letter saying I was sacked,' she later revealed. 'I couldn't believe it because the picture was really a very tender, romantic love story – and we weren't actually naked anyway, we wore body stockings.'

By the late sixties, though, with her career having stalled, she decided to take her chances in 'swinging' London. She claimed she left for England 'to join the National Theatre'. But the theatre has no record of her being there. 'If she'd appeared here we'd know about it,' says press officer Sarah Duncan. Later on, she also boasted that she had twice won the Actress of the Year award in her native Australia – but this, too, has proved impossible to verify.

Once in London, her good looks and outgoing nature opened a lot of doors that would have been closed to lesser mortals. And Cassandra – as she now began calling herself – was soon hanging out with the so-called 'smart set'. 'She was absolutely stunning,' says one friend who got to know her at the time. 'But she was also very bright. She had a great sense of humour, was fun to be with and had men buzzing around her all the time. She was much more than a pretty face.'

Photographer Joe Bangay, a regular contributor to the William Hickey column in the *Daily Express*, also got to know her well. 'She was tall, beautiful, had long legs and a very sexy mouth,' he recalls. 'She was a great socialite, very much a party animal and socially ambitious.' (Perhaps even more ambitious than Pierce when it came to money and fame.) She met actor Richard Harris's younger brother, Dermot, at one such 'smart set' party. He was a music publisher and a director of his brother's Limbridge Productions film company. It was a case of instant attraction for both, according to pals, and by 1970 they were living together at his beautiful home at 6 Child's Walk, Chelsea.

The street in Earl's Court Village, which has its own wrought-iron gate, has an intimate, Mediterranean-type feel, and flower baskets and terracotta pots vie for space outside the whitewashed houses with their Georgian-style façades. An estate agent describes number 6 – which boasts three bedrooms, three bathrooms and a fifty-foot garden complete with fountain and pond – as 'a unique property'. It was valued at £297,000 in 1986. Today it's worth even more.

Sandra went on to bear him two children in the space of a year – 'Dermot was keen for me to have babies,' she explained – and changed her name by deed poll to Harris. First to arrive was Charlotte – born on 27 November 1971 at St Teresa's Hospital, a private hospital in Wimbledon, which has since closed. Within days Richard Harris flew in from New York to see his new god-daughter. Christopher was born on 11 November 1972, also at St Teresa's.

However, it was to be a volatile relationship from the start, characterised by rows and bust-ups. Not that one old acquaintance was surprised, saying: 'Dermot was a piss artist and anyone living with him was guaranteed a rough ride.'

A new career as a model beckoned when Cassie was 'discovered' by Sammy Davis Jr. She was walking past the stage door of the London Palladium, where he was appearing, when he asked if he could take her photograph. The picture was published in a glossy magazine alongside the caption 'My Ideal Woman – by Sammy Davis Jr'.

Modelling work flowed in. She landed the part of the American Express girl in the television advert, becoming famous for uttering those immortal words: 'That'll do nicely.' Her photograph also appeared in Lord Lichfield's book, *The World's Most Beautiful Women*.

Her modelling also gave her acting career a much-needed boost. She won a part in Gerry Anderson's space series, *1999*; donned a red wig to play a villainess in *Dick Barton Special Agent*; and landed a role in the £3 million film, *The Greek Tycoon*, which starred Anthony Quinn in a story loosely based on Aristotle Onassis's rags to riches life. 'She played one of his girlfriends,' reveals a friend. 'But unfortunately the scene ended up on the cutting-room floor.'

Somewhat implausibly for a budding actress desperate for stardom, Cassandra also claimed in December 1976 that she'd turned down a part in the forthcoming Bond film, *The Spy Who Loved Me*, because it was too saucy. 'It's far too explicit and there are too many sex scenes of every kind – and I only got through half the script,' she said. Nevertheless, by the mid-seventies, Cassie had become a familiar face in the gossip columns of mid-market newspapers like the *Daily Mail* and *Daily Express*. 'She was beautiful, hung out with the beautiful people, and was just the sort of pretty girl whose picture brightened up a newspaper,' says one former gossip page editor.

But her worsening relationship with Harris filled ever-more column inches. In September 1975's *Daily Express*, the William Hickey page reported that Cassandra was to sue 36-year-old Dermot to get maintenance payments for their children, after she had left his Child's Walk house and set up home in a South Kensington flat.

'The nearest we got to marriage was last summer,' she told the paper. 'I felt we ought to get married for the sake of the children, and Dermot told me to go ahead and make all the arrangements at Kensington registry office. But we never went through with it. After that our relationship deteriorated. It's all very sad that this has happened because we both love the children. I hope the situation can be settled amicably.' She was subsequently awarded more than £1,000 a year maintenance at London's Marlborough Street Court.

But despite her undeniable beauty, the 'coolly elegant Cassandra', as she was usually described in the gossip pages, didn't enjoy the best of health. In the spring of 1976 she underwent heart surgery and spent four weeks recuperating at Guy's Hospital. The drama drew her and Harris together once again. 'I shall be staying at his house until I am fully recovered,' she told the *Daily Mail*. 'But I am not sure about the future.' By June 1976, the couple seemed to be fully reconciled. She spent six weeks relaxing with Dermot and their children at Richard Harris's holiday home on Paradise Island in the Bahamas. And the couple were finally planning to wed, reported a newspaper, adding: 'Friends are hoping the row-prone couple will actually tie the knot before the three-month notice expires.'

It was to be yet another false dawn, though. She and Harris never did make it to the registry office on time, and eventually she decided enough was enough and walked out of his life forever.

After ending her eight-year relationship with Dermot Harris in rather 'acrimonious circumstances', reported the *Daily Mail* in January 1979, 'actress Cassandra Harris has a new man in her life'. Little did Brosnan know it, but this was to be the first of hundreds of appearances in the gossip columns. 'We met at a party six months ago,' Cassie went on to reveal. 'Eventually we hope to marry.'

Looking back, Pierce describes her years with Dermot as 'very painful', adding: 'When I met her she was a woman who'd been hurt by a man who didn't quite know what he had in this wonderful lady and who was in pain himself. When I came along a lot of animosity was generated.'

He and Cassie moved in together just months after they met. Of course, getting involved with Cassandra meant becoming not just the man in her life – but becoming stepfather to the two children from her affair with Harris. Countless relationships have foundered on the tricky issue of stepchildren. Kids may not accept the new partner in their parent's life. The estranged parent may try to stir things up. Or a new lover may have little time for a partner's children from a former relationship.

Luckily, Pierce hit it off with Cassie's ready-made family straight away. 'When we started living together I was "Pierce" to them, then I became "Daddy Pierce",' he reveals. The children's youth helped them adapt to their new domestic situation. What's more, they had seen – and heard – the rows between their real parents. So when the likeable, easy-going Irishman appeared on the scene, memories of Harris – who would die of a heart attack in 1986 – soon faded. 'From the beginning Pierce was just Dad,' recalls Charlotte. 'I can't honestly say either Christopher or I ever had any difficulty adapting to a stepfather. We all had a lot of laughs.'

Within eighteen months, the couple had decided to marry – in happy contrast to Cassandra's protracted, on-off relationship with Dermot which was never formalised in law. 'I guess my Catholic morality caught up with me,' says Brosnan. 'I wanted marriage. I didn't want Cassie to be my girlfriend, I wanted her to be my wife. I wanted the children to be my stepchildren and any child we had to be legitimate. We could have gone on living together but we didn't want any loose ends.'

The marriage took place at King's Road registry office, Chelsea, the scene of numerous showbiz and high society weddings, on 27 December 1980. It was a fitting venue for an actor's – and Pierce's, in particular – wedding. For not only was Chelsea home to many screen stars, including his hero Laurence Olivier – but Ian Fleming had completed his first Bond novel, *Casino Royale*, a few streets away at Carlyle Mansions, Cheyne Walk. In fact, Chelsea was also the fictional home of 007 himself. The exact location is left vague, but the author tells us the spy 'lived in a comfortable ground-floor flat in a converted Regency house in a square off the King's Road. Parked under the plane trees was his 1930 four-and-a-half litre, supercharged Bentley coupé, which he kept expertly tuned so he could do a hundred when he wanted to.' Not in Chelsea, though, that's for sure.

A picture story about the wedding – showing Pierce in a fawn-coloured suit, Cassandra as stunning as ever in a matching skirt and top, and the two children in their best outfits – appeared in the following day's *Sunday People*. Brosnan was 27 and the caption said Cassie was '30'. In fact she was older, a lot older, some ten years older than her husband. (Had the paper known, it would no doubt have dubbed him 'her toyboy'.)

The day after the wedding Pierce's joy was complete when Cassie's children called him 'Daddy' for the first time – proof of his acceptance by the whole family. 'Now I think of them as my own,' he said proudly.

However, love and marriage didn't solve the problem of making financial ends meet. There were still mouths to feed and bills to pay, and Pierce was very much a struggling actor. One friend recalls: 'He was so impoverished in those days he couldn't even afford to bring a bottle of plonk to a dinner party.'

The couple rented a semi-detached Victorian house in Delamere Road, Wimbledon. Neighbour Jean Kirton, who had a daughter of Charlotte's age, got to know them well. 'Pierce was strikingly good-looking and Cassie was tall and willowy – they made the perfect couple. They were very much in love and Cassie made the house very cosy inside.

'They liked their wine but they didn't have a lot of money, and in between acting jobs Pierce would take any work he could get, be it helping out at the greengrocer's down the road or doing the odd job for my husband, Paul. I can still remember Pierce asking him, "You haven't got any work for me, have you?" He found him work as a labourer. They also drove a bashed-up old car which was always breaking down, so they'd often ask me to take the children to school.'

In 1980, Brosnan returned to the Palace Theatre, Westcliff, to star in Brian Clark's award-winning play, *Whose Life Is It Anyway?* This time he got a respectable £85 a week – nearly double what he'd been paid during his earlier stint at the theatre. The play highlighted a pressing moral problem facing the medical profession – the question of a patient's right to live or die. It also questioned whether it was right for a hospital to detain a patient against his will or forcibly inject him with drugs.

He played Ken Harrison, who has been so severely injured in a car crash that he is paralysed from the neck down with only his brain functioning. Kept alive by the miracles of modern medicine, he demands to be discharged from hospital, knowing full well that as soon as he's disconnected from a life support machine he will die.

Staging the play posed special problems for Pierce because he had to sit immobile in a hospital bed in front of the audience throughout the show, moving nothing but his head. 'The part was a tremendous challenge because Pierce could only move from the neck upwards,' says Dunham, who turned to a local doctor for advice on the medical and nursing aspects of the production. 'At first, he found it frustrating but he soon got to grips with the role and turned in a solid performance.'

The production also posed another unusual problem – what to do if the bedridden actor had to use the toilet? 'The interval gave Pierce a chance to pop out to the loo and stretch his legs,' says Dunham. 'And we agreed that if things got really desperate he'd just have to ask one of the "nurses" to bring him a bottle – and pretend it was part of the scene. Luckily, though, it never came to that!'

But Pierce relished the challenge of the part, saying: 'As an actor, if you get an itch on stage, you can usually happily scratch away. Or if a hair gets in your mouth you can simply take it out. But I can't do that in this role. I have to try to beat it through mind over matter.' Nor was he bothered by another potentially embarrassing scene in the play – where he had to be washed by a nurse. 'I think Pierce quite enjoyed being given a bed bath every night,' giggles Dunham.

Actor Tom Conti had very much made the part his own during *Whose Life Is It Anyway*'s West End run. And Pierce admits: 'It wasn't easy following in Tom's footsteps – I had to cope with the fear that I wouldn't live up to expectations.' But local critics gave both the play and Pierce's performance a resounding thumbs up.

Meanwhile, Cassie had landed a part as one of the Bond girls in *For Your Eyes Only*, playing Countess Lisl opposite Roger Moore. Within minutes of meeting, she and 007 are kissing in the back of his white Rolls Royce after he's offered to give her a lift home. Once there, she invites him to share some 'oysters and champagne' but, needless to say, they're soon carried away by their passion for each other. The following morning the couple are ambushed by a bunch of buggy-driving baddies while strolling hand-in hand along a beach. The Countess utters the familiar refrain of the 007 damsel in distress – 'Oh, James!' – before meeting her demise. Exit Cassie just ten minutes after appearing.

It's debatable how much of a career stepping-stone a part as a Bond girl is, but the role enabled Cassie and Pierce to find the down-payment for a mortgage on a big terraced house in Manor Road, Merton Park, near Wimbledon. What's more, it gave the family a free, six-week holiday in the sun.

Even now, Charlotte has fond memories of the trip. 'I remember Roger Moore sitting us all down and taking lots of photographs,' she says. 'He always seemed to have time for us, even though Mum told us not to pester him. I was allowed to watch some of the filming and the bit I always remember is Roger sidling up to Mum and saying: "Your nightie's slipping. And so is your accent, Countess." I was in stitches.'

More than a decade on, *For Your Eyes Only* is perhaps most memorable for Sheena Easton's theme song of the same name. But after 1979's disappointing *Moonraker*, the 1981 movie – shot against a sun-and-sea Greek isle backdrop that involved 007 in a race with Soviet agents to recover a lost secret weapon – got generally favourable reviews.

'One fast-paced chase follows another,' said one critic. 'It features some of the best stunts in the Bond series, though Moore is clearly getting a mite too old for all this.' Although London's trendy *Time Out* magazine put the knife in, blasting the film for having 'no plot and poor dialogue' and concluding that 'Moore's old enough to be uncle to all those girls'.

However, determined Cassie still dreamt of her husband becoming a TV and cinema star – and with that in mind encouraged him to take any screen part he could get, no matter how minor. One of his first small screen appearances was in an episode of *The Professionals*, the long-running (1977–83) British cop show starring Lewis Collins, Martin Shaw and Gordon Jackson. He played a radio operator in *Blood Sports*, which saw Bodie and Doyle going undercover to save the life of a foreign diplomat. He also landed a small part – a speaking part, no less – in an episode of the *Hammer House of Horror*, called *The Carpathian Eagle*, screened in 1980. The drama followed a writer, played by Anthony Valentine, who was trying to solve a series of mysterious deaths.

Pierce played a tracksuited jogger in a park whose eye is caught by a bimbo in a pink mini-skirt. 'Do you fancy some coffee?' he asks, employing a pick-up approach so brazen it could get a man arrested in today's politically correct climate. 'I fancy you, you fancy me. Why mess about?' But after going off with her, he vanishes, becoming another 'missing person'.

His first film part was in the classic 1980 British flick, *The Long Good Friday*. The taut thriller told the story of an East End gangland leader, brilliantly played by Bob Hoskins, with ambitious plans to redevelop London's docklands with the help of Mafia money. Suddenly his empire is threatened with extinction after a number of disasters are inflicted on him by mysterious rivals.

The film turned Hoskins into a star – but the same could not be said for Brosnan, who got to appear on screen for little more than a minute, although he did get to bare his famously hairy chest to a cinema audience for the first time. The actor played the part of an IRA hitman. But even though he'd have had little trouble with the accent, he didn't get to say a word. We first see him emerging from a swimming pool in a pair of skimpy black trunks, making eyes at one of Hoskins's lieutenants, who is homosexual. The gay gangster follows Brosnan into the showers – 'Hi,' he says – and Pierce smiles back, affectionately stroking the man's chest before ruthlessly knifing him in the stomach.

He reappeared in the movie's final moments when Hoskins unwittingly steps into the back of a hijacked limousine. As the car speeds off, a sinister-looking Brosnan turns round and points a gun in his face. 'Afterwards everyone asked me what Bob was like,' says Brosnan. 'But I never even met him! A piece of white tape was put on a camera box and I was told, "Act towards that".'

He also got one day's work on the film, *The Mirror Crack'd*, a whodunnit set in England, starring a veritable Who's Who of Hollywood stars, including Elizabeth Taylor, Rock Hudson and Tony Curtis.

'I didn't say a word and I looked like a King's Road hairdresser,' chuckles Brosnan. 'My hair is all frizzed up, I'm wearing a fancy silk shirt, I've got rouge on my cheeks and a beauty mark – and I looked like I didn't have a thought in my head. Worse, I arrived late on the set for my one day's work, which was a scene with Liz Taylor. It was a scene within a scene and she had to clasp me to her bosom and say, "Jamie, Jamie". In the middle of this she spotted a woman standing on the sidelines and snapped, "Get that bitch out of my eyeline".'

The movie got terrible reviews. 'It's obvious after five minutes it's a complete no-no,' said one critic. 'The cinema equivalent of a bellyflop,' scoffed another. 'A Miss Marple mystery masquerading as a Royal Command performance in which all the American stars look stoned,' commented a third.

At last, though, Brosnan was beginning to make headway – thanks, in part, to catching the eye of Rose Tobias Shaw, a shrewd, London-based New Yorker and casting director who saw in him 'hidden depths of passion' and 'a brooding sexiness'. The first requirement of all good casting directors is intuition, and the second is having the courage to act upon it – and Rose, who 'discovered' George Peppard and Telly Savalas, says: 'I really went out on a limb for Pierce.'

In May 1980, he starred in *Murphy's Stroke*, an entertaining, tongue-in-cheek ITV dramatised documentary, directed by award-winning film-maker Frank Cvitoanovich, about an Irish gang which a few years earlier had come within a whisker of swindling £250,000 out of the bookies.

Then, while holidaying with Cassie and the children during the making of *For Your Eyes Only*, he got word he was being considered for a role in *The Manions of America*. His agent telexed him the script, Cassie rehearsed it with him and he flew back to London for an audition at The Dorchester Hotel, London. 'The job's yours,' the casting director told the overjoyed actor afterwards.

The £3 million American-made saga – described as an Irish version of *Roots* – followed the adventures of a nineteenth-century Irish-American family. Shot in Ireland and the States in early 1981, it also starred David Soul, Simon MacCorkindale, Barbara Parkins and Anthony Quayle.

Brosnan played troubleshooter Rory Manion – the hero of the story – an Irish patriot who becomes involved in the movement to free Ireland from British rule and is eventually forced to quit his beloved homeland for a new life in the States. But it wasn't easy work. 'I'm black and blue,' groaned Pierce, during the making of the mini-series. 'I'm doing my own stunts and I was riding bare-back and fell off my horse.'

Critics dismissed *The Manions of America* as a glossy, grossly simplistic Tinseltown take on history. One dubbed it a 'sluggish mini-series of primary interest to Irish-Americans'. While *Variety* branded it an 'evening soap opera flinging itself from distress to despair with little to relieve it'. However, it proved to be a hit in America, and with its screening Pierce became a nascent sex symbol. 'The reaction was incredible,' he says. 'Women wanted to touch me in the street and I got a bag full of letters.'

His success in the part helped land him a role in *Nancy Astor*, another costume drama, this time made by BBC in conjunction with Time-Life Productions. The nine-part series – screened in early 1982 – starred Lisa Harrow, James Fox, Sylvia Sims and Nigel Havers.

It told the story of the colourful life of Nancy Langhorne – later Astor – who became the first woman to sit in the House of Commons. Born in America in 1879, she fell in love with and married the Bostonian, Robert Gerald Shaw (played by Brosnan), in 1897. However, for all his good looks, Shaw was a womaniser, a drunk and a bully. He slapped his wife, threw whisky in her face and carried on behind her back, as the series showed. All too soon, Nancy realised her mistake and fled.

Pierce grew a Clark Gable-style moustache for the series and his convincing American accent put some members of the cast to shame. But he was puzzled by the popularity of the character with the ladies. 'Shaw was a terrible boozer and gave Nancy a very hard time but women seem to find him a knockout nevertheless,' he said. 'I think he must bring out the motherly as well as the sexual instinct in them.'

The couple divorced in 1903. Nancy went on to marry Waldorf Astor and carve out a unique place for herself in history while Shaw ended his days in obscurity. Pierce was luckier. These two roles – particularly *The Manions of America* role – were to prove a valuable stepping-stone, even if they were to result in him being seen as the archetypal good-looking leading man. Of all the roles to be typecast in, it's probably not a bad one, and certainly a lucrative one, but such roles sometimes lack in interest what they have in glamour. '*Manion* and *Nancy Astor* proved his big stepping-stone,' admitted Cassandra. But even she could not have guessed just quite how big a stepping-stone.

7. MAN OF STEELE

But for Cassandra's drive and determination, it's questionable whether Brosnan would have taken his chances in America, and, in true storybook fashion, found fame and fortune with a lead role in a new prime time television series that would rival *Dynasty* and *Dallas* as a ratings success.

The couple borrowed £2,000 from their bank manager – supposedly to pay for the installation of central heating – and flew out to Los Angeles with their 'lunches packed in paper bags' in late 1981, after Pierce's London agent had lined up a Hollywood contact. 'I didn't want to take the risk but Cassie has a great sense of adventure and encouraged me to go,' admitted Pierce. 'Either I stayed in England and worked as a mini-cab driver between the few acting jobs I was being offered or I took a gamble. Looking back, we'd have been fools to stay. I'd have plodded on, doing costume drama for the BBC – and we'd still probably be in Wimbledon, having to get out and push the car every time it broke down.'

They hired a saloon from Rentawreck (where you can get an old banger for next to nothing) and Brosnan saw every agent and casting director he could in two weeks. Then he learned that producers were still looking for the title role in a spoof detective series called *Remington Steele*. He put in a call and his work in *Manions of America* secured him an audition. 'I arrived in this beat-up old Pacer, looking very dapper in my suit and tie,' he says. 'Maybe that clinched it for me – they probably thought that anyone who dresses like that and drives a car that looks like that must have style.' One casting director – unable to place Brosnan's Irish accent after his years in England – asked 'how he had come by such a marvellous French accent?'

'We then returned to London. There were phone calls to and fro and they asked me to go out for a second audition – in front of three producers, the director, casting director and ten network executives! It was horrendous. Then the waiting began. I knew I wasn't first choice but I got the part. I guess I was the right person in the right place at the right time. Call it the luck of the Irish, if you like!' There was one condition – he was told to get his teeth capped and shed fifteen pounds.

The Remington character, a millionaire playboy turned detective, was in some ways a Bond spoof himself. And Brosnan – who admits he prepared for the part by watching old Cary Grant and 007 films – says:

'In some respects my Remington Steele was a cross between John Cleese, Cary Grant and James Bond.' (Although many people might have trouble spotting the Cleesean element in the character – you certainly couldn't accuse Steele of having a funny walk.) But if you're handed a first script with only two words – 'charming' and 'worldy' – to help with characterisation, you have to look somewhere for inspiration.

Despite drawing on such obviously British characters to play the part, Michael Gleason, the show's co-producer, has since revealed: 'I never thought that Remington should be British.' (Apparently, the show's producers originally envisaged Steele as a 45-year-old American.) 'But two TV bigwigs did. Then Brosnan came in for his interview. He sounded British – and was perfect for the part.' (Ironically, his Irish background would subsequently be played up for the benefit of American audiences, even though the character couldn't have sounded less like an Irishman.)

The dashing Remington Steele and his employer, the smart, sassy Laura Holt – played by Stephanie Zimbalist – teamed up by accident, according to the scriptwriters. Opening a detective agency, she found that a woman's name did not bring in much work so she invented an imaginary boss – Remington Steele – and business boomed. The trouble was that wealthy clients kept wanting to meet the supersleuth whose name was on the door.

Then along came a suitably handsome, suave man with a mysterious past she thought she could pass off as her boss – so she dubbed him 'Remington Steele'. He bumbled a lot at first . . . ('Let me find the clients,' Laura tells him. 'You have no training for this sort of work. All you have to do is put in a appearance and look good.') But he learned the private eye trade quickly and soon showed that he was more than a good-looking front man for the agency. 'Now I do the work and he takes the bows,' moaned Laura.

Ever since, viewers were given to understand, the unlikely duo had been solving baffling high society murders together. Even though Steele, a fan of old Hollywood movies, took an unorthodox approach to his work, preferring to nail his man by playing out scenes from classic films like *The Thin Man*, *Notorious* or *Key Largo*. In addition, while the investigative business traditionally called for a low profile, Remington could hardly have been more conspicuous, accustomed as he was to cruising LA's sun-kissed streets in a stretch limousine.

The show was slick, mainstream entertainment down to its catchy score – as was to be expected, coming as it did from the MTM (Mary Tyler

Moore Productions) stable which had already brought hit shows like *Hill Street Blues* and *Lou Grant* to the small screen. When he flew out to Los Angeles early in 1982, Brosnan initially only expected to stay in America for a few weeks to complete the pilot – six episodes at most. But following a private screening, network bosses instantly sensed it had all the ingredients of a hit show and gave MTM the green light to make an entire series.

He and the rest of the family booked into Hollywood's luxurious Chateau Marmont – for once, money wasn't a problem, as Pierce was now being paid what must have seemed an astronomical £20,000 a week – while they looked for a house and braced themselves for whatever the future held in store.

However, nobody was prepared for the extent of the show's success. Lightweight and easy to watch, it combined two American obsessions – money and glamour – which helped make it an instant hit Stateside when it was first screened on NBC in October 1982. Every episode had a title with a pun on the word Steele – such as 'Steele Waters Run Deep', 'Signed, Steeled and Delivered', 'Thou Shalt Not Steele' and 'Steele Crazy After All These Years' – which might be corny but was in keeping with the show's feel. So popular did *Remington Steele* become that it was soon airing twice a week.

At first, Brosnan claims the show's runaway success frightened him. 'I felt such a fraud because it was nothing to do with being a fine actor,' he says. 'It was about having screen charisma.' However, the series proved the perfect showcase for his talents, turning him into a star literally overnight.

His handsome features were soon adorning countless magazine covers (including *Newsweek*) and smiling down at passers-by on the fabled Sunset Strip. He was popping up in the gossip columns, challenging the likes of Tom Selleck and Patrick Duffy for the honour of being TV's biggest heart-throb. And he was getting up to 500 letters a week from lovestruck female fans. Of course, Pierce had wanted the series to be a success, but he was amazed at just how quickly it took off. 'My following in America is amazing,' he said at the time. 'I've become a heart-throb, a sex symbol or whatever you want to call it.' Though he made no secret of the fact that he liked the attention, saying: 'It does the ego good.'

It's not hard to see why Brosnan made such an impact. For a start, he looked good, whether he was wearing a Savile Row suit, a tan jacket, black silk shirt and white trousers, or a woolly jumper slung casually over his shoulders. And with up to ten costume changes a show – surely a record for a male TV star – viewers could be forgiven for thinking Pierce swapped outfits more frequently that his co-star, Stephanie.

But not surprisingly, given his drama training, he took offence when some people assumed that he was a model – a mere clothes-horse – before landing the role. Unlike many TV stars, he also liked to do his own stunts – including fight scenes – whenever possible. He even performed his own fire-eating stunt in one show, a legacy of his Oval House theatre training.

The adulation he inspired is reflected in this gushing piece penned by a smitten woman writer on *People* magazine: 'His facial features are sculpted out of soapstone instead of granite, his blue eyes really do twinkle and his six-foot-one-inch physique does not boast goalposts for shoulders . . . he is the thinking woman's hunk.' However, Pierce was inclined to laugh off the sex symbol tag, saying: 'My kids certainly don't think of their dad as a hunk. I'm a buffoon at home.' And when it was suggested he pose for a poster that would appeal to teenage girls, he quipped: 'If I do, I'll be wearing a tuxedo not a pair of trunks.'

He also brought a welcome lightness of touch to the role. (For instance, he plays polo in one episode. 'I never knew you played,' says a surprised Stephanie. To which Steele casually replies: 'Charles and I used to have a go at it whenever I was in London. Of course, now he's married we don't play as often as we'd like to.') He was self-assured, always had an answer and possessed 'lots of sauce', as one pundit observed. And this, along with his quiet elegance and understated sex appeal, was soon winning him comparisons with a screen star from Hollywood's golden age, Cary Grant. 'I'm flattered,' said Brosnan. 'But it's really Remington Steele that people are comparing to Cary Grant, not me.'

However he did confess: 'It's the role closest to myself that I've ever played.' (Considering some of his previous parts – such as the ruthless IRA terrorist in *The Long Good Friday* or Robert Shaw in *Nancy Astor* – it wasn't that great a revelation.) 'He's a self-taught fella, this Remington. He's full of sophistication which certainly hasn't come from being born into money and he has a rather meagre background, a bit like me really.'

But Cassie pointed out that for every character trait Brosnan and Steele shared, there was a difference, saying: 'I think he's the opposite of Remington, very careful and conservative, very precise, not one to take risks.' And Pierce himself admitted there was a huge gulf between them in one particular respect, saying: 'He's a bit of a cad when it comes to women – I'm incredibly faithful.'

Nevertheless, Brosnan soon discovered that making an American TV series was no holiday. Shooting in Hollywood meant working up to eighteen hours a day, one show finishing at lunchtime and a new one beginning in the afternoon, a new director walking on to the set as the old one walked off. Each episode was shot in a week – and making the series took up nine months of the year. 'The schedule is punishing,' he said. 'It just gobbles you up. After a day in the studio all I want to do is flop on to the settee and watch television.'

Memorising scripts, at least, became somewhat less of a chore than it had been in Britain. For, having rented a beautiful house in the hills above West Hollywood, Brosnan could now sit in the sun on the patio and learn his lines as he looked down on Los Angeles and the kids splashed about in the pool. (Early in 1983, Cassandra discovered, to her delight, that she was pregnant – and the birth of Sean in September finally gave her and Pierce a longed-for child of their own.)

As in subsequent hit TV shows like *Moonlighting* and *The X-Files*, a vital ingredient to *Remington Steele*'s success was romance – or at least the whiff of romance – between the leading man and woman. And this helped to win the series a devoted female following. The romantic possibilities are hinted at during the show's opening sequence when Laura says: 'We never mix business with pleasure . . . Well, almost never.' And while she dismisses Steele as an 'amateur' when it comes to detective work, she – like every other woman he meets – is powerless in the face of his charm. But to her frustration, she, 'the great detective', can never get him to reveal his past. 'Who are you? Where did you come from?' she sometimes wonders, looking at his photograph in the privacy of her office.

Her secretary knows Holt is secretly smitten by the suave Mr Steele and confesses that 'if she were in the market for a heart-stopping, teeth-rattling fling' she would look no further than Remington. But Laura coolly replies, 'I'm probably the only woman he's ever met who didn't tumble right into bed with him.' Given half a chance, though, you suspect she just might.

Of course, Remington strings her along for all he's worth. When she questions his ability, he fights his corner by emphasising the advantages of working together as a team. It requires 'long hours in cramped quarters,' he says, with a knowing look. 'The possibilities are endless.' You can almost hear her heart skip a beat. And at the conclusion of a successful case, he's not averse to sharing a celebratory bottle of champagne with Laura in the privacy of his apartment.

If only their relations had been half as cordial off-screen. In fact, potential conflict between the show's two stars, Pierce and Stephanie (daughter of TV veteran Efrem Zimbalist Jr of *Sunset Strip* and *FBI* fame), was built into the series from its earliest days. For while *Remington Steele* was initially conceived as a star vehicle for her, he always got more mail and publicity. And his popularity soon prompted the show's producers to upgrade his second fiddle role to joint star status.

She was furious about the show's shifting focus and in 1983 told one interviewer: 'I have to do something or when this show goes off the air, all anybody is going to remember is that Pierce Brosnan starred in it.' (Of course, her words were prophetic because that's exactly what happened.) But if her relations with Brosnan were frosty, they were positively frigid with Cassie, who saw Steele as nothing more than a stepping-stone to superstardom for her husband.

Not that she was the sole driving force in their partnership. For while Pierce could turn on the famous charm at the flick of a switch, a fierce ambition lurked unseen beneath his calm, cool exterior. 'Ambition isn't a dirty word here,' he said at the time. 'In England they say "he's so ambitious", as though that's a bad thing, but why shouldn't you be ambitious? I don't want to pennypinch all my life. I know exactly what I want – and I'm not going to end up at forty living off BBC *Plays for Today* and touring stage shows. I've worked hard but the buck doesn't stop here.'

Most actors in a leading role are usually full of praise (at least, publicly) for their co-stars – to the point of claiming they can do everything but walk on water. But there was always an obvious reluctance on Pierce's part to compliment Zimbalist and vice versa. 'I'm not paid to like people,' he once commented tartly. 'I'm paid to do a job.' The actor freely admitted they had had their 'differences' and weren't 'bosom buddies'. He also spoke of the 'underlying tension' between them, going on to reveal they 'never socialised and I don't think we ever will'.

It was said Zimbalist 'was something of a prima donna'. And while Brosnan never said as much when quizzed by reporters, the ambivalence of his answers – 'Growing up in Hollywood with a famous daddy is difficult and creates a lot of pressure on some people,' was as far as he would go – left readers with little doubt as to his true feelings. Typically, though, Brosnan would pull back from the brink and try to laugh off reports of difficulties, unconvincingly adding: 'They're always good clean fights. We put the boxing gloves on first!'

However, their feud became so serious that in due course Brosnan, when asked to put his arm around Zimbalist for a photo-shoot, refused. And the gloves were soon off altogether. 'I've got no time to deal with awkward leading ladies,' he said. 'Life is too short for that. Stephanie is a product of California, brought up in the business. We are not alike.' Then for good measure, he added: 'Women can be difficult to work with – and I'd like my next project to involve men only. I think I'd like to do a war film where leading ladies don't exist. What bliss that would be!'

Further proof of the bad blood between them came when Pierce's Irish fan club innocently sent out a newsletter showing a picture of him and Stephanie together on the cover – little realising its 'error'. After seeing it, Brosnan allegedly raged over the phone: 'I don't want that woman having anything to do with me. It's my fan club not hers.'

The star had agreed to let Irish fans set up their own separate fan club during a visit to Eire to film *Remington Steele* in July 1984. It marked his first return to his homeland as a celebrity. 'Coming back has been quite an emotional experience,' he said at the time. 'The show is very popular there. I took my mother and stepfather from London with me as a treat and they were quite impressed by all the fuss. Until then I don't think they'd taken what I do very seriously!'

Cast and film crew descended on Dublin's famous Phoenix Park racetrack one afternoon, to shoot a scene for an episode – naturally with a pun in the title – called 'Steele Your Heart Away'. Brosnan was mobbed wherever he went. 'Now I know how the horses feel in the enclosure,' he joked. Women fell over themselves to get his autograph while 'behind him moved his co-star, edging her way politely through the crowds, ignored,' noted the *Irish Times*. Only when the crowd couldn't reach 'gorgeous Mr Brosnan' did they feel it might be worth asking for her autograph. As for Cassandra, 'she didn't move four yards from her husband's elbow' all afternoon, according to the newspaper.

Somewhat embarrassingly, Pierce later had to apologise for a scene in which Steele walked into a pub one morning and found the locals knocking back their first beer of the day. While there was no malice intended, the scene laid the producers open to accusations of reinforcing Irish stereotypes – and a number of complaints were lodged following its transmission. In an attempt to pacify critics, Brosnan went on record as saying the programme was 'not a true description of Ireland' – then added that he hadn't seen the particular episode himself, indeed, he walked out of the room whenever the series was aired. Hardly a ringing endorsement of the show!

That day, two adoring teenage girls, Gina Hetherington and Ursula Gormally, met up with Pierce at the racetrack and persuaded him to let them set up an Irish fan club. 'He was very pleasant, as was Cassandra, but I got the impression that she was the one who organised him,' says

Gormally. And once it was up and running, it was Cassie who took control. 'If we ever wanted something we had to pass it by her first,' says Gormally.

At its peak the club had some 200 members. Most were teenagers and it will come as no surprise to learn that '99 per cent were girls'. Members received the 'P.B. Chronicles' – a newsletter that contained titbits of information about the star. For example, fans got to learn that Pierce took a size 15½ collar and could only say two things – 'go home' and 'sit down' – in Gaelic.

A couple of letters written by Cassandra to the girls survive and show just how tight a grip she kept on the flow of information. This extract comes from a letter sent that year to Gina:

> Just a couple of points – as Pierce legally adopted Charlotte and Christopher when they were young, we never want any reference in the fan club newsletter to the fact that they are not Pierce's own.
>   The fan club here tried to do that and Pierce almost wiped them completely – in fact I have. You know about the father's side – leave all that out in any news.

The Irish fan club lasted about a year before it fell foul of Brosnan by printing the picture of Pierce and his *Remington Steele* co-star in the newsletter. 'Since then Pierce has refused to supply me with information,' Hetherington revealed at the time. 'So I've been forced to close the club.' That wasn't the whole story, though. 'The club wasn't very well organised,' says Gormally, who left after a few months because she thought it was being run 'autocratically' by Gina and she was being given 'the donkey work'. But she insists the two girls never short-changed members, adding: 'If anything, we ended up putting some of our own money into the club to cover the costs.'

More importantly, on that trip to Ireland, Pierce would get to meet his real father for the first time since he was a child. Tom – or Tommy as he was known by the Brosnan side of the family – had eventually returned to his roots in County Kerry, after a wandering, working life, much of it spent in England. He now lived alone in a little three-room, terraced council cottage in Tralee, worlds away from his son's fabulous LA home. Despite his marriage having broken down more than 30 years earlier, a faded photograph of he and May on their wedding day still took pride of place on the dusty mantelpiece, while a colour picture of Pierce, cut from a magazine, had been pasted on to cardboard and carefully framed.

He was 'a lonely, lonely man' with a simple lifestyle, according to a neighbour. 'He'd cycle up to ten miles a day – he liked to be outdoors – and then pop into the local pub for a few jars.' But Tom wasn't entirely alone, for his nephew Pierce (Wallace) and niece Mary Daly, along with their respective families, also lived in the Kerry town.

'He'd sometimes go to Mary's for lunch,' says Wallace. 'And he always had somewhere to go at Christmas. You looked forward to seeing Tommy, but after lunch when everyone was watching telly he'd say what's on the other side and . . .' Despite drifting off in mid-sentence, you get the impression old Tom Brosnan would soon outstay his welcome. 'As he got older he got worse,' says Wallace. 'After a couple of pints he'd start talking as if he'd had six or seven. A lot of people around Tralee took the mickey out of him. He'd never back off – he thought people were out to get him. Half the time, you'd dread bumping into him because he could yell out something that could be embarrassing.'

But Brosnan didn't shy away from bringing up the subject of his father in the press. In a series of interviews earlier that year, he told how he himself had turned detective – just like Remington Steele – to track down his long-lost father. 'I thought about it again and again,' he claimed. 'I was very curious about him.' Pierce says he searched through a County Kerry phone book but there were dozens of Brosnans. 'The name is like Smith in that area,' he said. 'None was the right one.' (It was hardly surprising because his dad wasn't even on the phone.) Eventually, though, in his version of events, he got a lucky break, tracked down a distant cousin and in due course, hooked up with his dad.

But that's not quite how Wallace remembers it. 'I read somewhere that Pierce claimed he'd tried to trace his father, which is a load of rubbish,' he says. 'That's always bugged me, because I was the one who contacted him after a relative saw a photograph of him in the newspaper when he was filming *Murphy's Stroke*.' After getting in touch with Brosnan, Wallace arranged for the old man to call Pierce from his workplace at a pre-arranged time. It would be the first time father and son had spoken in decades.

'It was very emotional,' recalls Brosnan. 'My father just kept uttering, "My son, my son" and then broke down. He talked about my mother, saying she was the only one for him and that he'd never remarried but they just couldn't make it together. He said he'd tried to see me when I was small but there were complications. I was stunned. It made my brain whirl round. Quite frankly I could have done without dredging up those echoes of the past.'

However, father and son exchanged addresses, and back in Holly-wood a few weeks later, Brosnan summed up the courage to write a six-page letter to his father, telling him of his lonely childhood, his marriage to Cassandra and all about his family and acting career. In due course, Tom wrote back, telling Pierce how he had been a carpenter but was now retired.

Knowing he was coming to Dublin in the summer of 1984 to film a *Remington Steele* episode, Wallace suggested the time might be right for a reunion. But as the day drew close, Pierce became hesitant, worried about the reaction of May and his stepfather Bill, who were staying with him and his family at the city's luxurious Berkeley Court Hotel. 'I haven't seen my father since he shoved off all those years ago and I've no recollection of him at all,' said Pierce Brosnan then. 'The thought flashed through my mind that he only wanted to know me again because I was making something of my life.'

As usual, though, Cassandra was making her influence felt behind the scenes. She rang Wallace to spell out Pierce's worries about 'opening up a can of worms', but added that she was doing her best to reassure him and was confident the meeting would take place. The negotiations were 'protracted', according to Wallace, but Cassandra finally won Pierce round by asking the searching question: 'What if Tom dies and you've turned away from seeing him?' Somewhat ironically, the old man himself – the cause of all the fuss – was by now nearing 70 and had no idea what was going on behind his back.

Finally, it was agreed that the hush-hush, private meeting would take place in the Berkeley Court Hotel at 11 a.m. on a Saturday – no earlier, or Tom might have bumped into May and Bill, who were returning to London that morning. Pierce and the rest of the family were leaving for the south of France later in the day but he had set aside 30 minutes to see his father, who would be accompanied by his nephew Wallace, and his wife Kathleen, as well as niece Mary Daly (Wallace's sister).

'We were all excited,' says Wallace. 'I won't deny that – after all, Pierce was a star.' He and the others were up by six that morning, washing their hair and getting ready for the occasion. Tom had splashed out on a £70 suit and bought a teddy bear for Sean. 'But we were also a bit apprehensive,' adds Wallace. 'We didn't know how Tom was going to react.' When they arrived at the reception area, who should be standing in front of them but Charles Haughey, the Irish prime minister. And with a politician's instinct for pressing the flesh, he instantly shook Tommy's hand – even though the two had never met.

The actor and his family were staying in the Fitzwilliam Suite. When Wallace and Tom Brosnan went up, Pierce – who was dressed in jeans and a casual shirt – opened the door and invited them in. Cassie and the three children were also present. The introductions were made and Tom gave Sean the teddy bear. 'We all sat down but nobody quite knew what to say,' says Wallace. 'So I suggested bringing up my wife and sister – and once they'd come up the atmosphere eased. Cassie passed around tea and biscuits and everyone started chatting. We talked about anything and everything – but nothing that really mattered.'

After a few minutes, Pierce took out a camera and started snapping away – so his cousins asked if he minded if they took pictures, too, and he replied it was fine. The meeting was only supposed to last half an hour but Pierce then suggested they adjourn to the bar. No one argued. Pierce was going to buy the drinks but Tom, anxious to show he wasn't interested in his son's wealth, said: 'Put away your money, Pierce, I'll buy the drinks.' It was a noble gesture, but a round of drinks couldn't begin to make up for the lost years.

When the meeting drew to a close, Pierce threw his arms around everybody and bade them farewell, finally turning to his father. 'I'll see ya,' he said affectionately. 'It was very emotional,' says Wallace. 'There wasn't time to discuss the rights and wrongs of the past but I'd only ever envisaged the meeting as a means of breaking the ice between father and son, and under the circumstances, I thought things had gone pretty well.' Now the family ties had been renewed, Wallace and his relatives hoped it would be the first of many such meetings.

However, within weeks, Brosnan put a very different slant on the meeting, saying: 'My father and some cousins visited me on my last day in Dublin. We had photographs taken but he was a stranger and I was a stranger. There were no echoes of anything. He'd left no mark. How can you miss something that's never been there? We sat down and had a cup of tea and ate cucumber sandwiches. I would have liked to feel a rapport but there wasn't much to talk about. It wasn't until we said our goodbyes that the situation became emotional. It was sad but it was quickly forgotten. As far as I'm concerned, Bill is my father, the children's grandfather and the only father I've ever known. I don't think I'll see Tom again. I'm glad I've laid that ghost to rest.'

Back in Tralee, Tom – oblivious to this broadside – could not contain his glee, telling people wherever he went about his son, the Hollywood actor. 'That's my fella,' he would say. But regardless of whether they believed him or not, many locals made fun of his unlikely story – and it became something of a standing joke. 'He was a funny old bloke,' says one neighbour. 'We couldn't help wondering what he was doing living in a little council cottage if his son was the great Remington Steele. It didn't ring true.' Others would mockingly call out: 'When are you off to Hollywood, then?' as Tom rode by on his bike and then wink at their friends.

'He was soon a bigger laughing-stock than ever,' says Wallace. 'People treated him like the village idiot and kids would chase him down the street on his bicycle.' Upset at the way Tommy was being mocked, he and Mary supplied a photo of the reunion to the local newspaper, *The Kerryman* – which put it on the front page – hoping this would prove their uncle was telling the truth. 'They promised that the picture wouldn't go anywhere else and no money changed hands,' says Wallace. Within days, though, the photograph had been syndicated to newspapers and magazines all over the world.

When Pierce and Cassandra realised what had happened, there was a furious row. Cassandra rang Wallace to accuse him of 'betraying' their trust. Her anger was obvious in this extract from a letter she wrote to Gina Hetherington that September. 'We must tell you NOT to contact Pierce Wallace. Pierce Wallace sold some photos to the local paper and spoke of an interview that was supposed to be private and confidential to the press – so we don't want any contact with that side of the family again.' Cassie, understandably protective of Pierce, and in the heat of the moment, must have forgotten Wallace would never have deliberately upset his cousin, or caused ructions between Tommy and his son. Indeed, *The Kerryman* has officially stated that 'the question of paying money for [the photos] never arose'.

The star himself accused his father's side of the family of 'shabby behaviour', furiously adding: 'It was as if Tom just wanted to prove he was related to this famous TV star. That was hurtful. As for my cousins, they just burned any bridges that might have existed as far as I'm concerned. Only the bloody Irish could do it! A little respect, that's all that was needed.'

Now Wallace concedes that he made a mistake but adds, reasonably enough: 'When I discovered how upset Pierce and Cassie were I immediately regretted giving the picture to *The Kerryman*. But we didn't know how the media worked. And Tommy didn't know anything about the photos, so it wasn't as if he was trying to cash in on his son's fame. Looking back, I still don't think it was that big a deal. What's the harm in giving a photo to a local paper? We just wanted people to know that Tommy wasn't crackers. We can be accused of being naïve but we had his best interests at heart.'

Of course, Wallace couldn't know that Brosnan had deliberately kept quiet about the meeting because he knew it would upset his mother and stepfather. 'Bill had a heart attack after the reunion and I'm not saying that caused it,' says Pierce. 'But in the midst of it all someone sent him and my mother all the press cuttings.'

Perhaps the biggest loser in all this was old Tom Brosnan. Shortly afterwards he told of his sorrow at the bust-up: 'Pierce doesn't want to know and I've heard nothing from him since. I think he sees me as a bit of a blabbermouth. But the photos in the paper were just to show people around here I really am his "Da". A lot of the fellas in town don't believe it – they think I'm a right chancer.'

Just who did flog the photographs? *The Kerryman*'s chief reporter, Conor Keane, insists the paper was not responsible for the pictures ending up in Ireland's national newspapers. 'We didn't have the technical facilities to even transmit the photos,' he says. 'Besides, if we'd given a commitment to the family, we'd never have gone back on our word.' Another local media source points the finger of blame at the rival weekly paper, *Kerry's Eye*.

But Jerry Kennelly who, besides running a photographic agency at the time, was the son of *Kerry's Eye* editor, Padraig Kennelly, refutes this. 'That's simply not true,' he says. 'I'd have dearly loved to get my hands on the pictures, but the family refused to give them to me.' And a trawl though the back issues of *Kerry's Eye* reveals that it never carried the famous photograph.

So the mystery remains – and perhaps we'll never now know who flogged the picture. What is indisputable, though, is that someone somewhere made an awful lot of money out of the photo, and drove a lasting wedge between father and son.

In June 1985, Pierce and his family returned to Britain to shoot another episode of *Remington Steele*. During their stay they caught up with family and friends, and Pierce saw Bruce Springsteen in concert. However, while he and Cassie were asleep at the Mayfair house they were renting, the ceiling collapsed. 'We heard this terrible rumbling, then suddenly the ceiling started caving in,' revealed Pierce. 'We were covered in plaster and water and were lucky not to be badly hurt.'

Ironically for Pierce, despite having spent most of his life to date in Britain – eighteen years, compared to just eleven in Ireland – *Remington Steele*'s massive Stateside success was never repeated across the pond (except in Ireland). It was first screened on BBC 1 in the autumn of 1983 and, sure enough, hit our screens with the usual fanfare. From

Cary Grant to Hugh Grant, newspapers and magazines in the UK have always worked themselves into a frenzy whenever a Brit (even if he was born in Ireland and had since done everything to emphasise his Irishness) has made it big in Hollywood, and the same became true of Brosnan. But after just one season, the Beeb axed *Remington Steele* (although Channel 4 later resurrected it, airing it from the summer of 1986 to January 1987).

The British perception of the character was neatly, if cruelly, summed up in the *Boxtree Encyclopaedia of TV Detectives*. 'Remington Steele was Mr Cool,' wrote author Geoff Tibballs. 'He didn't pick his teeth in restaurants or blow his nose on the serviette. He didn't have dandruff, hiccups or excessive flatulence after eating cabbage. He had style. He was so handsome he made Robert Redford look like the Elephant Man and had glamorous girls swooning at his immaculately manicured feet. In fact, he was more of a blockhead because for all his elegance he had the personality of a plank of wood.'

Such criticism was echoed in this bitchy piece in the *Sun* in September 1983 by columnist Margaret Forwood:

> Once upon a time there was a good-looking Irish actor called Pierce Brosnan who made a minor impact as Nancy Astor's first husband in the BBC 2 series. And then ended up on the dole. So he went to Hollywood and became a star. Instantly. Overnight. Just like that. The sort of star who gets mobbed by frantic women wherever he goes. And all on account of his face. It doesn't matter if he can act or not – and it's difficult to tell when someone is wading up to their waist in rubbish like *Remington Steele*. It doesn't matter if he is required to speak dialogue that sounds like the twitterings of a deranged budgerigar. He's a star. The show itself is about a girl who invents an invisible male boss because people won't take a woman seriously. And to discuss it any further would be dignifying it with an importance that it does not deserve. It is the pits of the earth.

Such criticism wasn't unusual, although other newspapers were predictably a little less forthright in their views. Tibballs concluded that it flopped in the UK because 'its superficiality did not sit well with British audiences' and 'after 72 episodes the producers ran out of puns'.

In truth, the show's superficiality wasn't the only reason for its less than spectacular showing. After all, plenty of British and American shows have been just as superficial but proved a hit with viewers. Indeed, some might argue the more superficial the show, the greater its chances of success. Nevertheless, British viewers simply didn't buy the smooth, suave Englishman that Brosnan portrayed in the series. In essence, his character was an American caricature of the typical Englishman – and one that, for better or for worse, was light years away from the reality. But whereas such a character might have struck a chord with British viewers in an earlier era, it failed to do so in the eighties.

Of course, Pierce didn't agree with all his critics, but even he was ready to concede that a show like *Moonlighting* had a distinct edge over *Remington Steele*, saying: 'I was sad the series never had the same sort of mass appeal in Britain – but it just didn't have enough guts.'

A simple analysis of TV ratings hits and misses suggests that British audiences favour hard-hitting cop shows built around larger-than-life characters. For instance, two US cop shows from the seventies – *Kojak* and *Starsky & Hutch* – fulfilled both these criteria and became huge, not just in Britain and America, but around the world. In contrast, *Remington Steele* was more in *The Rockford Files* tradition – amusing enough but lacking that killer punch. The truth is that *Remington Steele* already looks dated. And when the history of twentieth-century television comes to be written it's unlikely to be up there with classic cop shows like *Hawaii Five-0*, *Kojak*, *Starsky & Hutch*, *The Sweeney* or *NYPD Blue*.

During its long run, Cassandra made several guest appearances as Steele's ex-mistress and expert conwoman, Felicia. 'Some husbands and wives hate working together but we love it,' she said. 'We'd like to be able to do so more often.' And Charlotte and Christopher had cameos in an episode filmed in Acapulco. While a number of then-unknown actors who guest-starred on the show – such as Sharon Stone and Geena Davis – went on to find fame.

By 1986, though, the series was running out of steam. No TV show can stay on top forever. Sooner or later, every story angle and character trait has been explored, viewers become bored and ratings slip. Originally airing on Friday nights, it was switched to Tuesdays for most of its run, and then moved to Saturdays in a last-ditch effort for high ratings – but nothing could stop the slide.

Relations between the show's two stars were no better, though for once, both agreed that something had to be done to shake things up. But the producers' one notable idea for invigorating the series – having the pair get married – infuriated them equally. 'If they force us to marry, they can find someone else to play Laura,' stormed Zimbalist. 'That is not the character I signed up to play.' Brosnan was no happier. 'They were quite vocal when it came to their characters,' recalls Gleason. Despite Stephanie's threat, Steele and Holt were married in that season's final episode. 'There was a lot of tension on the set that day,' recalls an insider. But the wedding still did nothing for *Remington Steele*'s ratings – and it was duly axed.

Critics felt part of the reason the show didn't exactly sizzle on-screen – compared to *Moonlighting* – was the lack of sexual chemistry between its two stars, a point Brosnan doesn't dispute. 'You never quite believe Remington and Laura,' he says. 'They pussyfoot around a situation – having a little kiss here and little kiss there. But things never got adult enough. It was too prissy, too cute.'

Just as *Remington Steele* was going through its death throes, a wonderful new opportunity presented itself. After thirteen years, and seven Bond pictures, Roger Moore had announced his decision to hang up his Walther PPK. Within days, there were reports in the press that Brosnan – by then 33, and a star – was set to take over the Bond role. 'It seems almost certain he will be the new James Bond when the latest 007 picture goes before the cameras this summer,' reported one tabloid in May 1986.

He and Cassie had often joked that he'd make a great Bond and when, following her role as a Bond girl, they were invited to 007 producer Cubby Broccoli's estate, Brosnan allowed his daydreams full rein. 'On the way home in our car, I kept turning to her and saying: "My name's Bond, James Bond." We laughed all the way home.' Newspapers had also latched on to the Bond-like qualities of Remington Steele and predicted that he'd be just the man to one day step into Moore's shoes.

There were a flurry of meetings and screen tests in the summer of 1986, and when Broccoli offered him the part he eagerly accepted. Playing the part would fulfil a long-term ambition – and he and Cassandra hurriedly started laying plans to return to London. 'I've asked myself again and again if I really want the role,' he said at the time. 'Do I want to get locked into another character after all those years as Remington Steele? And the answer is "Yes". I think I can bring something fresh to the part. And it does seem a natural progression to go from Remington Steele to James Bond.'

Thinking he had closed a chapter in his career, he took to trashing *Remington Steele*, saying: 'I thought it was a load of twaddle. After the first year I was bored with the character but they just wanted to press the button and keep making more money. It became too much like working in a factory.

'But I did it because it seemed a bit of fun. I thought I'd just do it, no one would pick it up and then I'd go back to London to see my mates and say, "Well, I've done Hollywood!" Then, when the pilot was picked up, my wife and I said to each other, "God, they're serious about this!" We were quite depressed. But I'd signed a contract to do the show – a seven-year contract, as it happens. Playing it was more of a stepping-stone than a life's ambition. But it's brought me wealth and success and at the end of the day that's what life is all about – surviving.' Clearly, to Pierce, once a small boy living with relatives, educated in a tough environment, with the mark of an outsider, survival is what it is all about. Survival is essential. Pride in one's work would just be a bonus. A bonus that was to elude him for a while.

The press even descended on poor Tom Brosnan to find out how he felt about his son landing this dream role. But that morning he must have got out the wrong side of his bed, for when newsmen knocked on his front door all they could hear was him moaning: 'Pierce Brosnan . . . Pierce bloody Brosnan . . . Pierce damned Brosnan.' And he was no more gracious when he opened the door, looking the worse for wear. 'Why on earth should I talk about him? He hasn't bothered to write to me for years!' fumed the old man. 'Talk to him in his Hollywood mansion but leave me alone. I just don't want to know. All this James Bond that and James Bond this makes me sick. It's all so much foolishness. It's like he's being treated as some kind of royalty. But I'll tell you this – there are far better actors than my son. I wish I didn't have a son, not a famous one. It's all too much hassle.'

It's hard not to feel some sympathy for Tom. He'd suddenly been catapulted from obscurity to a surreal sort of fame – all thanks to the son he'd barely seen in 30 years. And so much for the big reunion, he must have thought – he hadn't heard so much as a whisper out of Pierce since.

Of course, he couldn't have known that his comments would end up in newspapers the world over, but the outburst was typical of the man. It was just another example of him 'saying something out of turn' and 'making things hard on himself', as his relatives would have said. His problem was that he didn't think before he opened his mouth. 'It was unfortunate,' says Wallace. 'He didn't mean any harm but actors like John Wayne and Burt Lancaster were the heroes of his generation.' Not surprisingly, his actor son wasn't so forgiving and described the outburst as 'very sad'.

Meanwhile with the surge of publicity surrounding Pierce's probable 007 casting, NBC showed renewed interest in *Remington Steele*. On the strength of him being the new Bond, reruns of the show were getting much-improved ratings in America. And unknown to him, there was a clause in his contract which was about to put paid to his plans. Despite the series having been axed, the small print gave MTM 60 days to try to resell the show. Proof, if needed, that 'sod's law' really did exist, came when MTM sold a new series of the show to NBC – which would involve shooting six more episodes – on the 60th and final day of his contract pick-up.

'My first reaction was to tell them to shove the *Remington* contract,' says Brosnan. 'But they had me by the short and curlies and there was absolutely nothing I could do – they'd nailed me to the wall. In truth, I felt numb. The thing I find hardest to forgive is the way the television network resurrected the show without even having the courtesy to tell me. What is it with these people? But Cassie, despite being so strong, took it more on the chin than I did. She was heartbroken. I went out and played a lot of tennis. That's how I got some of the anger out of my system.'

After getting the news, Brosnan vowed: 'I might go down in history as the man who couldn't be Bond – but my agents are going to hit MTM hard and make them pay. There's a lot of blood left to squeeze out of them.'

The Bond role subsequently went to Timothy Dalton and Pierce publicly wished him well. Deep down, though, he was still bitter. 'One afternoon, I was driving along the Pacific Coast Highway, a few miles from my home, and I started thinking about what could have been and what I should have been doing,' he reveals. 'I became so angry that I had to stop the car. I ranted and raved and shouted to myself along a quiet stretch of the road, with just the sound of the gulls and the sea. I thought to myself, "You've lost it, Brosnan. This is it. Don't let them get to you. Just get back in the car and drive on." Eventually, I did. Very slowly. That's when I came to terms with the fact that not getting Bond was never going to leave me. However spectacular my career might be, I'd always be known for "nearly being Bond". It was a deeply depressing thought, yet I was going to have to come to terms with it in the years ahead.'

A year or so later, he was forced to watch the film against his wishes. Trapped in a jetliner over the Atlantic, the steward announced the movie would be *The Living Daylights*. His inclination was to pick up a magazine, tune into a music channel and blot it out. But his son wanted to watch so reluctantly he, too, clamped on the headphones and sat through the flick. 'I thought the story was a bit convoluted and I suppose I did think "If I'd done it . . ."' he says diplomatically. But you sense it was not an experience he wished to repeat.

Did anything good come out of the fiasco? Was it a blessing in disguise? Pierce must have been hard-pushed to put a positive spin on things at the time – but he was touched by the public's sympathy for his plight. 'People started coming up to me in the street, shaking my hand and telling me how sorry they were that I hadn't got the role,' he says. 'And I had dozens of letters of sympathy from all over the world.'

The only other good thing to come out of the whole sorry episode was that Brosnan found himself a superb personal trainer. When he was on the point of being signed up to play 007, the film company hired a keep fit expert to get him in trim. But, of course, as soon, as *Remington Steele* was revived, they stopped paying the bills. Despite the cost, Pierce kept him on – and never again had to worry about his weight.

Ironically, once it emerged that Brosnan would not, after all, be playing Bond, the ratings for the *Remington Steele* reruns fell once again – as anyone with half a brain could have predicted. Only six more hours of the show were ever shot, and despite the fact that Remington and Laura at last consummated their relationship, the shortened fifth season was not a success – and the last-ever episode was broadcast in February 1987.

After the show was finally cancelled for good, he said: 'I can't exactly say I'm sorry. In fact, I'm relieved because I don't have any emotional ties to it anymore. But I'm still proud of what we achieved. It's been a success and that's been, in part, thanks to me.' Asked, though, if he envisaged teaming up with Zimbalist again, he commented dryly: 'I'm sure we wouldn't kill ourselves to work with each other again.' As for missing out on playing Bond, that would soon be the least of his worries.

8. SHATTERED IDYLL

By the time Brosnan landed his breakthrough Remington Steele role, newspapers and magazines were just beginning to wake up to his and Cassandra's media potential as 'the most committed couple in Hollywood'. They were young, they were good-looking and glamorous, they embodied wholesome family values, they were about to become rich – and dashing, dark-haired Pierce would soon have the world at his feet. Untouched by a whiff of scandal or controversy, they were a publicist's dream.

One of the first of a multitude of fawning articles appeared in the *Daily Mail* in the summer of 1982. In a fashion spread, headlined: 'There isn't a smarter act to follow', the handsome star and his wife were pictured in a variety of summer outfits. 'Honey-blonde Cassandra' told how she favoured flat shoes as well as cool blues, whites and creams, in sheer georgette, soft cotton or easy sweatshirt fabrics in the summer'. While Pierce – 'a strapping 6 foot 1' – revealed: 'Cassandra prefers me in well-cut slacks, maybe a tie and a jacket – smarter than just jeans.'

Their move to Los Angeles in 1981, swiftly followed by the acquisition of a glamorous wealthy lifestyle, seemed to embody the aspirations of people everywhere. And over the next few years the showbusiness world's 'most glamorous young couple', as they were also dubbed, would generate page after page of invariably squeaky-clean, favourable picture spreads in glossy magazines, documenting the latest happenings in their exciting celebrity lives.

Unlike so many stars who have one topic of interest – themselves – Pierce's favourite role was that of family man, and he seemed happiest talking about his home life. 'I like to spend my days off at home with Cassie and the children,' he said in 1987, five years after moving to the States. Indeed, his life revolved around them. 'We're very much a solid family unit, so much so that we've never really become part of the Hollywood set. I cherish my home, I cherish Charlotte, Christopher and Cassie – and being a family man makes what I do worthwhile.' One friend suggested: 'Part of the reason his family is so important to him is that he didn't really have one for the early part of his life.'

Rarely can a man have spoken in such glowing terms so frequently about his wife. 'I never stop counting my luck when I think about Cassie,' he once said. 'She has dignity, beauty, humour, intelligence and humility – and has been my inspiration and my support. It just feels organically right that I should be with this woman and share my life with her, and her with me.' It was an extraordinarily close and happy marriage. Although, like any couple, they had their disagreements but were able to talk them through. For both, the marriage was an emotional refuge after uncertain, troubled childhoods – something Brosnan seems to acknowledge: 'Before I met Cassie there was a lack of a sense of family, I suppose, in my life.'

Unlike many – perhaps most – male movie stars, he wasn't embarrassed to admit that he, for one, planned to stick to his wedding vows. It may not have been cool to say as much in Hollywood's fast-living celebrity circle of the eighties, where drugs, alcohol and easy sex were a way of life, but Brosnan was more than happy to confess: 'I believe in fidelity – why get married unless you do?

'I have a beautiful wife who is a great mother, a great lady and a great lover. Some guys I've worked with go off on location and end up going out to clubs, pulling the birds and jumping into the sack. Then their ladies show up on the set the next week and they act as if nothing has happened. I find that hard to take. Sex is a very important part of our relationship and I have no need to look elsewhere.' He and Cassie even bought each other pink Russian wedding rings as a symbol of their mutual devotion.

Such loyalty was rare indeed in America's cinematic fantasyland and, as one Tinseltown insider put it: 'You can count on one hand the truly handsome male stars here who are faithful to their spouses.' Quizzed time and again about how he felt about being 'a sex symbol', Pierce would reply with a laugh: 'The only woman I want to consider me sexy is Cassandra.' He liked to spend Sunday evenings alone with his wife – and see her whenever possible during the week. 'We make sure that we have lunch two or three times a week on the set,' said Cassie. 'And if he's working late, the kids and I go down on location.'

While admitting that, like every other red-blooded man, he could not help but admire a beautiful woman, he drew the line at touching. 'Of course I flirt,' he once said. 'You have to keep certain things alive. The fact is, though, Cassie is very attractive and could find another partner very easily if she wished – and if I were unfaithful and she ever found out, I don't think she'd hang around.'

Is it any wonder women everywhere thought he must be God's gift to the fair sex? Not that Brosnan thought there was anything exceptional about his love for his wife. 'I know people who've been married a lot longer than us and feel the same way about each other,' he said. 'We just love being with each other and we're the best of friends.'

The happy family routine was no public relations gimmick either, confirm the children. 'My parents really did have a wonderful relationship,' says Charlotte. 'To me and my brothers it was just natural having a mum and dad who were so devoted, so family-orientated. They were always kissing and hugging, going horse-riding with us and planning surprises. After he'd been filming all day, Dad would come home exhausted wanting to spend the evening with us.'

Until she was eighteen, Charlotte – and Christopher – would regularly slip into their parents' king-size bed in the morning – with Pierce invariably being dispatched to the kitchen where he would play chef, and bring up wholemeal toast, jam and orange juice, serving breakfast in a funny foreign accent. However, Charlotte also caught sight of her father's 'Irish temper' – usually when playing tennis. 'Dad and I would always play Mum and Christopher at mixed doubles,' she says. 'If you were playing with Dad, he was fine and would be really encouraging. But he didn't like losing and if you were playing against him you could find out that he has some temper!'

The birth of his and Cassie's own child – christened Sean William – in 1983 was a cause of yet more celebration. 'I decided if I couldn't work and had to sit there and be a mother I may as well have another baby,' said Cassandra, by then over 40. It was a smooth birth – 'there was no panic' – and Pierce was there to provide support and cut the baby's umbilical cord. 'Having our own child just made everything complete,' he said. 'We both wept.

'If it wasn't for the success of *Remington Steele*, there's no way we could have afforded to have a baby. But now we're in the lucky position to be able to contemplate having another child, although I think next time we might adopt, as Cassie and I are keen for her to get back to her acting career.' Of course, her real age would have been another – unspoken – factor in such a decision. As it happened, they never did adopt a child.

They also took their parental responsibilities very seriously, worrying about the effect of Tinseltown – 'teenagers and Hollywood don't mix,' said Brosnan – and their itinerant lifestyle on their offspring. 'They couldn't travel with us, they had to go to school, and it just became a nightmare,' revealed Cassie. So at fifteen, the two older children were packed off to Millfield boarding school in Somerset (in 1995 the fees were £13,000 a year) because Pierce and Cassandra wanted them to appreciate their heritage. 'Sending them back to England was the best thing we ever did,' said Cassie. 'It gave them that bit of Englishness back again.'

Despite splashing out on a public school education, the couple were keen to ensure the kids didn't become archetypal Hollywood brats – turning up at school in their own sports cars and blowing a fortune on clothes at designer stores with gold credit cards borrowed from their millionaire parents.

'Keeping the kids level-headed in the face of the incredible materialism they see around them is a problem but we keep them on a fairly tight rein,' admitted Pierce. 'Luckily, Cassie and I are pretty down to earth – and Charlotte and Christopher have a fairly good balance because they saw me in London scraping together pennies to pay the milkman and remember the times we couldn't always afford to put petrol in the car. But Sean's only ever seen everyone driving round in limousines.'

They were also very conscious of the danger posed by drugs like cannabis, cocaine and speed that were freely available to Tinseltown's rich kids. 'Within any school there's a certain amount of experimentation these days,' said Brosnan. 'But Charlotte and Christopher tell us exactly what's happening. I've told them that I experimented when I was younger – but I've also seen people get badly screwed up by drugs.' Of course, this was another good reason to keep the two well out of harm's way, deep in rural Somerset.

Brosnan also drew on his own experience to give the kids the love and support he felt he did not enjoy in his own youth. 'It's taught me not to take their feelings for granted, to listen as hard as possible to what they say to me and to try to understand what it's like to be their age,' he said. 'I know how fragile our existence is and how the little day-to-day incidents that happen in life can colour a child's development. So I give Charlotte, Christopher and Sean as much love as I possibly can – to make up for my own lack of nurturing. This town can be especially rough on children because so many marriages end in divorce.'

New man that he was, Pierce even shared the cooking chores with his wife and a hired help. 'When we first married, Cassie was working more than me so I got some practice,' he said. 'I do the odd leg of lamb, pasta – and a good ratatouille.' Living in health-conscious California, he also found the strength to kick smoking. 'When I started on *Remington Steele*, I was on two packs a day, but after the first month of filming, I lit a cigarette and thought, "I don't like doing this" and stopped.'

What's more, in a business where going to church was considered less than hip – unless you were the wrong side of 40 or a member of one of California's wackier fringe religions – Pierce liked to go to Mass on a Sunday. 'I'm not fanatical about it,' he said. 'And to this day, I don't like obsessive Christians – they make me sick.' (A legacy, no doubt, of his strict religious schooling in Ireland.) 'But in my heart, I'm still a Catholic, and I need to talk to the Man Himself for a bit of comfort and strength.'

He certainly enjoyed his money, though, splashing out on a black Corvette and going into partnership with pools heir Robert Sangster to buy an Irish-bred racehorse, Salidar, for a six-figure sum. But Pierce still insisted that wealth and fame hadn't really changed him. 'I'm basically the same guy – but a little richer, I guess,' he would say, usually adding that he would willingly swap his jet-set lifestyle for the tranquillity of the Irish countryside. 'I'm a simple peasant at heart.

'Making all this money doesn't feel real – it's like talking in telephone numbers. Funnily enough, the money that means most to us is the few thousand we've made in repeat fees from a commercial that Cassie did in England for American Express. It's kept in a separate account and it feels like a fortune, because it's difficult to grasp the reality of what you're paid if you're a successful actor here.' Besides, there was always good old Cassie to keep his feet firmly on the ground. 'She stops me getting too pig-headed,' he would joke.

The couple soon became an essential part of Malibu's glamorous social circle which included former *Dallas* star Larry Hagman, Bruce and Andrea Dern, and film producer Jerome Hellman (*Midnight Cowboy*, *The Mosquito Coast*) and his photographer wife, Nancy. And they loved to entertain friends – US-style – by throwing a big barbecue. What did these people see in Brosnan – besides his obvious star status? 'There's still a lot of the little boy in Pierce,' said Hellman. 'There is a nice, attractive level of uncertainty, a certain degree of insecurity. You want to nurture the guy.'

The couple's rise to riches was a Tinseltown-style tale of good fortune – but life in LA wasn't perfect. Sure, Hollywood stardom brought perks like secretaries, nannies, maids and the freedom to jet off at a moment's notice for a luxury weekend break. And Pierce spoke in glowing terms of 'the space, the freedom and the supermarkets'. But he also admitted: 'All the clichés you hear about it are true – it's a company town in the business of entertainment and if you lose your sense of humour and perspective, you'll end up down the plughole.'

Being rich and famous, and living in a candyfloss, air-conditioned world of swimming pools, luxury mansions and limos did not shield one from the harsh realities of life – as the children, in particular, discovered when their beloved black labrador, Albi (who'd been flown over specially from England), was killed one night by the coyotes that howl in the Hollywood Hills.

There was also the violence. 'We were petrified when we first arrived,' said Brosnan. 'Absolutely terrified.' Within months he saw a man die a violent death. 'I was filming downtown when a guy staggered over to a cop on the other side of the street. He pulled up his T-shirt and he had a knife sticking out of his chest. His back was torn to ribbons and he just went over to the sidewalk and died.' But this being LA, the cameras continued to roll, because otherwise the TV company would have had to pay overtime. It must have seemed a long way from Wimbledon's leafy streets.

It also took time for Charlotte and Christopher to adapt to their new lifestyle. 'They were so excited when they first came here,' said Pierce, who indulged the pair after the lean years by taking them to rock concerts and movie premières. 'What child wouldn't be, with the swimming pools, surfing and Disneyland?' But unlike London, where they played with pals in the street, there was 'only the pool'. They were also teased by other kids for their English accents. 'Having been uprooted myself as a child, I saw myself in them a lot,' says Pierce. 'There's no denying they had a difficult first year but we all pulled together and they came through it with flying colours.'

As for being a heart-throb in a town famous for its sex-hungry, man-eating women, that was anything but a joke. 'The women in Hollywood frighten me,' he said. 'They're ferocious. They even attack me in the street. My wife might be standing beside me but they ignore her. It's so rude. Hollywood's such a strange place, especially if you're a celebrity. Suddenly, all sorts of people want to be your friend for all sorts of reasons and you have to wise up. If I were single and without a family I'd have burnt myself out by now.'

That wasn't the only disadvantage. 'I might be regarded as a sex symbol, but sometimes I'd just like to sit back, get fat and enjoy myself,' he said, only half-jokingly. 'I do have to watch the "old weight". I enjoy all the bad things in life. I enjoy beer. I love bread and butter, and sugar and cream cakes.' But his favourite snack of all was cornflakes – and he would sometimes tuck into five bowls a day.

'Instead I've got to spend my life watching my weight. I work out at the gym and run a few miles every day. In California people treat their bodies like gods. There's a constant pressure to look wonderful. As soon as we got a place to live in America we had a sauna, Jacuzzi and gym built. It's just the way you're expected to live. As soon as you're out of shape in America you're out of work. But at least Cassandra and I can sit back and laugh about it. It isn't an obsession with us. If we were both enormous, we'd still love one another!'

Of course, there were things about England that Pierce and the family missed, particularly their friends. 'We've got some great mates in London, and there isn't even time to write to them and tell them how much we miss them,' said Brosnan. 'Sometimes they come to visit, which is great, but they often think that Hollywood must change you, that you aren't the same. That's hurtful because it's not true.' They also missed the culture, the pubs and those 'silly things like hopping on and off buses, and having the milk and papers being delivered in the morning,' said Pierce, adding: 'I miss the music scene and the nightlife, too – because although Cassie and I have been out boogying a couple of times, LA's not a night person's city; it's culturally starved. It's got the movie industry and very little else. You can't beat London as a hothouse for the arts.' He even confessed to sometimes getting bored with California's endless sunshine.

'There is still a sense of coming home to England,' said Pierce, who now stayed 'en famille' at The Savoy whenever he visited the metropolis. 'But when I'm in London I kind of miss LA. I guess you romanticise things and when you go back it's not like you remembered it at all. There are times when I'm travelling so much I feel as if I'm in limbo. At the moment Cassie and I are still wandering, I suppose. We love LA, we have an enviable lifestyle but it doesn't give you everything – and I constantly find myself looking for a way out. It lacks substance and colour and character. If it all ended tomorrow, we'd just sell the house and move back to England. I'm sure we could survive without things like an electric gate and a swimming pool.

'The chances are that if I'd been brought up an Englishman, I might have seen my future with the National Theatre or the Royal Shakespeare Company. But the way my life has panned out, I've gone wherever my work has taken me – and I consider wherever I'm living home, really. Besides, America's been good to me and I get a buzz out of working here.'

In the summer of 1988, Tom Brosnan passed away – a sad, lonely old man forgotten by all but his immediate family. In his final years, he'd compensated for the loss of his son by lavishing attention on the children of his nephews and nieces. There's little doubt that young Sean would have adored his colourful grandad – if only they'd had a chance to get to know one another.

His health deteriorated in the last year of his life, and he was admitted to Tralee General Hospital in late July. Two weeks later – on 11 August – he died in his sleep – and at last found the peace he'd never found in life. He was 72 years old. The cause of death on the death certificate was given as pneumonia – but he was also suffering from Alzheimer's disease. The funeral took place at St Brendan's Catholic Church, Tralee. Only 50 mourners attended the service at the lonely, rainswept cemetery where the old man was laid to rest alongside his mother – and Brosnan was not among them. Tom's nephew, Pierce Wallace, says: 'We let Pierce know about the funeral but we didn't really expect him to come, so we weren't disappointed that he didn't turn up.' However, they were upset that the fabulously rich star couldn't find it in himself to send flowers . . . or even a card of condolence.

After the burial, Wallace told of his sadness at the actor's attacks on his father. 'I would very much like to meet Pierce once more, if only to set him straight on a few facts. It may suit him to think he was abandoned by his dad but that is not the case. It's disgraceful that the memory of a decent, generous man should be sullied like this. No one is pretending Tommy was a saint, but he does not deserve to be remembered so scandalously. He had it rough, too. If anyone paid for a broken marriage it was him – he endured thirty years of loneliness.'

The old man left little in the way of personal possessions. But when his relatives went around to his small council cottage to gather up the family keepsakes, they discovered he'd touchingly scrawled on the back of a kitchen prayer card this message: 'Please pray for me always. God bless all my relations. And neighbours too . . . Forgive me, Tom.' It was the nearest he would come to an admission that he, too, had made mistakes and perhaps not been the man he'd wanted to be. It was a sad but somewhat fitting epitaph to an ultimately unfulfilled life.

However, by then, Pierce had other things on his mind – for in December 1987, Cassie was diagnosed as suffering from ovarian cancer. She first suspected something was wrong when her stomach became swollen and she felt unusually tired. But a specialist told her not to worry, it was 'just that one of her ovaries had slipped'. It wasn't until she visited a second gynaecologist a few months later while in London, en route to Los Angeles from India, that the truth emerged. They arrived on a Sunday, Cassie went into the Portland Clinic for tests on the Monday, and on the Wednesday they learned the terrible truth.

'Life,' says Pierce, 'turned around on a dime.' Surgeons discovered a malignant growth on her ovaries. 'From day one, we really had a fight on our hands. This was not a shadow or a small tumour – this had invaded Cassie's being.' There are few early warning signs of ovarian cancer and the tumour was already quite large. In such cases, the five-year survival rate is less than 40 per cent. 'I remember asking the doctor how long she had to live,' recalls Pierce. 'And he said, "Ohhh . . . well, it's hard to tell" and left the room.'

Even now, the children can vividly remember the day they got the shocking news. 'At the end of the school term, Dad picked up Christopher and I from the train station and the minute I saw him I knew there was something wrong,' says Charlotte, then sixteen. 'He got us into a taxi, put his arms around us and told us Mum was ill. He didn't have to tell us it was serious – and we went straight to see her at Portland Hospital.'

Too sick to travel, Cassandra offered to stay in England while Pierce went back to the US to finish filming a *Remington Steele* episode. But he wouldn't have it, telling her: 'I'm staying with you, as long as it takes. We're going to fight this thing all the way – we're a team and nothing is going to beat us.' From that moment on, Brosnan handled everything. The couple had rented an apartment in London but saw no reason not to celebrate Christmas in style, as usual. 'Pierce made sure we had all the festive trimmings,' said Cassandra, 'and he even cooked Christmas Day lunch himself.'

Within days, she began undergoing punishing daily chemotherapy which made her hair fall out. After each session she would go to bed until the nausea had passed. 'The treatment was psychologically and physically brutal but she showed great dignity, courage and humour', according to her husband. Sometimes Sean would play nurse and that would cheer her up. She also began treating the cancer herself through meditation and a fat-free diet. 'My husband and children all went on my diet to help me stick to it,' said Cassandra. 'Instead of them eating one thing and me another, we were able to share our dinners as a family. It was their way of showing me how much they supported me.'

In addition, Cassandra read all there was to know on the illness, wisely questioned every prescribed treatment and decided which ones to take and which to reject. 'She had to,' insists Brosnan. 'As frightened as you are, you have to second-guess the doctors. I was the quiet party but I was always there for her.' Cassie even looked into the idea of joining a cancer support group but eventually decided against it. 'We decided we were stronger being by ourselves,' he explains.

About six weeks after the surgery, she returned to their Los Angeles home. Unable to hire outside help because his wife's immune system was so weak, Brosnan played mother and father for the next six months, turning down acting roles in favour of nursing his wife back to health. 'He cooked, he cleaned, he helped look after the baby, he just did everything,' said Cassandra. 'His sense of humour often lifted my spirits. I would be so tired and weak and he'd always pull me up. Late one evening I woke up and found him sitting in a chair reading a cookbook on organic Italian cuisine, and the next night he prepared the most wonderful pasta dish. He looked so proud when he served it. I told him, "If all your adoring female fans could see you now, slaving over a hot stove, they'd love you even more than they do now – but not nearly as much as I do."'

At first, Brosnan tried to keep his wife's illness a secret, but in due course it leaked out. 'Of course, it's been difficult for us,' he reluctantly told the press. 'But Cassie has a wonderful passion for life. As for the children, they've handled things extremely well. There have been times when they've had their own kinds of "breakdowns" but they're coping. When these things happen you just have to get on with life. We're a very strong family and we can win.'

However, his relationship with the press – and, in particular, the tabloids – never fully recovered from the way in which they covered 'the story' of Cassie's illness. In today's incredibly competitive media world, newspapers, magazines and TV networks care about just one thing – getting the story – and they're willing to stoop pretty low to achieve their ends. Unfortunately, the feelings of their victims do not come into the equation. Until then, Brosnan had by and large been treated with kid gloves by the press. Now he would discover what it was like to be the target of unwanted attention. 'It was inevitable that "the rags" would get hold of the news,' he said at the time, showing a rare flash of anger. 'Since they did, we've been hounded by people asking us all sorts of questions. How dare some lowlife inveigle his way into my life to get a story!'

In the summer of 1988, while Cassandra was having major surgery again, to take tissue samples to see if the cancer had gone, Brosnan was offered the part of Phileas Fogg in the TV mini-series, *Around the World in 80 Days*. But he refused to even consider the job, because it would have involved three months filming – on location in Hong Kong, Thailand, Yugoslavia and England.

'He insisted on staying with me,' she said. 'He told me "You're far more important to me than my career." Only after I'd called the doctors and they had promised him that they would see me through things did he agree to make the series – but even then he called me constantly to find out how I was feeling.' That operation, her second, revealed that

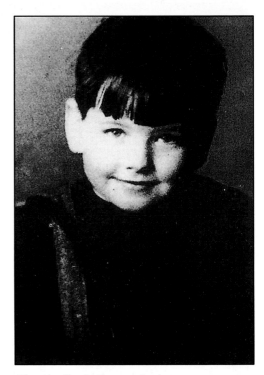

aby-faced Brosnan on a family
easide holiday *(msi)*

Already displaying a winning
smile for the camera *(msi)*

With his Aunt Rosie and beloved grandfather, Philip *(msi)*

Left Pierce in his Sunday best

Above Boyne Crest Cottage – where Pierce lived briefly with his grandparents

Below 2 St Finian's Terrace (second house along), where Pierce spent his early years

Teenage days. Pierce and a skinhead mate, Dennis Tritton, in a
Fulham back alley

lebrating Christmas with his mum May *(right)*, stepfather Bill *(front centre)* and best
nd Stuart Turner *(back centre)* in Fulham c.1970

Early 1970s. Underground and overground – it's showtime with
Busker Brosnan *(Colin Curwood)*

Wearing a tutu in Brighton
(Colin Curwood)

Out for belly laughs in a
Bradford street theatre festival
(Colin Curwood)

Rebecca McKenzie, 1973. This was Pierce's favourite photo of his then girlfriend

Pierce waiting for a train at Liverpool Street Station. 'He scoured jumble sales for Fair Isle jumpers,' says Rebecca

Even at drama school, Brosnan *(centre)* had that Bond charm

Student actor as future
star, Highgate Cemetery,
1974. Pierce sporting the
'new Clark Gable' look

Pierce as a brilliant but absent-minded professor in a children's
show, *The Dragon Who Came to Tea*, 1974

Christmas 1975,
with Rebecca at
his parents' house
in Raynes Park,
London

One Sunday in
spring at Camden
Lock, London,
1976

Pierce Brosnan and Amy Nissen in *Wait Until Dark* at the Theatre
Royal, York, August 1976 *(Theatre Royal, York)*

Standing tall in David Storey's play *The Changing Room* at the
Palace Theatre, Westcliff, 1977 *(John Alexander)*

Cassie *(right)* – young and beautiful in Australia, with her best friend Denice Reynolds

The Happy Day – Pierce and Cassandra tie the knot in Chelsea, 1980. Joining them are her two children, Charlotte and Christopher *(msi)*

With Stephanie Zimbalist, his sparring partner in *Remington Steele (Rex Features)*

With Jeff Fahey and a lawnmower in *The Lawnmower Man,* 1992 *(Rex Features)*

Brosnan plays the hard man in *Death Train*, 1993 *(Rex Features)*

With his wife Cassie and
their son Sean
(Rex Features)

Smiling through the
tears. Pierce with *(from
left to right)* Charlotte,
Sean and Christopher
after Cassie's death
(Rex Features)

'The name is Bond, James Bond …'
(Rex Features)

The *GoldenEye* première, with Keely *(left)*, the new woman in his life, and Sean, Charlotte and Christopher *(Rex Features)*

Above As producer and star – on the set of *The Thomas Crown Affair* (*Rex Features*)

Right With Keely and son Dylan (*Rex Features*)

Cassie still had faint traces of cancer, so she underwent another six months of chemotherapy.

By the spring of 1989, the couple were convinced she had conquered the killer disease. 'The doctors are pretty confident that my next test won't turn up any signs of cancer,' said Cassandra. While Pierce was saying: 'Cassie is doing extremely well. She's in great hands and has wonderful doctors. The situation has been addressed and she's clear.'

After 'winning' her fight for life, she and Pierce celebrated by arranging a 'saucy surprise' at a birthday party for Charlotte, eighteen, and Christopher, seventeen, at London's Savoy Hotel in October 1989. Guests roared with laughter as a male and female strippogram – dressed as police officers – stripped to matching G-strings and then pretended to arrest the startled youngsters for under-age drinking. 'It was a typical Pierce prank,' said a friend. 'But it was also a chance for him and the family to have some fun after a couple of very difficult years.'

Shortly afterwards, Brosnan and his wife first set eyes upon the sprawling £3.5 million fieldstone and stucco Malibu Hills house, then owned by one of the Getty clan, that was to offer them such comfort in the years ahead. Despite her 'recovery', Cassandra was still undergoing chemotherapy and 'was feeling rotten that day', according to Pierce.

The drive up to the house is like a scene out of a Hollywood movie. The sun glints off the cobalt-blue ocean, which flows and ebbs on the sandy shores along the stretch of Pacific Coast Highway between Hollywood and Malibu. You take a turn off the highway and climb a winding road. Twisting and turning, through the shade of trees, you glimpse white pillars, clapboard porches and verandahs hidden behind electric gates and bottlebrush trees. It's an area that has been home to some of Tinseltown's biggest stars – including Steven Spielberg, Barbra Streisand, Olivia Newton-John, Johnny Carson, Sly Stallone, Ali Mac-Graw and Rod Steiger. Finally, you take a steep curve and there is the seven-bedroom house, named Redtails after the redtail hawks that inhabit the area. Hidden from view by trees and flowering bushes, this hilltop eyrie is set in six lush acres, overlooking the Pacific Ocean. The interior is equally impressive. The living room is huge and high-ceilinged while marble passages lead to unexpected little rooms and terraces. An oasis of peace, it was the perfect place to escape the lunacy of Los Angeles. The Brosnans sat down beside the pool and, despite the price tag, made the decision to buy it with their *Remington Steele* money. 'It was love at first sight for both of us,' says Pierce.

The purchase symbolised the couple's renewed hope in the future and Cassandra declared defiantly: 'The important thing is to never give up hope, never quit fighting, never give in to pain and despair. If you believe you can beat cancer – and work with your doctors and have the love and support of your family – you can achieve miracles.' At last, it looked as if the couple's long nightmare was over. In fact it was just beginning.

9. BIG SCREEN DREAMS

His anger at missing out on the Bond role at the eleventh hour, together with the 'empty-headed image' he feared that *Remington Steele* had lumbered him with, left the actor more determined than ever to prove himself in the movies.

'Films are my future,' said Pierce optimistically. 'I could be just as good as Cary Grant or Clint Eastwood if I made the move at the right time. I want a long-term career in the pictures – but not as a manufactured sex symbol or poster boy.' After five years as Remington Steele, he was equally determined not to get trapped in a long-running television role, saying: 'My work before then was always diverse. I was trained for other things. I've proved I can do TV – now I want to see if I can make it in the movies.' But as all too many stars of the small screen have discovered – most recently, *NYPD Blue*'s carrot-haired cop, David Caruso – making it in the world of television is no guarantee of big screen success.

His first project, *Nomads*, shot during a break in the making of *Remington Steele* in the late spring/early summer of 1984, was an intriguing fantasy-cum-horror film, written and directed by New York-born John McTiernan. Pierce starred opposite the lovely English actress Lesley-Anne Down; pop star Adam Ant also appeared. The schedule was tight – Brosnan had to be back on the *Remington Steele* set by Monday 4 June – but he was excited about starting work on his first film in which he was the star.

The movie, set in modern-day Los Angeles, opens with a bearded Brosnan lying on a hospital bed with a bloody face and torn shirt, yelling his head off and looking like countless other LA 'crazies'. When Down, playing a doctor, shines a light into his eyes, he leaps up, knocks her to the floor, and promptly dies. After an opening sequence sure to grab the viewer's attention, the story unfolds via a series of flashbacks. Contrary to appearance, it turns out that Pierce's character is not a bum, but a brilliant French anthropologist, fluent in half a dozen languages, who after travelling the world has decided to settle in the City of the Angels with his wife. One night, a gang of vicious street punks – led by Ant – daub the words 'pigs' and 'kill' on the walls of their new home.

Meanwhile, Down starts having visions and proceeds to relive Brosnan's last hours. After the graffiti attack on his home, we learn that he followed the gang to a derelict warehouse, where he saw them murder an innocent man. He secretly took a number of photographs but on developing the film, finds that Ant and his accomplices have miraculously vanished. It turns out that the gang are the vengeful spirits of a nomadic tribe the Frenchman has encountered during his travels in a far-off land, and soon turn his life into a nightmare. In one memorable scene, Brosnan and his wife look down on LA from a viewing platform on the roof of a skyscraper, when a Nomad sidles up to him. Fearing for his life, Pierce throws the villain over the side of the building, while his wife and the other sightseers remain oblivious to the struggle.

Having incurred the wrath of this secret society of malevolent ghosts, the Frenchman's only escape is to leave LA for good. His demise is just a matter of time after his stubborn decision to stay. However, Lesley-Anne Down and his wife are luckier. They take heed of the danger and flee California. But who should they pass at the state boundary? A sinister-looking, leather-clad Brosnan, sitting astride a Harley Davidson, reincarnated as a wicked Nomad.

The look Brosnan adopted couldn't have been further from his squeaky-clean Remington Steele persona – his hair was lank and long, and he grew a scruffy beard, while the convincing French accent he adopted was meant to put further space between him and the suave TV detective. (The actor was attracted to the part, according to an insider, by the parallels between the Frenchman – who in one scene tells his wife: 'We have wandered so far from home' – and himself.)

Afterwards, Lesley-Anne Down gushed: 'Aside from his talent, Pierce is one of the best-looking men I've ever seen.' While he was equally complimentary about her, saying: 'She was great. We found out we were at neighbouring schools at the same time in London. I was at Elliott School and she was at Mayfield Comprehensive.' Pop star Adam Ant, making his big screen début, recalls Brosnan's concern that he might have hurt him in a fight scene. 'Pierce had to hit me over the head with a tyre iron,' he says. 'It was a fake, made of rubber, but we both got a bit carried away and afterwards he was really apologetic. He struck me as a real humble kind of guy.'

The film, shot in down-at-heel parts of LA, was aimed fairly and squarely at a youth audience. And despite its low budget, Hollywood moguls had high hopes for it. After the movie's British première, Brosnan joined a star-studded launch party at London's Limelight Club, where he was joined by two beautiful women – his wife and co-star. (Was it any wonder he was the envy of men everywhere?)

Reviews were mixed, though. One described Nomads as 'a thought-provoking and chilling shocker'. While another branded it 'stylish nonsense', adding: 'It would have been more striking if it hadn't been

500th in line.' The film was not a box office smash, though it would have a long shelf life in video stores. In hindsight, Brosnan says: 'I think I was so anxious to get away from my Remington Steele image that I went too far – growing a beard and wearing my hair long. I loved the film but it disappeared very quickly.' The real winner was McTiernan, who went on to direct three blockbusters in a row – 1987's *Predator*, starring Arnie Schwarzenegger, 1988's *Die Hard*, which established Bruce Willis as a macho big screen star, and 1990's gripping submarine thriller, *The Hunt For Red October*, which gave Sean Connery one of his biggest post-Bond successes, although some critics still consider *Nomads* McTiernan's most individual film.

After trying his hand at something so different, Pierce returned to more familiar territory in the old-fashioned £8 million Cold War thriller, *The Fourth Protocol*, based on Frederick Forsyth's bestselling book. Little could Forsyth (also an executive producer), or anyone else involved in the making of the film, have guessed that within a few years the long postwar struggle between East and West would be as much a part of history as the Russian Revolution.

The backdrop to the story was a treaty signed on 1 July 1968 by America, Britain and Russia to halt the spread of nuclear weapons. 'Four secret clauses – or protocols – were added,' claimed the novel. 'The most secret and dangerous was, and remains, the Fourth. Now someone is trying to breach it!' That someone is Major Valeri Petrofsky (Brosnan), a crack Soviet agent, despatched to England by a renegade spymaster, who wants to reignite the Cold War. His mission is to blow up an atomic bomb inside a US Army base.

The star of the film, shot in England in the spring and summer of 1986, was Michael Caine, playing retired SAS agent John Preston, on whose shoulders rested the the future of the Western Alliance. It was directed by John Mackenzie, who also made *The Long Good Friday*. And it had a strong supporting cast that included Ian Richardson (best known for his starring role in the hit TV series *House of Cards*), the late, great Ray McAnally (whose TV credits include *A Perfect Spy* and *A Very British Coup*) and the American actress Joanna Cassidy (who starred in *Blade Runner* and *Under Fire*).

The Soviet agent Brosnan plays first appears – wearing a long grey military coat not dissimilar to the old RAF coat he wore as a teenager – on the snow-covered Russian steppes, where he's given a top secret briefing. A ruthless killing machine, within minutes of the film opening he's claimed his first victim, an innocent Russian soldier doubling up as his driver.

Once in Britain, he swaps his uniform for a suit, tie and beige raincoat, adopts a perfect English accent and hires every boy racer's favourite car, a Ford Escort XR3. (Of course, he would in time graduate to an altogether more stylish Aston Martin.) The cold-hearted communist kills a homosexual who approaches him in a public toilet, spurns a sexy neighbour's amorous advances for fear of jeopardising his mission and shoots dead the female KGB agent (Cassidy) sent to assemble the bomb minutes after they've made love. As if that's not enough, he then calmly washes while her body lies lifeless in the bath.

It was one of those films where you just know straight away that the Russians haven't a hope in hell. A team of British agents, led by Caine, storm the house where Brosnan is hiding out seconds before he's due to detonate the bomb – and the two end up in a fight to the death. No prizes for guessing who wins.

To research the part, Pierce met a KGB spy 'of extremely impressive height who turned up with two minders who he pretended were interpreters'. He also learnt to ride a motorbike which he 'almost came off a couple of times'. As for Michael Caine, he 'was nothing but supportive', according to Brosnan. The two men struck up an instant rapport. Their wives already knew one another from their modelling days and the actor said afterwards: 'Michael, like me, takes Hollywood with a pinch of salt and plenty of humour.'

However, reviews were patchy. 'Despite being convincingly mean, Brosnan seemed to be after the record for the fewest lines of dialogue in a starring role,' said the *Washington Post*. Another review branded *The Fourth Protocol* 'a competent but somehow old hat espionage thriller'. While *Time Out* magazine singled out Pierce for criticism, saying: 'He poses and pouts so much that there are hopes of the film developing into a Bond-like spoof.' Being a movie star must have seemed a thankless task at times. Nor did *The Fourth Protocol* exactly set the box office alight. The Cold War furrow had been ploughed too many times to appeal to an eighties cinema audience weaned on the exploits of celluloid superheroes like Arnie Schwarzenegger, Sly Stallone and Bruce Willis. And the mysterious Middle Eastern businessman, Wafic Said – who hit the headlines in 1996 with a £20 million donation to Oxford University – reportedly 'lost a bundle' on the film.

His first real post-*Remington Steele* lead movie role was in *Taffin*, a low-budget gangster thriller set in Ireland. Shot on location in Wicklow and Dublin in the summer of 1987, Pierce played handsome loner Mark Taffin, a professional debt collector in a small town, living on the fringes of the criminal world. He drove a convertible red Mustang and had a way with words: 'I'll be back and I won't be selling subscriptions to *Reader's Digest*,' he warned one local who dared to cross him, while telling another: 'I think you need a change of scenery.' He swapped the playboy look and designer suits of *Remington Steele* for a fashionably scruffy style, sporting a two-day growth of stubble, shoulder-length hair, black leather jacket and cowboy boots; he also got to wear an earring for the first time on screen.

Within minutes of the film opening, he finds himself a gorgeous girlfriend – in true, movie-star style. Having 'put the squeeze' on her big-headed nightclub boss, worldly-wise barmaid Charlotte (played by ex-model Alison Doody, who went on to star in *Indiana Jones and the Last Crusade*) asks him for a lift home. He drops her off and she coyly asks: 'Are you coming in?' and the action shifts to her bedroom (if only it were that easy).

The story revolves around a plot by unscrupulous British businessmen and an Irish crime syndicate to build a dangerous chemical plant on the outskirts of town, and pocket a fortune when land prices rocket in value – even though it could have a catastrophic impact on the environment.

A former teacher at Taffin's Roman Catholic school, O'Rourke (Ray McAnally), leads the fight against the greedy Brits who are in league with corrupt local councillors. However, he and the other townsfolk soon discover that peaceful protest has no influence on the 'vicious, corrupt men' they're up against. So despite reservations about his methods, they eventually call on Taffin, who in Robin Hood-style goes to the rescue of the defenceless community.

One night he is ambushed and beaten up by thugs led by a tough-talking mobster (Irish actor Jim Bartley). The fight sparks a bust-up between Taffin and Charlotte, who's moved in with him after their night of passion. She storms out, muttering, 'I had a life before I met this guy and I'll have a life without him' – but you know they'll be reconciled before the end of the film. However, falling victim to the gang does nothing to weaken Taffin's resolve. Things soon turn even nastier. An upper-crust British businessman (played by Jeremy Child) is killed in a bomb blast and Taffin, who is suspected of being behind the outrage but is innocent, is deserted by the community. A hitman is hired to dispose of Taffin, who hunts down the gang and proves in the climactic final scene that 'mind can overcome might', according to the movie's makers.

The film, directed by Irish-born Francis McGahey, was sold to the public as a cross between a thriller and a modern-day Irish western. And Brosnan said: 'There's a western feel to it – Taffin is a quiet man, a loner with a conscience, a kind of Irish Clint Eastwood. It's a great character, it has some substance to it. And it fits like an old shoe. I'm Irish, it's my country, the sounds that I make are Irish sounds – and Taffin is a sort of Irish Dirty Harry.' As for the violence, he claimed the character used it 'in a very cerebral way, believing that the threat is far more terrifying than the act'.

Aside from the sentimental appeal of returning to Ireland, it's hard to see what Brosnan saw in the project. Slow-moving and predictable, *Taffin* has the look and feel of a seventies British cop show. Critics gave it short shrift. 'A confused and unexciting thriller . . . rarely generating any real tension,' said *Time Out*. 'The character of Taffin is too complex for Brosnan's limited acting talents, though he's good in the action scenes and displays his coarse good looks to advantage. Equally unconvincing is Taffin's passionate affair.' But *Halliwell's Film Guide* dismissively branded it 'a dull thriller that never rises above the mundane'. The film bombed.

Just about the only people who must have been happy with the movie were the Irish Tourist Board. For it featured some magnificent panoramic shots of the country – and one scene in particular, showing Brosnan and Doody lying side by side on a grassy slope in front of a castle framed against a perfect blue sky, looked as if it belonged in a travel brochure, not a gangster picture.

Later that year, Pierce travelled to India for ten weeks to make *The Deceivers*, based on the John Masters novel. Set in the British Raj in the 1820s, it was a typically lavish costume drama from the Merchant-Ivory film-making team – who were responsible for bringing *A Room With a View* to the big screen. Part-financed by Channel 4, it incorporated a number of trademark Merchant-Ivory set pieces. Such as the grand ball showing the officers and their wives dancing in their exquisite Victorian outfits, and a superbly-staged British cavalry attack reminiscent of *The Charge Of The Light Brigade*.

The film cast Brosnan – who likened its story to Joseph Conrad's classic *Heart of Darkness* – as Lieutenant William Savage, an English army officer with a conscience, who witnesses at first hand a massacre by a religious cult of murderers called Thuggees (Hindi for 'deceivers'), who rob and murder travellers on the road. Savage rounds up the locals, determined to root out the killers, but his commander disapproves of his methods, and asks for his resignation – leaving him, he feels, no option but to break colonial taboos by dyeing his skin and infiltrating the Thuggees in a bid to clear his name.

He gains entry to the mysterious cult after interrogating a Thug called Hussein (played by the Anglo-Indian actor Saeed Jaffrey) who becomes a friend. With his turban, robes, dark Celtic features and bushy black beard, Pierce makes a convincing Indian. And the Thuggees, whose password is 'Greetings, Ali, my brother', soon treat him as one of their own. But drawn ever-deeper into the cult, which worships Kali, the Goddess of Destruction, he is forced to turn killer himself. 'It's a bleak film and Pierce didn't shy away from that,' said the director, Nicholas Meyer. 'He embraced it and should get full marks for not wanting to make the character an out-and-out good guy.'

The movie was shot in the 'pink city' of Jaipur, a desert oasis in Rajasthan; and Khajuraho, a small town surrounded by forests in central India, famous for its erotic temples. Filming took place in the autumn/winter of 1987 when temperatures were more bearable. And the role offered Brosnan the chance to put yet more distance between himself and Remington Steele.

He travelled to India with his wife and their young son, Sean. 'If you're on location on your own, it can become lonely and depressing,' explained Brosnan. 'To be able to talk to Cassie at the end of the day helped to get everything in perspective.'

As was to be expected, Pierce – dressed in a red army jacket and white trousers, and sporting the big bushy sideburns that were fashionable at the time – was perfect in the part. 'He looked effortlessly regal,' says Jaffrey. 'Indeed, he was so much better-looking than the local maharajah (prince) that we nicknamed him the "Maharajah of Jaipur".' However, Meyer observed: 'It's very rare that an actor who is as handsome as Pierce is so devoid of narcissism. That's what he has in common with Cary Grant – he wears it so lightly. What you end up with is a man's man who women like, too.'

During the shoot, Jaffrey got to know the Brosnans well. 'We spent some lovely evenings together, meeting for drinks and playing snooker,' he says. 'Pierce was great to work with, and was as nice a person inside as he looked outside.' Ismail Merchant spoke of his devotion to 'his work, his wife and family'. While another actor comments: 'The tightness of the connection between them was quite wonderful.' But he adds: 'While Pierce was warm, affectionate and friendly with people he knew, he could also be somewhat mercurial.'

The film got its first screening at the 1988 Montreal Film Festival, and Pierce and Saeed Jaffrey attended its official première in New York. However the critics gave it a pasting and the public stayed away. One magazine described The Deceivers as a 'shock-horror costume caper';

another attacked 'the opening set of clichés – a tiger hunt, a *Gone With the Wind* dance and a regimental wedding'. A third reviewer claimed it made 'India look like something out of a travel brochure' and blasted 'its Hollywood-Viennese musical score'. While a fourth described it as 'slow-going' but reluctantly conceded 'it has its moments'.

Cast and crew were deeply disappointed by the movie's lack of success. Why did it bomb? 'I don't think the *Remington Steele* audience accepted poor Pierce as a nineteenth-century British soldier,' offers Jaffrey. The sort of people who went to Merchant-Ivory films were also unlikely to be *Remington* fans. So Pierce's casting would have given the film little extra appeal in their eyes. The film may have been more successful too if, à la *Howard's End*, it had featured an all-star ensemble cast. Its box office failure may have also reflected the sad fact that Western audiences have little interest in films with a largely ethnic cast. In the final analysis, though, Jaffrey is perhaps closest to the truth when he says: 'The success of any film is a gift of God.'

The movie was Pierce's fourth box office flop in a row. Surely he deserved a hit? In 1989 he made *Mister Johnson* on location in Nigeria, a movie which echoed *The Deceivers* in a number of ways. Again, it was a period drama; again it was set against the backdrop of the British Empire; and again Brosnan played a stiff-upper-lipped British army officer. Co-starring Edward Woodward (who starred in the hit TV series *Callan* and *The Equalizer*), it was another movie about a white master and a black servant from the Australian director, Bruce Beresford – whose previous film, *Driving Miss Daisy*, scooped the best picture award at the 1989 Oscars ceremony. (Of course, he'd also worked with Cassandra many years before on *Five Days*.) The story was adapted from Joyce Carey's novel for the big screen by author William Boyd.

Set in West Africa in the 1920s, it told the story of a naïve and feckless native clerk, Mister Johnson (played by Maynard Eziashi). A cog in the great imperial machine, he attempts to be more English than the English, but destroys himself when he gets into debt and has to take ever more drastic action to find a way out of the hole he's dug for himself.

With his distinguished air, military bearing and neat military moustache, Pierce looked every inch an army officer, and brought to mind classical British actors like Robert Donat and David Niven. With his clipped English accent he also sounded like an army officer. As in *The Deceivers*, he was also a decent, honourable man, refusing to allow prostitutes to be flogged, as was the local custom.

Life in the village of Fada in semi-barren West Africa was difficult for both District Officer Harry Rudbeck (Pierce) and the local natives. But he tried to keep up appearances, doing his best to celebrate Christmas in a traditional way by tucking into plum pudding despite the searing heat. After a while he was joined by his wife, but she had difficulty adapting to her new lot – and to 'delicacies' like peanut soup. 'Do you like it?' asks Rudbeck innocently enough. 'It's just peanuts in hot water,' she answers icily.

The film fared better at the hands of the critics than most of Pierce's past efforts. The *Observer* commented: 'A very generous, thoughtful and affecting movie.' Another critic said it was 'a deftly-acted tragicomedy of human fallibility and colonial attitudes'. While *Time Out* thought it 'eminently respectable'. Most tellingly of all, the Queen found it so touching that she reportedly shed a tear at its royal première in April 1991. 'It was a beautiful film and being chosen for it renewed my confidence as an actor,' says Brosnan. 'It was a rebirth.'

Unfortunately, *Mister Johnson* was not to have the crossover appeal of *Driving Miss Daisy* and only got a limited release. As with *The Deceivers*, a number of factors conspired against its success. The large ethnic cast – and the fact that the lead role was played by a little-known African (Eziashi), even though Brosnan got star billing – did little for its commercial appeal. But even more crucially, the film's distributor, Avenue Entertainment, was going belly up at the time and didn't have the money to promote *Mister Johnson*. The result being 'that about twelve people saw the picture,' says Brosnan sarcastically. 'It kills you when that happens.'

In contrast, his next project was the forgettable, low-budget *Live Wire*, which cast him as an FBI explosives expert. 'I did it because Cassie said it would be good to do,' he says. Cassie of course, was hugely involved in his career and his choices. This was not perhaps her best piece of advice. The film opened with footage of the wreckage of the Pan Am jet at Lockerbie, Scotland, and the following passage: 'Over the last decade over 3,500 lives have been lost through terrorism around the world. Nearly every country has had its share of kidnappings and bombings – the one exception has been the USA. Until now . . .' Of course, the movie-makers had no idea that America too would soon fall victim to hate-filled fanatics, leading to a string of outrages such as the World Trade Center, Oklahoma and Atlanta bombings.

Otherwise, *Live Wire* was a run-of-the-mill action thriller. Pierce played Danny O'Neill, an Irish-American cop with – guess what? – a marital problem. His wife, Terry (Lisa Eilbacher), had left him for slimy senator Frank Traveres (Ron Silver). 'My character carries quite a lot of emotional baggage,' he said at the time. 'As well as discovering that my wife is having an affair, I have a daughter who has drowned. So there's quite an emotional side to it, too.'

But Brosnan soon has to confront an even bigger problem in the shape of a mad terrorist leader – played by British actor Ben Cross. (In these politically correct times, a baddie only seems acceptable in Hollywood if he's British. But Cross was in good company, having trod in the footsteps of Steven Berkoff, Alan Rickman, Anthony Hopkins, Jeremy Irons and Joss Ackland, to name but a few.)

Somewhat bizarrely, despite his public school accent, Cross played a character called Mikhail Rashid, presumably an Arab, who thinks he's been cheated out of $10 million by three senators in an arms deal that's turned sour. With the help of an ingenious liquid explosive ignited by stomach acid, Rashid eliminates two senators – and vows to get the third, Traveres. In spite of his understandable animosity towards the crooked senator – 'You touch my wife again and I'll separate you from your body,' he tells him – O'Neill has a duty to protect Traveres from this terrorist threat. In the climactic showdown, though, everything is resolved. Rashid swallows his own poison and blows himself up; Traveres is thrown off a rooftop by the force of the explosion and impaled on a wrought-iron fence; while O'Neill survives and, following a reconciliation with his wife, presumably lives happily ever after.

Once again, the film – which got lukewarm reviews – bit the dust at the box office. Pierce had made six films and had six flops. It was an unenviable track record. Nor was it as if they were of great artistic merit: of the six, only one, *Mister Johnson*, really stands the test of time.

Ironically, despite his efforts to prove his versatility as an actor, he was still unable to lay to rest the spectre of James Bond. In 1989 it was claimed he'd been offered £1 million to play the secret agent in a breakaway 007 film. Apparently, the actor held a secret meeting with producer Kevin McClory in Dublin to discuss his appearance in a proposed £10 million movie, *Warhead 8* – based on a film script McClory had written with Bond's creator Ian Fleming 30 years earlier. However, the talks came to nothing. And just weeks later a newspaper was saying that Cubby Broccoli had approached Brosnan to star in the next Bond film because the current 007 – Timothy Dalton – was 'too dour'. Would he never escape 007's shadow?

For all Pierce's efforts to become a movie star – 'to get a body of work behind me that will redefine my career, screen persona and territory as an actor' – it was the small screen which continued to provide his bread-and-butter work. And even though his big screen offerings had largely sunk without trace at the box office, he continued to attract huge audiences on both sides of the Atlantic in the mini-series and movies that he shot for television.

The crucial difference between the two formats was that while most of his cinema work was characterised by low budgets and bad marketing, his small screen projects were invariably well-financed and well-publicised, and were chasing the maximum possible television audience.

One of the most successful mini-series of the eighties – to the dismay of many critics – was *Noble House*, the eight-hour, £10 million, mini-series based on James Clavell's best-selling saga of a shipping firm's fight for survival. Just weeks after missing out on the Bond role, Brosnan took delivery of a fat, 6-inch-thick script from his agent, an adaptation of Clavell's 1,110-page blockbuster. 'It came at a point where I'd just gone through the Bond and Steele business,' he says, 'and it seemed a good idea to do something that would distract me for a few months.'

He played the part of Ian Struan Dunross, the powerful *tai-pan* (leader) of Struan and Company (also known as Noble House), an old and influential Hong Kong trading house. In the novel, Dunross is a married man with two children. But in the mini-series, he's a widower – which opened the way for Brosnan's romantic involvement with Casey Tcholok (played by Deborah Raffin), a high-powered executive with a US firm who's visiting Hong Kong to discuss a joint venture with Struan's. Other key players in this *Dynasty*-style tale of corporate intrigue include Casey's boss, Linc Bartlett (Ben Masters), who is thinking corporate takeover instead of joint venture, and Quillan Gornt (John Rhys-Davies – who Pierce had worked with at York's Theatre Royal). The Welshman played Dunross's arch-rival, who hoped to turn Bartlett's venture to his own advantage. As usual, the shaven-headed Chinese actor Khigh Dhiegh – a sinister villain in *Hawaii Five-O* – was playing a bad guy, while Gordon Jackson (*Upstairs, Downstairs*), Denholm Elliott and the exotic Tia Carrere (who later found fame as the *Wayne's World* 'babe') appeared in supporting roles.

The action unfolds over a six-day period in which Dunross has to fight to re-establish the financial stability of his company amid conspiracies left, right and centre. Woven into the plot are several strands of Hong Kong mystique. For instance, when Dunross becomes *tai-pan* he is entrusted with a set of half-coins, and has to agree to grant a favour to whoever presents him with the other half.

As part of the research for the role, Brosnan met up with the *tai-pans* of real trading houses. 'Until I got there I thought Clavell had made it all up,' he confesses. 'But once I was in Hong Kong I realised how close to the truth it was.' Despite appearing in almost every scene of the series, he now claims: 'Hong Kong was the real star of the show.'

Within half an hour of *Noble House* starting, the dashing hero has seduced Casey. 'I think I know what you're going to do next,' she tells him as they recline on a sofa. Then he kisses her and she adds: 'I was right.' But perhaps the series' most memorable moment came when a floating restaurant caught fire. The blaze, on a specially built, fire-resistant structure, was fed by more than a hundred gas cylinders. 'It was incredibly hot and if anything had gone wrong, there was only one way to go – over the side,' says Brosnan. But he applauded the action of the BBC in cutting a scene in which a man is savagely smashed over the head with a shovel. 'If violence is part of the story and not gratuitous, then that's fine,' he said. 'But I don't like violence for the sake of it. That particular scene was rather bloody and I didn't like it at all. I don't want to be known as a tough guy actor associated with blood and guts and shootings and murders.'

Afterwards he said: 'It was a brooding piece and I played a brooding guy. Everything that can go wrong does go wrong, but everything that should go right does go right in the end. I enjoyed doing it up to a point – but it's not really my kind of material. The character was a very calculating guy who kept his cards close to his chest. Having done it, I realised I'd rather play characters with a little more humanity and vulnerability.' And judging by his less than flattering comments about 35-year-old co-star Deborah Raffin – 'I had no say in her casting but she may have been a little old for the love interest' – one gets the feeling they didn't exactly bond.

Once it had been screened, and he'd been paid, Pierce spoke even more frankly about the mini-series. 'I enjoyed making *Noble House* but it just didn't come out the way I wanted it to, and I never saw it,' he confessed adding wistfully, 'My heart's always in my work but there are just some things you don't want to see afterwards. I suppose I don't like a lot of work I do . . .' You can hear him sigh very slightly, look down and then, remembering that survival is what matters, brighten and smile.

The drama was but one of several mini-series and movies that Brosnan shot for the small screen during this period. He also starred in *Around the World in 80 Days*, reprising the David Niven role of the 1956 cinema film. The 1989 small-screen remake with Pierce became one of the ten most watched mini-series in television history – shot, fittingly enough, around the world in England, Macao, Hong Kong, Thailand, the USA and Yugoslavia. 'After *Noble House* I said I wasn't going to do another mini-series but it had a delightful script and great family appeal,' explained an embarrassed Pierce at the time.

His character, Phileas Fogg, is the quintessential nineteenth-century English gentleman. He wears a top hat and tails, a cravat and a white shirt buttoned up to his chin, takes his tea in the bath, reads *The Times* and is a great believer in punctuality. But in a card game at his London club he makes a gentleman's wager that he can travel around the world in 80 days – or 1,920 hours, or 115,200 minutes – and so the adventure begins . . .

The trip's no plain sailing: Fogg's train to Paris is commandeered by revolutionaries. He is propositioned in the French capital by a prostitute well past her prime. He flies a balloon over the Alps, hires an elephant in India, is taken hostage in the Burmese jungle, survives a shipwreck in the China Sea and is attacked by Red Indians in America's wild west. But he somehow overcomes one obstacle after another in his epic race against the clock. He is joined on his travels by his faithful French manservant, played by *Monty Python* star Eric Idle, and trailed by the bumbling Detective Fix, played by Peter Ustinov, who wrongly suspects Fogg of netting more than £50,000 in a daring daylight raid on the Bank of England.

The mini-series, based on the Jules Verne classic, was never likely to win great praise from the critics but it certainly made entertaining viewing – thanks in part to cameo appearances from Robert Morley, Roddy McDowall, Christopher Lee, Patrick MacNee, Jack Klugman, Lee Remick, Jill St John and Robert Wagner.

Brosnan also made *The Heist*, a comedy drama in which he played a security firm boss who is framed for theft and leaves prison bent on revenge; *Victim of Love*, in which he played a handsome widower caught in a love triangle with a therapist and one of her patients; and *Murder 101*, a whodunnit thriller in which he plays a university lecturer who turns detective to track down the killer responsible for a high society murder.

However, his television performances were slated as much, if not more, than his movie performances. And the critics, not for the first time, used his matinee idol appearance as a stick with which to beat him about the head. For instance, the *Daily Mail* spoke of his 'pretty boy looks' eclipsing the beauty of Raffin in *Noble House*. While columnist Peter Tory laid into him with all the subtlety of a sledgehammer in his *Daily Express* review of the mini-series. So vitriolic was the piece that it's worth quoting in full:

Pierce Brosnan is quite absurdly, ludicrously good-looking. He is also quite dauntingly uninteresting. Wet, even. He is a very nice chap – but as an actor, utterly dreary. How on earth he could have been offered the role of James Bond is difficult to imagine! Behind the God-like features and the startling blue eyes nothing whatsoever appears to be happening. He is not there. Out to lunch, as they say. For he represents a great host of successful, handsome actors who are similarly incapable, in the words of Hamlet to the players at his court, of "suiting the thoughts to the action". Brosnan never looks particularly angry or loving or wistful or even the slightest bit anxious. He just simply looks.

While few would argue that *Noble House* represents the finest body of work in Pierce's career, it's debatable whether such invective was justified. Good looks are not a crime, after all.

The Drama Centre's principal, Christopher Fettes, is quick to take issue with the critics. 'The English always knock actors who are talented and good-looking,' he thunders. 'They said the same thing about Vivien Leigh, for God's sake! You can't expect any actor to shine in two-dimensional parts like Remington Steele or Ian Dunross. They're "nothing roles" compared to playing a character like Laertes. I *know* that Pierce has an extremely wide range. And had he stayed in England he'd be a leading stage actor, at the pinnacle of the profession. The truth is that he's never really been given the chance to show his range as an actor.' This sentiment is echoed by the school's other leading light, Yat Malmgren, who dismisses those critics who imply that Pierce's looks alone have been responsible for his success. 'That's such nonsense,' he says. 'Of course, he's good-looking. Name a leading man who isn't? But looks alone don't make an actor. Thankfully for Pierce, he's always had looks *and* talent.'

As for Brosnan, he reacted to the criticism by saying: 'I came to Hollywood to do movies, thinking I was hot, angry, intense and vital and what did I get? This suave playboy. But after doing *Remington Steele* I got a bit jaded creatively – it was like going into a factory day in day out. Now I just follow the course. I am an actor and this business is very fickle. Sometimes you have to look at your bank account and make up your mind to take the dross.

'If you care about your work, though, as I do, you're never satisfied. I've always been pretty tough on myself, but as I get older I'm beginning to let go a little more. I'm beginning to say, "Forget it. It's not worth it. You did the scene well enough." I still find that I give my best performances, not in front of the cameras, but alone in the car, driving home afterwards! I just coast along, I'm a journeyman.

'The truth is there are many kinds of actors. There are the brilliantly gifted actors like Daniel Day-Lewis or Gary Oldman, who leave their mark every time they touch the screen. I wish I could shine as brightly as them and share their commitment and passion but perhaps I don't have their reverence. I've got the talent that I've got – it's like a little piece of gold you polish.'

Perhaps this more relaxed approach reflected an acceptance on his part that you couldn't have everything – and that, for better of for worse, he was now typecast in the eyes of Tinseltown as a dashing leading man. Not that it didn't rankle occasionally. Despite obviously benefiting from the suave good looks which helped him land the lead role in *Remington Steele* and a host of films, TV movies and mini-series, Brosnan increasingly felt they were a mixed blessing. 'The looks get in the way as much as they benefit in some ways,' he said. 'People say "he's too good-looking" but I am who I am. It does rankle when people call me "pretty". No man wants to be called pretty. It's demeaning.' Then typically, he added self-mockingly: 'But I suppose I do scrub up well for an Irishman!'

If anything, though, it was Charlotte and Christopher who were his fiercest critics. 'They'll say, "Daddy, you were good" or "Daddy, you were bad",' he revealed. 'After watching me as Phileas Fogg in *Around the World in 80 Days*, they just looked at me and said, "Daddy, what are you doing?" '

As the nineties dawned, some critics felt that he was cursed to live out his days as a B-movie hunk; a male version of America's TV movie queen, Jane Seymour (another Brit who'd found fame and fortune across the Atlantic); a slab of prime-cut beefcake who was guaranteed to put female bums on seats during peak-time viewing. There were worse fates – but it can't have been a particularly attractive proposition for a proud man like Pierce.

However talented a thespian he might be, though, no actor's mask would be able to disguise the heartache he would feel in the difficult years ahead.

10. TRAGEDY

Tragically, after going into remission, Cassie's cancer returned with a vengeance in the spring of 1991. And the 'disgusting, insidious disease', as Pierce called it, would rule the couple's lives for the rest of their days together.

They learned that her mother, who died of ovarian cancer when Cassie was in her teens, had probably passed on a genetic susceptibility to the disease. Cassie wasn't the only Hollywood celebrity to have ovarian cancer and she became involved in a much-needed informal support group which would be of great comfort to all its members. Funnyman Gene Wilder's wife, Gilda Radner, who was also suffering from the disease, would phone Cassie daily, though they never met. And Jill Ireland, who lived near the Brosnans in Malibu, was another faithful friend. But when Gilda died in 1989, and then Jill a year later, the Brosnans were devastated. 'Still Cassie's resolve never diminished,' says Pierce proudly.

Their magnificent house provided a sanctuary for her in those desperate last months. 'It was such a comfort,' says Pierce. 'The serenity of it gave Cassie so much joy.' And even when she was very sick, recalls close family friend Jerome Hellman, 'you'd come into that house, and all would be wellness. The kids would be screaming, leaping into the pool and doing somersaults while Cassie watched from her chair.'

Living in the disease's shadow was 'very strange', according to Brosnan. 'I'd work fourteen hours a day on a film, then sleep at the hospital.' He also travelled to Nigeria to make *Mister Johnson* against his wishes. 'I wouldn't have gone unless Cassie had been so supportive,' he says. 'But she said, "Darling, you've got to do this picture. I'll be able to handle myself." But the separation was painful, really painful.'

During the the ten-week shoot she suffered a relapse in his absence – and there was only one phone in the remote village where he was filming. 'Each night I'd race to this phone after work, telling Cassie how much I missed her, wanting to find out how she was doing,' he says. 'Sometimes there were long silences and we'd say nothing. Just knowing she was alive and well was enough.'

As time went by, and he endured the agony of seeing his beautiful wife lose her hair and grow weaker by the day, the outcome became increasingly clear – but Brosnan refused to accept the inevitable, insisting: 'There has to be something that can be done to save her. I'd give up everything if my wife could get better. If someone said, "Pierce, you'll have to be a sheep farmer for the rest of your life," I'd reply, "Okay. Let's do it. Right now." When someone you love and cherish dearly with all your heart has a life-threatening illness, everything else pales in comparison. Whether I am a successful actor isn't important any more – I just want to see my wife get better.

'If it had been me, I'd have given up fighting a long time ago. But Cassie has remained vitally involved in life. We do our best to treat the cancer as an inconvenience. We don't sit around moping; we still try to get the most out of life. And when the pain becomes unbearable we've just sat down and hugged each other.'

The actor set up a studio next to their bedroom where he would paint – but in time the strain began to take its toll on him, too. He hardly slept, lost weight and some friends thought at one point he looked almost as ill as his wife. 'He looked deathly pale and far older than his years,' said one. And Brosnan himself, at one particularly low moment, said: 'When you sit there in the hospital waiting room and they tell you the grim facts – that they have found another lymph node, or the blood count is very low, you just feel so impotent.

'Sometimes I've let myself down, let that Irish melancholy creep over me and just asked, "Why is this happening?" Fortunately I have a partner who doesn't let me indulge in such frivolous thoughts, and so you struggle on.' There's no doubt Cassie appreciated she was married to a man in a million. 'I only wish everyone suffering from cancer could have someone like Pierce with them,' she said.

As her life drew to a close, their wealth counted for less and less and they learned to appreciate the simple things in life. 'We always loved being with each other,' says Pierce. 'And we let go of a lot of things – of striving for so much, wanting success, always thinking ahead instead of just living for the moment. We became conscious of being in the here and now, of stopping and smelling the roses.' Sometimes friends – they had a small, steadfast group of about twenty – would come over, and they'd have a barbecue by the pool and exchange Hollywood gossip. The one thing he never asked Cassie was if she was scared of dying. Some terminal patients are comforted by such talk – but as far as she and Pierce were concerned, to even contemplate the possibility seemed an admission of defeat. Only once did she raise the topic, and then with tongue firmly in cheek, teasingly saying to her husband: 'If I ever move on, I want you to behave yourself, no running off and getting married straight away, I want a nice long period of time, thank you very much!'

Despite fearlessly battling the disease for so long, the day came when both she and Pierce knew the war was ultimately lost. He says: 'I was painting and she was downstairs on the phone to the doctor, and then she came up to me and said, "Things don't look good for me. But, please darling, don't worry. It's okay. It's just a life winding down. What can you do?" And that was the only time we wept together. Up until then there was always something new, some new treatment. But the options gradually got fewer and fewer.'

On 2 December 1991, she was admitted to the Kenneth Norris Jr Cancer Hospital in Los Angeles for the last time. She was in terrible pain and was put on a steady morphine drip. Her body began to close down, but she had told doctors that she didn't want to be resuscitated by any machines. 'I'm dying,' she told Pierce. 'Yes,' he replied and they held hands and prayed. 'I realised I was losing my Cassie – and it brought me to my knees.' He kept a vigil by her side, 'cherishing each moment with her as though it was a precious jewel in time', according to a friend. Hospital spokesman Gordon Cohn said: 'Pierce spent practically every waking minute with her – watching over her, sitting next to her while she slept and talking to her whenever possible. He even slept in her room in the bed next to hers for the last three weeks of her life.'

Occasionally, exhaustion would overtake him, and Cassandra or the nurses had to tell him to get some sleep. He would – but only after making sure she was comfortable. Leaving nothing to chance, Pierce hired private nurses and told them: 'My wife is drifting in and out of sleep. When she opens her eyes, whenever that is, I want her to see my face.'

On 15 December – Cassie's birthday – he threw a surprise birthday party for his wife in her hospital room. One of the nurses took Cassie out of her room for a few minutes. In her absence it was decorated with balloons, streamers and a banner. When she returned, friends and members of her family were waiting. 'She said it was perhaps the most memorable birthday of her life,' comments Cohn.

Both Cassie and Pierce knew she'd never see another birthday. And a friend reveals that in a touching bedside talk she told her husband: 'I want you to marry again – I want you to have a full, happy life.' But he told her in a broken voice: 'There will never be another woman I could love as I love you.'

It was obvious that Cassie, who by now had wasted away to under six stone, didn't have long for this world. On Sunday 22 December Pierce called a local priest, who prayed with the couple (Cassie was also Catholic) and left behind some pamphlets, one of which was the Book of Revelation.

Pierce began reading aloud from it as he stood at the foot of his wife's bed. But because he was under so much stress, the words just spilled out in a jumble until he stopped and said: 'Darling, I'm making a pig's ear of this. Here I am, an actor, and I can't even get these words out in the right order.' She whispered something but he couldn't quite hear so he put his ear to her lips and she repeated: 'Always an actor.' Those were her last comprehensible words. 'It was a poignant moment,' says Pierce, who thinks she also meant 'always a man, always a father'.

That Christmas was tough for the whole family, according to Charlotte. 'Everything about our home was different, muted, without Mum there,' she says. But Cassie had been determined to see in her and Pierce's eleventh wedding anniversary – two days later – and she did. By that evening, though, while still conscious and clinging to life, she had 'begun her journey', as Brosnan puts it, to the other side.

Both Charlotte and Christopher had spent many hours at their mother's hospital bedside – but as the end drew near they decided to let their father share the precious few remaining hours alone with his beloved wife. He spent that last night – which saw the coming of the rains in California after six long years of drought – holding his wife close to him. 'I wanted her to hear my heart beating against hers,' he told a friend. 'I didn't want her to feel alone and frightened.' At about 10 a.m. the next day, 'she began to go,' says Pierce, 'it was time.' The phone rang and it was Charlotte. 'I'd lain awake all night and, suddenly, I knew I should ring,' she says. 'It was like telepathy with Dad, like he wanted me to call.' He told her that her mother was dying. And she said: 'It's okay, Daddy.' For a moment, neither spoke. In that moment he, his dying wife and their daughter were together in their thoughts.

At 10.20 a.m. on 28 December 1991, Cassie died in her husband's arms. He sobbed his heart out and held his dear wife's body close to him for several minutes, whispering, 'I love you' over and over. 'Cassandra fought her cancer until the end,' said Cohn, following her death. 'She fought it bravely with the support of her family. She was not an ordinary patient and attracted great loyalty from the people who treated her. Everyone here is devastated by her death.'

It was the end of the fight, the day Pierce had prayed would never come. As well as losing his wife, he'd lost his best friend, his soul mate and the guiding light in his life. That afternoon, he went home to tell Sean the heartbreaking news. 'I sat him on my lap and told him Mummy had died,' he says. 'The tears came to his eyes but they never fell. He just said, "It's for the best, Daddy, she's not in pain anymore".'

Newspapers around the world carried reports of her death, in most cases putting her age at 39. In fact, she was 50.

Shortly afterwards, Cassie was cremated. Pierce and the three children paid their respects to her at a private Catholic Church in a low-key ceremony in Santa Monica, near their Malibu home, attended by only twenty friends and relatives. Among the mourners was Dermot's brother, Richard Harris. The letters that arrived following Cassie's death, from fans and friends, took two weeks to open. There were also numerous tributes. One of the most moving came from tough guy actor Charles Bronson, still grieving from the death of his own wife, Jill Ireland, to cancer. 'Pierce and Cassandra were the most loving couple I've ever known,' he said. 'Theirs was the greatest love story in Hollywood. No love story in fiction can come close to the love that existed between them.'

11. ALONE AGAIN

The death of Cassie was the most traumatic event to have taken place in Pierce's life – punching a gaping hole through his heart and soul. Overnight his world collapsed and it would take him years to come to terms with the tragedy. 'All I think about is Cassie, Cassie, Cassie,' he admitted six months after her death. 'I've screamed at God – Why? Why Cassie?' And there are those who question whether, five years on, he had still fully come to terms with her death.

He took to wearing his dead wife's ring on a leather thong around his throat and placed Cassie's ashes in a little shrine at the home – but still seemed desperate to avoid the grim truth that she had gone forever. Within days he had vowed he would never marry another woman, saying: 'No one could ever replace Cassie – I'll always be married to her.' His wife's memory filled the house, and a large portrait of Cassie in her modelling days hung on the living-room wall, alongside the last sad photographs of her, being carried up the driveway in her husband's arms, a frail figure swathed in a head scarf and long skirt.

Most evenings at his house he pretended, just for a while, that she really was with him. He changed nothing in their bedroom – and every item of clothing was there in her dressing room just as she had left it. 'I go in there and talk to her,' he said. 'She is with me there. It feels like a two-way conversation. There's a dialogue that goes on, some days more than others. But some days you just feel terribly alone, terribly adrift.' He even visited a therapist – not that there was anything unusual about that in California – to make sure he was doing the right thing. However, he was too private a man to really share his innermost feelings with a stranger, albeit a professional, preferring to write his thoughts down in a secret journal. 'It's all for therapy,' he said. 'I just write whatever's there, what's in my head. I've always been a great believer in putting things on paper and letting your thoughts flow out.'

Unlike all too many men, though, he was not ashamed to show emotion. 'I weep every day,' he confessed. 'The children have seen me weep and I don't hide that. But I don't go around the house weeping, either. The pain is there but you've got to go on. You have to face the day, you just have to keep faith with yourself. I ask myself how I cope every morning of every day – but, you see, wherever I go, Cassie's always with me.'

The death of Cassandra also brought back memories of his unhappy childhood. 'Since she died, I've been sifting through my past and I realise just how much emotion I buried as a boy,' he said. But the tragedy also drew him and his mother May closer. 'There's been a lot of growing up between us. She has lots of regrets about what should have happened in my childhood.'

He admits that his first reaction after losing Cassie was to just 'take off' – perhaps travel the world – and while he may have done just that if he'd been single, he had responsibilities. So he remained at the Malibu house with Sean, the five family dogs, a housekeeper and gardeners – and he confessed that being there helped him to keep his 'mind and body together'. Whatever problems Pierce himself encountered in coming to terms with Cassandra's death, family and friends agree that he was a wonderful father to the children in the months ahead – and they became the pride of his life. But he was keenly aware of the heavy burden of responsibility that his wife's loss placed on his shoulders.

'Being a single parent can be quite overwhelming at times,' he said. 'The first year of bereavement I just felt numbness. Then the blood comes back and you realise you have survived – and that you're alone and have to make these decisions. Having to play mother and father has been one of the biggest challenges I've ever faced. Making the choices for the family becomes frightening. Whether to sell the house or stay? Wondering what's best for the children? But I've found great strength in taking care of the family. You have to be strong for them.'

He turned down an opportunity in 1993 to renew his stage career by appearing on Broadway in the play, *Somebody To Watch Over Me*, for the children's sake. 'We talked about it very seriously but it would have meant basing myself in New York for a year and uprooting Sean,' he said. 'I have to think about him.' The two elder children were of less concern – 'they're on their way,' as he put it – although Brosnan still tried to speak to them on the phone whenever possible. They were in fact to prove pillars of strength, helping him to accept his loss. 'Charlotte is a little Cassie,' he said. 'She has wisdom and beauty, and tells me, "Go ahead, Dad, cry. It's fine".' Christopher also rallied round in support, delaying his return to boarding school when Brosnan told him he needed him there at home. 'He nestled down on the bed and said, "Daddy, I'm staying",' says Pierce.

However, Brosnan feared that young Sean might bury his emotions – much as he himself had done as a child – in an attempt to cope with the trauma of the loss. So he encouraged the 8-year-old boy to put pen to paper in a form of self-therapy.

'I've encouraged Sean to express his feelings in drawings or by painting,' he revealed. 'I sometimes see the pain in his eyes and I can see it in the silences in his conversation. Cassie was ill for four years and he can barely remember a time when she wasn't ill. He's very stoic. There's a lot in him that will probably not come out until much later in life. I tell him not to bury it. But you can't push too far. You just have to be there to love and to hug.'

While readily admitting that he spoiled the children – particularly Sean, being the youngest – Brosnan could be tough with them when the need arose. 'I'll give Sean a slap if it's called for, whereas some American parents get upset about that kind of thing,' he said. Somewhat ironically, given the fact that Sean had been brought up an American citizen and even had an American passport, Pierce also revealed that he hoped to send him to Millfield School one day.

Despite the horrors he experienced as a child at the hands of the Christian Brothers, he remained a Catholic and found his faith a great comfort following his wife's death. 'I believe in God utterly and absolutely,' he revealed. 'I don't usually say prayers. I say thank you. If you'd had my life you'd spend more time saying thank you than asking for things. I have a lot to be thankful for – I cherish Charlotte, Christopher and Sean.'

Having lost his wife to ovarian cancer, Brosnan was absolutely determined that everything should be done to prevent Charlotte from contracting it too. He was painfully aware that if doctors had diagnosed Cassie's illness earlier she might still be alive. So Charlotte had check-ups every six months, including a CA125 blood test which could detect the disease. She was also advised that she should have children by the time she was 30 and then have a full hysterectomy.

'She is very aware of it and I am making sure she is not neglected,' said Pierce. 'The doctors are also aware of the vulnerability. It's not a pleasant thing to be told but she has great spirit and is just getting on with her life.'

The most effective tranquilliser in dealing with his grief was sheer hard work – and over the next couple of years Pierce threw his energies into work, any work. 'Before she died, Cassie made it clear that she didn't want me to mope around the house in a state of depression,' he said. 'So I picked myself up and got on with things.'

After struggling for so long to make his mark on the big screen during Cassie's life, largely without success, Brosnan cannot have failed to appreciate the irony of his next film being a box office hit. A surprise smash in the States, *The Lawnmower Man* hit the No. 2 slot in its first week of release and went on to gross nearly £90 million ($130 million) worldwide. 'Cassie would have relished this,' he admitted.

The British-produced movie, actually shot before his wife's death, explored for the first time the mysteries of virtual reality – a new technology which gave the user the impression of actually being inside a futuristic video world. Made in only 35 days for £6 million – small beer alongside the £45 million splashed out on the making of Arnold Schwarzenegger's *Terminator 2* – it recouped its costs within days of opening. And thus netted London-based Allied Vision, part-owned by rock promoter Harvey Goldsmith, a tidy profit. 'We're overwhelmed by its success,' said executive producer Ed Simons, who brought *The Stud* to the screen in the seventies.

Based on a Stephen King short story and directed by Brett Leonard, *The Lawnmower Man* is about a driven, obsessive scientist, Dr Angelo (played by Pierce), who experiments with computer-generated virtual reality to increase the strength and intelligence of monkeys.

When his funding is withdrawn, he uses the gentle, mentally retarded lawnmower man of the title, Jobe (played by *White Hunter, Black Heart* star Jeff Fahey), as a guinea pig, exposing him to virtual reality teaching technology and powerful drugs which accelerate his learning ability, transforming him into a genius. But when a mercenary Cybertech executive tampers with the experiment it has terrible consequences. The lawnmower man becomes a power-crazed psychopath, suits up to have 'cybersex' with the town beauty and takes control of the local community.

'I enjoyed making the film,' says Brosnan – who found Charlotte and Christopher summer jobs in the production office – though he wasn't crazy about the futuristic rubber suit he had to wear, because it accentuated his skinny legs. 'It was a good script. The research Angelo is doing is for the benefit of mankind – it's just that he opens the lid on Pandora's box a little too much.'

He was so intrigued by the chain-smoking character – described by one critic as a 'suburban Frankenstein' – that he carried out extensive background research into the pioneers of virtual reality. 'A lot of them came across as sixties-style, anti-establishment "pot-heads",' he says. 'One guy, a white guy, even had dreadlocks. So I dug out my old earring, stopped shaving, put Angelo in shorts and gave him a certain goofiness. What I liked was the vulnerability, the flaws and the cracks in his character.'

Working with computer-generated special effects posed Pierce a particular challenge. 'A lot of it was new to me,' he admits. 'I'm a bit of a dinosaur when it comes to this stuff and didn't know what virtual reality was until I started work on the film. I'm not technically minded at all – I can barely put a tape in a video recorder! There were moments when I was standing there, with 80 crew members looking at me, and I was looking at nothing at all, having to pretend I was really looking at a guy being blown up in front of me!'

Most critics were suitably impressed by the 'mind-blowing special effects' and 'dazzling computer animation' upon which the film's box office success was pinned. Although one reviewer pointed out the irony that 'almost nothing that matters actually depends on, or takes place within, virtual reality'. However, it was generally felt that the actors had been 'upstaged by the special effects'.

Unable to make the film's British première, Pierce was represented by Charlotte and Christopher, who also attended the after-screening party at London's Langham Hotel. Despite what the critics might say, though, Charlotte – who worked as a PA on the film – proudly defended her dad's performance, saying: 'The scene that sticks in my mind is the one in which Dad, in his silver suit, is racing against the clock to get out of a building before a bomb goes off. Just watching his sheer professionalism was stunning.'

Paradoxically, despite the success of *The Lawnmower Man*, Pierce went on to make several disappointing films before landing a supporting role in his first real blockbuster. He starred in two TV movies based on Alastair Maclean stories, *Death Train*, and a sequel, *Night Watch*. His character, Mike Graham, a tough weapons expert and member of a United Nations anti-terrorist force, was originally a Bond-type clone, whose favourite tipple (vodka martini straight up with a twist) echoed 007's taste in alcohol. Joining him in both films, shot in the former Yugoslavia at the height of the civil war, was Alexandra Paul, best known as one of the '*Baywatch* babes'.

Graham's first assignment was to stop a hijacked train armed with a nuclear bomb that is travelling through Europe en route to Iraq. And Brosnan – accurately enough – described *Death Train*, as 'boys' own stuff', adding: 'It's everything I've wanted to do – run along the top of trains, shoot guns and climb in and out of helicopters.' One of the most memorable scenes featured a breathtaking stunt in which Brosnan hung on to a helicopter flying 350 feet above the ground, without so much as a safety net for protection, just 40 miles from the war zone. Admitting he put his life 'on the line' for the stunt, he adds: 'I've woken up since and thought "My God, if anything had happened!" but I knew I could handle it.'

A pivotal sequence in which the anti-terrorist squad, led by Graham, captures the train inside a tunnel, also proved a testing experience. 'They would crank up the engine, smoke would billow up and roll down the walls, and everybody would be suffocating,' he says. 'This went on for four days and by the end of the shoot tempers were seriously frayed.'

It was the first production filmed in the newly independent states of Croatia and Slovenia since the outbreak of civil war in the former Yugoslavia. And the off-screen action was almost as hair-raising as the on-screen action. 'We saw jets screaming across the sky and heard guns being fired,' says the actor. 'We travelled though a bombed-out town and that was chilling. I couldn't help shivering as we went down the streets. You could smell the war.' Despite the danger, Pierce took his nine-year-old Sean with him, hiring a tutor. But it's debatable whether the boy would have been any safer had he remained in Los Angeles – for the night they flew out, the infamous riots exploded which left 58 people dead.

The second film, *Night Watch*, centred on a North Korean plot to sabotage communication systems and spark a meltdown on the Hong Kong Stock Exchange. Once again, cast and crew took their lives into their hands in the scenes filmed in war-torn Yugoslavia. As one technician on the film put it: 'Here in Croatia, the word "shoot" means a lot more than just pointing a camera.'

This time Brosnan played the part with scruffy long hair and a moustache, but still needed his wits about him – regardless of whether the cameras were rolling – quickly learning the unpredictability of a people hardened by war and hate. 'One night I was in a Croatian bar when a drunken soldier came in, pulled out a grenade, stuck it in an empty glass and started hitting it with his bayonet.' He also had to carry a genuine Kalashnikov rifle in his role as a member of a United Nations crime-busting team.

Both TV movies made entertaining enough television viewing but neither represented a real step forward for Brosnan, other than confirming what the world already knew – that he had what it took in the looks and physical fitness departments to make a convincing action hero.

He also starred in a couple of other run-of-the-mill TV movies – *The Broken Chain* and *Don't Talk to Strangers*. In the first he played Sir William Johnson, a flamboyant Irishman and emissary to King George II, who worked for the well-being of the Iroquois tribe in eighteenth-century America. While in the second, set in contemporary America, he played a seemingly regular guy caught up in a bitter custody battle between his wife and her boorish ex-husband. However, Pierce's character turns out to be an even nastier piece of work.

On the big screen, Pierce played second fiddle to little-known Judd Nelson, a young Al Pacino lookalike, in the 1993 romantic thriller, *Entangled*, which was thin on romance and thrills. The Franco-Canadian production opens with a shot of a bandaged man lying on a hospital bed. Pierce opens the door and asks a nurse, 'What are the chances of survival?' He then slips a few francs into the pocket of her coat, adding: 'Keep me informed.' We then go back in time a few months to when a young American author (Judd) arrives in Paris and falls in love with Annabel, a beautiful French model. All too soon, though, he fears she is having an affair and accidentally kills the man he suspects of being her lover.

It's a B-movie in every sense of the word – and in this case the 'B' doesn't just stand for 'boring', but plain 'bad'. Playing a wealthy businessman, Brosnan sports a wispy beard, gets to wear some fancy clothes, smoke cigars and speak a few dozen lines, the most memorable of which is: 'With love, there's nothing more painful than having it, and nothing more painful than losing it.' To cut a long story short, the model dies in a car crash and the lovestruck writer ends up killing himself. Not until the closing seconds of the film do we discover the twist in the tale – namely, that Brosnan has orchestrated the suicide to avenge the murder of his gay lover, who Judd thought was having an affair with his girlfriend. By then, though, it would be a miracle if anyone cared about the outcome.

It's a shame, because with a bigger budget and better direction it could have been a good film. Why did Pierce appear in it? If one is cynical, one might speculate that it was the lure of going on an expenses-paid trip to Paris and a five-figure pay packet for a few days' work. Otherwise it's a mystery.

Following the release of *The Lawnmower Man*, Pierce had said: 'I've finally realised that what I really want to do is light comedy.' And in 1993 he got his chance to show his comic skills on the big screen, when he was cast in the Robin Williams vehicle, *Mrs Doubtfire*. 'I read for the part and thankfully got it,' he says. The film, directed by Chris Columbus, went on to become one of the biggest box office hits of the nineties, grossing over $220 million (£150 million) at the US box office alone.

Based on an English children's book, *Alias Madame Doubtfire*, the movie is about a divorcing couple, Daniel and Miranda Hillard (respectively played by Williams and Sally Field). Voice-over artist Daniel's 'principles' (New Age posturing) and 'love of life' (childishness) prevent him holding down a steady job. His exuberance makes him a hit with his kids but has exhausted the patience of his killjoy, career-orientated wife, who tells him their fourteen-year marriage is over, sues for divorce and gets custody of his beloved children.

Desperate to spend more time with the youngsters, Daniel, with the help of his make-up artist brother and and his own voice skills, creates Mrs Doubtfire – an elderly Scottish lady – who lands the job of housekeeper and nanny to the children. Playing against type, Pierce appeared as Miranda's smarmy new boyfriend, Stu, who looks set to sweep her off her feet – until Mrs Doubtfire intervenes.

'What are his intentions?' she asks. 'No, she cannot allow him any overnight stays! Does he not realise that Miranda is a married woman?' Says Brosnan: 'I am confronted by this nanny and know things look and sound a little odd. But I want to settle down so much with Miranda that I'll put up with anything.' But despite playing the suave smoothie to Williams's clown, his character still manages to emerge as a nice guy. 'Terrible things are done to my character but he's no wicked stepfather; he's a genuinely sympathetic character.'

At their first meeting, Stu, trying to be friendly, generously says: 'Miranda's been raving about you.' To which Mrs Doubtfire frostily replies: 'Odd, she's never mentioned you.' And when she discovers that the Mercedes parked outside is his, she bitchily says: 'Well, they say a man who has a big car is trying to cover up for a small . . .' Mrs D does her best to put Miranda off the hunky new man in her life. 'Stu?' she scoffs. 'That's more of a thick soup than a name.'

Later on, Stu (Pierce) emerges from a swimming pool, runs his fingers through his dark hair, lightly towels his tanned shoulders and smiles at Miranda and the children. Mrs Doubtfire takes one scornful look at his swimming costume and says: 'I see the water must have been very cold.' Then there's the classic moment when Mrs D, who's quietly getting sozzled at the poolside bar, hurls a piece of fruit at Stu's head. But Daniel eventually goes too far, smothering Stu's restaurant meal with ground pepper – knowing full well he's allergic to spices – causing him to choke on a prawn.

On the film set, Brosnan and Williams instantly bonded – even though the comic is a non-stop practical joker. 'It was great to work with Robin but a big challenge,' he said. 'He's a crazy man and all my scenes with him were improvised. It was a bit like free-falling. The clapper would go down and we'd be off. The ad-libs didn't bother me. I'm not in Robin's league because he's like quicksilver but I just about held my own.' The two men formed something of a double act – with Pierce playing the straight man to his joker – whether or not the cameras were rolling. 'I look at Pierce and think "handsome",' said Williams, during a break in filming. 'But I didn't realise that the guy could be so funny. Whenever I wanted to ad-lib, his expression didn't change and he'd come back at me with a line.' To which Brosnan replied with a laugh: 'My face didn't change because I was concentrating on your mouth, waiting for your lips to stop moving, so I could say my line!'

During a rare serious moment, Williams added: 'We wanted someone whose good looks were beyond question but who also has a sense of humour. How many guys in Hollywood can you say that about?' One of the biggest challenges facing Brosnan, though, was trying to keep a straight face during his scenes with Williams. 'Robin really made me laugh,' he says. 'I was just a hair's breadth away from cracking up most of the time.'

The critics are usually a bit sniffy about any film which has 'blockbuster' written all over it, as *Mrs Doubtfire* so obviously did. (They condescendingly seem to think that any movie with mass appeal can't be that good – after all, what do the public know about the cinema?) Several accused Williams of appearing in a 'sub-standard *Tootsie* role', but most agreed that he was still 'one of the funniest performers around'. And Pierce picked up some good reviews for a change – with the *Daily Mirror*, among others, declaring 'Brosnan's comic talent is a revelation.'

During a promotional group interview, it emerged that a foreign journalist was under the misconception that Pierce, like Daniel, was divorced. And in an attempt to be funny, he asked the actor who was going to get the Cadillac, him or his wife. 'Even if Brosnan hadn't been a widower, it would have been a monumentally tacky question,' says a showbusiness writer who was present. 'A lot of stars would have stormed out of the interview there and then and nobody would have blamed Pierce had he done so. But instead, much to everyone else's embarrassment, he corrected his questioner firmly but politely. He displayed great restraint under the circumstances.'

Following the movie's release, Pierce, who was accompanied by Sean to the movie's US première, said: 'Until now only one of my films, *The Lawnmower Man*, has made any impact. So I turned down TV work and took time to be selective and wait for the right role. I suffered financially but getting this part made it worthwhile.

'It's actually the first studio film I've been involved with – all my previous movies were independents, shot in India or Africa, or on the back streets of Los Angeles. Now people are patting me on the back and it feels great. I've always wanted to work with good people, and do work that will last and have resonance. Now it's finally happening. I think this film is truly a turning point.'

Publicly at least, Pierce was even more excited about his next project, *Love Affair*, even though he was to play the 'second banana' part. The film, starring real-life husband and wife Warren Beatty and Annette Bening, was a remake of 1957's classic weepie, *An Affair To Remember*, with Cary Grant and Deborah Kerr. The two stars play a couple – Mike Gambril and Terry McKay – who meet and unexpectedly fall in love, the only problem being that both are already engaged to other people. (Pierce played Bening's fiancé.) To discover if their love is the real thing, both agree not to see each other for three months. But on her way to the rendezvous, Terry is injured . . .

The picture, with its all-star cast – Beatty even charmed Katharine Hepburn into making an appearance – and Ennio Morricone score, seemed to have all the ingredients of a box office hit. But everything went wrong. The obsessive Beatty tried to take complete control of the picture, various writers came and went and the film simply 'didn't happen', to quote one critic.

It appeared that cinema-goers simply weren't interested in seeing Beatty and Bening kiss on screen. *Love Affair* grossed just $5 million in its first week on release in the US in October 1994, and subsequently sank without trace. Following this disaster, it went straight to video in much of the world, including Britain. But having a mere supporting role, Pierce could hardly be blamed for its failure.

Following Cassie's death, Pierce became a target for any number of gorgeous young women, eager to comfort him in his grief and put a smile on his face. And despite saying he 'planned to take things slowly and find out exactly who I am', the actor was subsequently linked to a number of glamorous women, including Roy Orbison's widow, Barbara, model Tatjana Patitz, television reporter Kathryn Kinley and rock star Bruce Springsteen's ex-wife, Julianne Phillips. 'After I lost Cassie I was in an arena I have never been in before and I received certain proposals which were very flattering,' he admits. And it is not uncommon, and certainly understandable, for a bereaved partner to occasionally seek solace, or distraction, in the arms of others simply to dull the sense of loss, and to pass interminable, lonely evenings.

One such proposal came from Denise Beaumont, the 35-year-old widow of a millionaire Hollywood hairdresser, who was introduced to him at a party by a mutual friend, film producer Bob Evans. Like most women, she found the actor 'polite and charming'.

'He was extremely shy and reserved at first,' says the sultry brunette, who had a thirteen-year-old daughter, Destiny, from her marriage. 'But he invited me to his Malibu home a few days later and I began to see more of him. He had a great sense of humour. He told me he'd spent a lot of time painting since Cassandra's death and showed me the part of the garden where he would sit with his wife.

'A few days later he invited me to his house again. His children were there and it was a little awkward, but then he sat us all down and and said to them "I need you to be okay with this. You knew this was going to happen sooner or later. I've met someone I like and I know you want me to be happy so this is a start." His kids were fine with me after that. We spent more quiet evenings together and I was madly in love with him by this time.'

Contrary to what Denise may have expected, the heart-throb star appeared reluctant to make the first move and end his self-imposed celibacy. 'Maybe he was thinking about his wife, maybe he was just shy,' she says. 'But once I took control it was great. He had a hard and supple body and was in great shape for a man of his age – and we made love inside and outside the house. He was a gentle, kind lover but everything I expected him to be in bed. I was the first woman he had made love to since the death of his wife.'

Their six-week romance looked as if it could develop into a loving, long-term relationship but then came a bombshell. It turned out that Beaumont was anything but the classy, sedate widow with a taste for conservative clothes that she had appeared to be. In fact, she was a retired porn queen – who'd starred in a blue movie called *High Heels* about a sex-crazed hooker – famous for throwing outrageous parties and dancing in nothing but a tight-fitting top and micro-skirt.

She had been told to leave the Pompeii disco in Palm Springs after writhing around on the dance floor semi-naked and the owner had threatened to call the police. She had also been thrown out of the Jehovah's Witness church in Palm Springs because of her 'devilish ways'. Former lovers included superstars Jack Nicholson and Warren Beatty. Beaumont's speciality was apparently 'bending over in front of men and exposing her naked backside'. It didn't take long for the tabloids to come up with a suitable nickname for her – 'Miss No-Knickers'.

'I used to throw what I called "tits and ass parties", but there didn't seem any point in telling Pierce about that side of my life,' says Denise. 'When he found out he asked me all these questions about my past. I tried to smooth things out, explaining that whatever I'd done was history, but nothing worked. He was furious and our relationship was over, just as suddenly as it had begun. I shall never forget our idyllic weeks together but I don't think his career would have survived the scandal of having me as his lover.'

Afterwards, Pierce – and you can't really blame him – tried to play down the relationship, claiming: 'I simply had dinner with a woman called Denise Beaumont and it got blown out of all proportion.' Nevertheless, it was a cautionary tale and made Brosnan more careful than ever about the women he dated – but how was he to know about Beaumont's seedy past? Several years later he had this to say about a fling he'd enjoyed at the time – presumably with Denise Beaumont. 'In the spring of 1992 I fell in love with somone who was just toxic. It was a really poisonous relationship. I knew I was on the wrong train to start with but for maybe nine months the lust factor got the better of me.'

Soon afterwards he stepped out with eighteen-year-old Yugoslav tennis player Monica Seles at a Los Angeles showbusiness bash. But it was Roy Orbison's beautiful widow, Barbara, with whom he would enjoy his next serious relationship. She, too, lived in Malibu, and had occasionally dropped in to give Cassandra encouragement in her fight for life. Following her death, the 41-year-old offered Pierce a shoulder to cry on, and the two would go for walks along the beach. She herself knew all about losing a partner. For singing legend Orbison – who'd penned classics like 'Pretty Woman', 'Crying' and 'Only The Lonely' – had dropped dead three years earlier after suffering a massive heart attack, aged just 52. Ever since, Barbara had dedicated herself to charity work.

The platonic relationship slowly developed into romance. 'She started out as my friend,' Brosnan reportedly told a pal. 'Now she's the woman in my life.' The couple would have dinner at little beach restaurants and Barbara invited Pierce and Sean to her house for dinner. After quietly dating for several months, they finally went public at a Beverly Hills charity gala in aid of cancer research, in early December 1992. 'They only had eyes for each other,' said one onlooker. 'They held hands and sneaked quick kisses when they thought no one was looking.'

However, the relationship fizzled out and within months a new woman entered his life. She was Tatjana Patitz, a stunning six-foot Swedish model-turned-actress who appeared in the £1 million Vauxhall TV advert alongside Naomi Campbell and Kate Moss, before landing a small but memorable part in *Rising Sun* opposite former 007 Sean Connery.

Unlikely as it may sound, Pierce met the 28-year-old at a cowboy dancing class in Los Angeles. 'He kept looking over at Tatjana,' says dance instructor C. C. Morgan. 'And when the music stopped he asked her to join him for a drink.' One of Tatjana's friends, model Laurinda De Le Pina, said shortly afterwards: 'They're head over heels in love.'

In May 1993, Tatjana and her mother joined Pierce at his 40th birthday bash. A surprise party was organised at Jimmy's, one of the actor's favourite Los Angeles restaurants, by his English-born PA, Mary O'Connell. More than 90 people attended, including tough guy actor Charles Bronson, singer Julian Lennon, and Pierce's mother, May. The four-foot-by-two-foot cake, trimmed with Emerald Isle green icing, was in the shape of a giant '40'. In the course of the evening Pierce told a friend: 'For the first time since my wife died I've really felt love for another woman.'

However, by the autumn the romance was over. Tatjana wanted some kind of commitment – which he could not give. 'It was just too soon after Cassie's death,' he explains. While Tatjana, who was subsequently linked to actor Johnny Depp, among others, says: 'I realised from the start that things might not work out. After all, he was still getting over the death of his wife. But was I wrong for daring to think I might be the one to take her place? The romance is over, but Pierce and I remain friends.'

In late 1993, he was linked to another beauty, Kathryn Kinley, a showbusiness reporter for a New York-based cable TV station. He met the glamorous blonde – who bore a resemblance to his late wife – while promoting *Mrs Doubtfire*. Twenty minutes into the interview, the 32-year-old claims she found herself falling in love with the suave actor. 'We just clicked,' she says. 'I'd interviewed just about every Hollywood star imaginable – including Sean Connery – but never felt any attraction. With Pierce, though, it was instant.'

The hour-long interview stretched into tea for two and then long into the night. 'What happened that evening is private and not for discussion,' says Kinley. 'But it will never leave me. It was a wonderful night, and believe me, Pierce is a healthy, passionate male.' Again, though, Brosnan was keen to play down the romance, saying: 'Kathryn and I are just having a good time together.'

The couple became an 'item', as they say, but all too soon, this romance, too, came to an end and the couple decided they 'would no longer be exclusive to one another'. By March 1994, just a few months after they had met, Kinley was saying: 'It's over between us. I made a major mistake in thinking Pierce was ready for marriage again. I'd met his children and got along with them great. I was even planning to leave New York to join him in California. Then Pierce just told me he couldn't handle it yet. I'm not sure Pierce knows what kind of woman he is looking for. Nobody could replace Cassie in his eyes.'

She went on to say: 'There's been no earth-shattering break-up and we're still in touch. But I don't think Pierce and I were perfectly in sync; we've both very much into our careers.' As to reports linking him to other women, she said: 'They aren't important; it hurts a little when you hear he's been dating someone else but you go on. Mind you, I'd have to be dead not to feel a little hurt.'

Before long, though, Pierce was enjoying the company of stunning 33-year-old ex-model Julianne Phillips. Her marriage to Bruce 'The Boss' Springsteen – one of the actor's rock idols – had ended in 1988 because he'd wanted children while she wanted an acting career.

Both Pierce and Julianne had been involved with other partners when they first met at a celebrity sports tournament in 1994. But a friend was reported as having said: 'Pierce took one long at Julianne and his heart skipped a beat. Julianne is a strong, take-charge woman, very similar in nature to Cassandra, and they had a long conversation and got on really well.' Their relationship soon flowered and by April the source was saying: 'Pierce is serious about Julianne. Both have had difficult times and fought through them – it's a bond they share.' But this relationship, too, inexplicably died a death.

Being a Hollywood star, Pierce never had any trouble getting a date. As one LA-based showbusiness writer says: 'I've yet to meet a woman who didn't find Brosnan extremely attractive – he's everything most girls are looking for in a man.' But after so many false starts, he must have wondered sometimes whether he would ever find true love again.

In late 1994, though, nearly three years after Cassie's death, Pierce met Keely Shaye-Smith, the former face of Estée Lauder's organic, cruelty-free cosmetics range, Origins. Their first encounter took place in Mexico, where she was on an environmental assignment for America's *Entertainment Tonight* with the 'Clean Oceans' campaign manager and actor, Ted Danson.

'He was reading and I was working and we said hallo,' says the brunette, who had her own home in LA where she grew organic vegetables. 'I asked him for an eco tip and he told me that he recycled glass, plastic and newspapers, and I thought, "Good for you".' As for Pierce, he recalls: 'This beautiful girl came up to me and we just hit it off.'

The couple spent time together writing poetry, swimming and walking along the beach near his Malibu home. She also liked listening to Brosnan play the flute. (One of the many hobbies Pierce seems to have picked up and tried out in an endearingly enthusiastic way.) Asked if Keely was the new lady in his life, Pierce smiled but would only say:

'She is a lovely Californian girl who has been a good companion and friend to me.' Within months, though, it was obvious that she was the most important woman to come into his life since Cassie's death. The two older children, in particular, got on well with her – even though Keely, at 30, was just a few years older than Charlotte.

12. LICENSED TO THRILL

In April 1994, Timothy Dalton announced that he was quitting the Bond role. 'I believe the time has come to seek new challenges,' he said, speaking in Charleston, South Carolina, where he was filming *Scarlett*, a TV sequel to *Gone With The Wind*. His departure was not a total surprise. He'd never seemed entirely happy in the role – and the disappointing performance of his second 007 film, *Licensed To Kill*, which grossed just over $156 million (about £100 million) worldwide, had left a question mark over his future.

Immediately, speculation began as to who would win the race to play the new Bond. Having come so close to landing the part eight years earlier, Brosnan quickly emerged as the favourite. But a lot had changed in the intervening years. The Bond films no longer generated the old excitement – the formula was beginning to look jaded; it seemed as if the franchise was being milked for all it was worth; and Dalton had failed to breathe new life into the character. Action-packed, big-budget blockbusters like *Die Hard*, *Speed*, *The Fugitive* and *True Lies* now reigned supreme at the box office. Audiences had been conditioned to expect fantastic stunts, hair-raising chases and mind-boggling blasts. And many critics felt that, in contrast, 1989's *Licensed To Kill* just hadn't packed enough of a punch. Any new Bond film would have to be really spectacular.

The great big bear of a man who masterminded 007's transition to the big screen, Cubby Broccoli, was hoping to persuade a big-name star like Mel Gibson to don Bond's tuxedo and give the aging spy a shot of adrenaline. He had the looks, charisma and sex appeal – 'the sheer machismo' – to fill 007's shoes and Broccoli reportedly offered him £10 million to sign on the dotted line, but he declined, saying the role was 'too boring'. Irish actor Liam Neeson was also approached – although, as one pundit said, he looked a bit 'rough and ready' for the role. But Neeson was still basking in the success of Steven Spielberg's harrowing concentration camp drama, *Schindler's List*, and announced that playing Bond was 'too frivolous' for his taste.

There were a number of other contenders. Harrison Ford had proved one of the cinema's most enduring stars. Despite being in his fifties, he had been dubbed 'a Bond for the nineties' following his starring role as Jack Ryan in *Patriot Games*; while Britain's Hugh Grant had shot to overnight fame in *Four Weddings And A Funeral* and was perceived as another possible candidate – even though it was hard to imagine him beating up the bad guys. As it happened, Ford wasn't interested and Grant, though screen-tested, declined the role. Dashing Ralph Fiennes, who appeared in *Schindler's List* and *Quiz Show*, and *Batman* star Michael Keaton were also mentioned as possibilities. And two up-and-coming British actors, Jeremy Northam and Jason Isaacs, were screen-tested – but were too little known to be in with a serious chance of landing the part.

In the coming weeks, the tabloids would have a lot of fun speculating on who might step into 007's shoes. It was suggested that the secret agent could be given a sex change for the nineties and return as 'Jane Bond'. Sexy Sharon Stone, who rose to fame in *Basic Instinct*, or Oscar-winning actress Emma Thompson could presumably step into the spy's newly-bought high-heeled shoes, thought one newspaper. There was even a wild claim that Denzel Washington was set to play the part – thus becoming the first black Bond. Things soon got even sillier, with bookies William Hill taking bets on who would be the next 007. Among the outsiders were prime minister John Major (200-1) and camp comic Julian Clary (250-1) – though you can't help wondering what sort of people were placing such stakes. However, the odds-on favourite, at 8-11, was Brosnan.

Finally, after weeks of feverish speculation, a press conference was called at the Regent (now the Landmark) Hotel in Marylebone Road, London, on Wednesday 8 June 1994, to announce the identity of the man – or woman – who would succeed Sean Connery, George Lazenby, Roger Moore and Tim Dalton.

More than 350 reporters from around the world packed into a vast ground-floor function room. The James Bond theme music piped up, and Pierce stepped out from behind the screen. (It was a case of *You Only Live Twice*, Ian Fleming might have joked.) Dozens of cameramen yelled out 'Pierce! Pierce!' and started flashing away. It was a dream come true for the actor, yet he says: 'Nothing could prepare me for the pandemonium. It was as if everyone wanted a piece of me. All I could do was smile and try to be gracious.'

Ironically, the Bond who appeared before the world's press that day – dressed in a black Armani suit, blue shirt and grey, polka-dot tie – bore little correlation to most people's mental picture of the suave secret agent. For Brosnan was sporting a grey-flecked beard and long hair in preparation for a starring role in a CBS TV drama, *Robinson Crusoe*, that was due to film in the South Seas the following week.

It was first rumoured that Brosnan would be taking over from Roger Moore as the next 007 way back in 1984, prompting denials from all concerned. The story, it was claimed, had originated from an American magazine's poll to discover its readers' choice for the next Bond, with Pierce topping the list. At the time, the actor joked: 'Why should Roger ever give up? He could go on playing James Bond forever. It's a piece of cake.'

After being cheated of the role in 1986, Brosnan said that even if Dalton quit the role and 'Cubby Broccoli got down on bended knee', he wouldn't be tempted. 'I could never play Bond now,' he insisted. 'That would be foolish. I've dipped my toes in the water once and couldn't go through all that again. It would be stale – like going back into an old cupboard with too many ghosts.' He went on to question whether 007 even had a long-term future, asking: 'The films have been going for something like 25 years and you have to wonder how long the character can survive.'

However, saying you would turn down a role theoretically offered to you, and doing so in practice, are two very different things. And despite what had happened, Pierce jumped at the opportunity to play Bond when he got a second chance in 1994. It was a role that had meant so much to him – and Cassie – for so long. 'I didn't think twice,' he says. 'It was unfinished business.' His children were equally happy. 'I was so pleased,' says Charlotte. 'It's special because Mum was a Bond girl.' While little Sean excitedly asked: 'Does that mean we can have a rollercoaster?'

The decision to offer the part to Pierce was taken following a series of meetings between Broccoli, his 34-year-old daughter, Barbara and stepson Michael Wilson – both of whom were to be producers on the forthcoming film. The job wasn't simply Brosnan's for the taking, though. Part of the reason Broccoli had offered him the role eight years earlier was because he'd proved such a hit with the American public in *Remington Steele*. By the nineties, he wasn't the fresh young star that he'd been. His Remington days were far behind him and his subsequent career had been patchy, to say the least – with only two of his big screen ventures, *The Lawnmower Man* and *Mrs Doubtfire* – really making their mark. And both could be branded flukes.

To therefore cast him as Bond represented a risk, a bigger risk than some in the Broccoli camp would have liked. Once again, though, the public tipped the balance in his favour. The movie-makers carried out extensive research which showed that the clean-cut actor was a big favourite with women – a vital factor in the Bond films' earlier success. Just as crucially, when 30,000 viewers of a US television show took part in a telephone poll in May 1994, to choose the next James Bond, a staggering 85 per cent voted for Pierce; Hugh Grant could muster only 3 per cent and Mel Gibson a mere 7 per cent.

After more than 30 years of dreaming about playing the character, Pierce finally took the all-important call informing him that he'd got the part at 12.35 p.m. on 1 June at his Malibu home. The sky was blue and the sun shone down that afternoon. Could it be a lucky omen? His agent, Fred Spector, was on the other end of the line. 'Hello, Mr Bond, you've got the part,' he said warmly.

Eight years earlier, Pierce might have whooped with joy. But older, wiser – and a little sadder – he now simply savoured the moment that had been so long in coming. Shortly afterwards, the telephone calls began. His mother May called from her home in Wimbledon, 6,000 miles away, to offer her congratulations. He was then joined by his girlfriend Keely and son Sean, home from school. 'Life then went into full throttle,' says Pierce. 'But I really had no idea of what was to come.'

In 1952, Eton-educated Ian Fleming, a former Reuters journalist and naval intelligence officer, sat down to write 'the thriller to end all thrillers'. He was 44. The result was *Casino Royale*, the first 007 novel, published the following year. He never wanted to write a great literary work – instead, his stories revolved around scantily clad girls, fast cars, fiendish despots, guns, exotic locations and a silky smooth English spy. 'The target of my books lies somewhere between the upper solar plexus and the upper thigh,' he once said. 'I write for warm-blooded heterosexuals in railway trains, aeroplanes and beds.'

Despite being named after an American ornithologist who had written a book about birds (the feathered variety) of the West Indies, Fleming's hero was a composite. He was largely based on his friend Fitzroy Maclean – another old Etonian, who joined the SAS in 1942 and carried out daring wartime raids behind enemy lines in North Africa, parachuted into Nazi-occupied Yugoslavia and had close links with the intelligence services – and on his own debonair self.

Just how close to Fleming's original blueprint was Brosnan's Bond, though? In *Casino Royale*, the author dubs Bond a 'not particularly attractive, blunt instrument of Government policy', describing him as having 'grey-blue eyes, a short lock of black hair that would never stay in place and a thin vertical scar down his right cheek' which made him look 'faintly piratical'. In stark contrast, Pierce's Bond would rarely have a hair out of place. But in all probability, he wouldn't have got the part if he'd had a spot, let alone a scar, on his cheek.

The author also spoke about Bond 'lighting his 70th cigarette of the day'. Aside from the fact that Britain's top agent wouldn't be around today – unless he was hanging on to life via a respirator – if he'd been puffing away so furiously, today's health fears made it unthinkable for a Bond of the nineties to be a chain smoker.

When it came to women, Fleming's suave secret agent was sexist to the core, like his creator. Just read the following passage in *Casino Royale*, which shows 007's somewhat less than politically correct reaction on learning he's been assigned a – naturally beautiful – female assistant:

> 'What the hell do they want to send me a woman for,' Bond said bitterly. 'Do they think this is a bloody picnic?' He sighed. Women were for recreation. On a job, they got in the way and fogged things up with sex and hurt feelings and all the emotional baggage they carried around. One had to look out for them and take care of them.

It wasn't just attitudes that had changed since the fifties. In one passage in *Casino Royale*, the Bond 'girl' tells 007: 'I did so want to be gay. And I am gay.' Needless to say, our understanding of the word 'gay' bears no relation to its use then. Our first reaction would probably be, 'What use could a lesbian Bond girl serve in a 007 movie?' The very notion of what being British involves has also changed beyond recognition. In the fifties, Britain still had an empire, and counted itself a superpower. (Only the USA, the Soviet Union, and perhaps China, were more powerful.)

One can't help wondering what Fleming – who died of a heart attack, aged 56, in 1964 – would have had to say if told that a lad from a humble Irish background would one day play his upper-crust secret agent. Despite Brosnan's very different start in life to Bond – one privileged, the other impoverished – the answers he gave at that June 1994 press conference showed he was very much in touch with the character.

'We're going to go back to basics,' Brosnan told the media. 'My Bond will be charming and sophisticated – but also utterly ruthless. There's a lethal quality to him and I want to bring out the flinty side of the character. After all, he's a trained killer and is licensed to kill.' He dismissed any supposed similarities between the secret agent and Remington Steele, saying: 'There's no comparison. With Bond we're talking about a man who has lived, whereas Remington was somebody who just got by – he didn't even like carrying a gun.'

He also vowed to dispense with the character's sexist overtones, saying: 'We are still looking at how we're going to shake things up. One of the things that originally turned people on to Bond was sexism. The sexism is a bit outdated and that has to be addressed. This will be a Bond for the nineties.' However, for all the talk of toning down the sexism, the last thing he planned to do was make Bond a new man. Heaven forbid! 'Making 007 too politically correct would make him boring,' he explained. 'He has to have some bite, some edge.'

Unlike the austere Dalton, though, who was also keen to get back to the Bond of the books, Brosnan realised a sense of humour was especially important in the nineties, in view of his character's anachronistic tendencies. He too showed a ready wit. 'A Guinness would be rather good now,' he observed at the press conference. When a Japanese journalist enquired if he had hair on his chest, he joked: 'Yes, I stuck it on this morning.' And pressed as to whether 007 would still go around bedding girls, he quipped: 'I'm sure Bond will be issued with the best condoms – they'll probably even glow in the dark!'

In addition, Brosnan wanted 'to peel back the layers and look at the demons in Bond's soul' and warned that he would make no attempt to disguise his soft Irish brogue. 'Sean Connery is Scottish and kept his accent so I'll keep mine,' he said. But when pestered to say: 'The name is Bond, James Bond', he narrowed his steel-blue eyes and told his inquisitor politely but firmly: 'You'll just have to wait for the film.'

He signed on the dotted line with Broccoli's Eon Productions for a reported £1.5 million. And his first Bond picture, *GoldenEye*, was set for a 1995 release. Perhaps not surprisingly, co-producer Barbara Broccoli told journalists she was delighted Brosnan was on board for the latest 007 adventure, saying: 'He's perfect. He has all the qualities we feel Bond needs. He's got charm and charisma and he's very sexy.' Put another way, if desire for the role had anything to do with being a successful Bond, Brosnan 'clearly had the credentials', one reporter commented.

The press conference duly generated headlines around the world. Just about everyone seemed to agree that Pierce was the man to save Bond from oblivion. Only one person had any doubts: Brosnan himself. That evening he lay on the bed in his hotel suite and thought: 'What the hell have I said yes to? Oh, God, Cassie, Cassie! Are you up there? Can you hear? Am I supposed to feel this shitty?'

Filming on *GoldenEye* had originally been due to start in the autumn of 1994. But it was put back four months after executives reportedly saw the state-of-the-art special effects in Arnold Schwarzenegger's summer smash, *True Lies* – which some critics dubbed a 007 spoof – and realised Bond's comeback movie needed beefing up.

In early 1993, after a long legal battle between MGM/UA, the studio that funded the films, and Broccoli's Eon Productions, which owns the 007 franchise, Broccoli had commissioned Michael France (who penned the screenplay for the Sly Stallone film, *Cliffhanger*) to write the script for *GoldenEye* – the name of Fleming's Jamaican beach house. France had travelled to Russia, even interviewing KGB agents, to observe the current state of military intelligence and delivered a screenplay in April 1994. But following the Schwarzenegger-inspired attack of the jitters, it was decided to pump at least £5 million more into the film. Another writer, London-born Jeffrey Caine, was invited to add his own ideas. And further revisions were later made by two more screenwriters. After this last-minute tinkering with the script, and the addition of several spectacular sequences, the *GoldenEye* screenplay finally got the green light.

Ironically, Bond's regular home at Pinewood, Buckinghamshire, with its purpose-built 007 stage, was unavailable after a sudden upturn in the number of pictures being shot in Britain. (Julia Roberts was filming the Jekyll and Hyde drama, *Mary Reilly*, at the studio.) An intense search for the right studio setting followed, with the infamous Greenham Common air base even being considered. But in June 1994, Eon took out a one-year rental contract on a former Rolls Royce factory – opened in 1940 to manufacture the Mosquito bomber – at Leavesden, Hertfordshire, about twenty miles from London. Among its advantages were the 1.25 million square feet of interior space and a 1,000-yard disused runway. It was so big that a week after filming had begun, Pierce was still complaining: 'I can't find my dressing room.'

There were a couple of other last-minute hitches. Brosnan had been training hard for the big role, working out with weights and kick-boxing at his Malibu home; perhaps too hard. In December 1995, he was admitted to Cedars-Sinai Medical Center in Los Angeles – under the alias Philip Picano – in terrible pain. Doctors diagnosed a herniated disc in his lower back and he underwent a three-hour operation. The surgery was a success and he was released from hospital two days later. Then he severed several tendons in his fingers. He couldn't even hold a gun properly, and despite daily physiotherapy, filming was delayed by a week. It was rumoured that he'd injured himself in a manly, all-action pursuit like hang-gliding. The truth was somewhat less glamorous. The injury was caused when a porcelain towel-rail he was using as a support to get out of the bath snapped. 'I felt such a prat making that one public,' he later confessed. (His reputation as the fledgling new all-action superhero suffered another dent shortly afterwards, when he was relieved of his wallet on the set of the film. Security was subsequently stepped up.)

Filming could have been delayed even longer if the makers of *The Lawnmower Man* had got nasty and things had boiled over into a *Remington Steele*-style legal fight. For Brosnan had been lined up to appear in the follow-up movie, *The Lawnmower Man: Jobe's War*, with shooting planned to start in late 1994. But having landed the 007 role, he had quit. Although no contract had been signed, there was an assumption at movie-makers Alliance Vision that Brosnan would do the film, and when he pulled out, executives were said to be 'absolutely furious'.

However, *The Lawnmower Man's* producer, Ed Simon, commented: 'Initially we were very unhappy because we had a commitment from him and we considered going to court. But Pierce has always wanted to play Bond, and the last thing I want is to engage an actor in a film he doesn't want to be in. Of course, I'm disappointed, but we'll just have to find another actor. In any case, the special effects were what made *The Lawnmower Man* a hit, not Pierce Brosnan.' This may have been the case, but the sequel bombed at the box office.

True to tradition, *GoldenEye* opened with a stunning visual sequence – some would argue the most spectacular opening sequence of any Bond film. Dressed in a no-nonsense black jumpsuit, 007 plunges more than 600 feet from a huge dam into a top secret Soviet nerve gas facility deep inside the Arctic Circle, with just a bungee cord for support. He then fires a piton gun into the concrete roof of the plant and literally drops in on a Red Army soldier reading a newspaper in a toilet cubicle. 'Beg your pardon, forgot to knock,' he quips.

The world's longest-ever bungee jump, it was actually shot from the top of a 70-storey high dam in Locarno, Switzerland – at a cost of £100,000. Although Brosnan liked to do his stunts, he was not foolhardy enough to try *that* particular stunt – so dangerous that the Oxford University bungee jump team warned the movie-makers: 'You're jumping into the unknown.' It was actually performed by top stuntman Wayne Michaels, who became the first man to abseil from one jet to another in mid-flight in *Cliffhanger*.

On gaining entry to the base, Bond teams up with his 006 secret service colleague, Alec Trevelyan (played by *Sharpe* star Sean Bean, with an uncharacteristic upper-crust accent). 'For England,' says Alex, as they go into battle. But their cover is blown and the Red Army's General Ourumov (Gottfried John), leads a counter-attack.

It's a desperate situation and Trevelyan is captured. 'Come out with your hands up,' orders Ourumov, who sees himself as the next iron man of Russia. 'How original,' mutters Bond sarcastically. He has a choice – to abandon the operation or try to fight his own way to freedom. Of course, the word 'surrender' doesn't figure in 007's vocabulary and he doggedly fights on, despite facing impossible odds. He sets the explosive charges, jumps down a chute and ends up on the runway. A light plane is taxiing to take-off on the edge of a sheer drop. Bond jumps into the cockpit but in the ensuing struggle both he and the pilot fall to the ground. A soldier on a motorbike who is giving chase swerves and crashes. Bond picks himself up, jumps on to the riderless machine and roars after the plane.

Just as it disappears over the precipice, Bond does the unthinkable – he accelerates and sends himself and the bike hurtling after it, into the abyss. Going into freefall, he manoeuvres himself towards the plane, grabs the wing-strut and hauls himself into the cockpit. With the ground hurtling towards him, he pulls out of the dive at the last minute and just clears the jagged rocks, as his bomb rips apart the plant . . .

The first day of filming took place on 16 January 1995. Pierce had rented an elegant five-bedroom Georgian house in Hampstead, London, for the twenty-week shoot. Each day a chauffeur-driven Mercedes would pull up at six o'clock in the morning and whisk him to Leavesden, three miles from the M25. Rehearsals would start at eight o'clock.

The first thing to get right was the look. For while Pierce undoubtedly lived up to the public's perception of how Bond should look, it was still vital to get the details right. Consequently, the first person he would meet at the studio or location each morning was make-up supervisor, Linda DeVetta, who insisted the star never have a close shave during the shoot because his features were 'a little too perfect'. She explains: 'I wanted him to keep some stubble to rough him up a bit – otherwise he'd have looked too young and too smooth.'

He also acquired a wardrobe second to none, thanks to costume designer, Lindy Hemming, who says: 'We wanted him to look modern, but not trendy like some advertising executive.' His £135 shirts came from Bond Street, his £1,850 Brioni suits – a total of eighteen were bought – came from Italy, and his £160 shoes came from top British bootmakers, Church's. All in all, his clothing budget approached £100,000 but, as one insider says: 'It was worth every penny – Pierce had to look the part.'

He had tried hard to make the movie a family affair. His stepson, Christopher, was working on the production as a runner. He also acted as a 'hand double' for his dad – and it's his hands we see in close up, not Pierce's, when Bond pulls on a hand-brake and flips open a glove compartment. 'I can't tell you the comfort it's given me, having him around,' said Pierce. Sean attended a local school for the duration of his father's stay in England.

In preparation for the part, Brosnan browsed through Fleming's novels and watched the first two Bond films – *Dr. No* and *From Russia With Love* – both of which starred Connery. But for all the earlier talk of creating a new Bond for the nineties, when it came to the crunch, Brosnan had few worries about how he'd play the part. 'He drinks the drink, gets the girl and finds himself in dangerous situations,' he said. 'I didn't want to think of a special twist or new angle – I just wanted to keep him as simple, direct and as exciting as possible.'

He was also grateful for the words of encouragement he received from his predecessors. 'Roger sent a lovely telegram which just said, "From the old James Bond to the new James Bond – kill 'em, sport",' reveals Pierce. 'Sean complimented me as an actor in an interview, which I thought was high praise, coming from him. And Tim sent a note wishing me luck. It was nice to be acknowledged by the guys.'

However, he was still nervous when he arrived at the studio that first morning. 'All I was thinking was that I didn't want to mess it up. Apart from the stakes being high, I wanted to get it right for Cassie. If I'd messed up and killed Bond, she'd have said, "Well, it took an Irishman to do it!" I knew I'd be judged against my predecessors, Connery and Moore, and they were big shoes to fill. I know the knives are out and the cynics say Bond is finished. It's up to me to prove them wrong.'

The film, directed by New Zealander Martin Campbell, is set in a world where the Hammer and Sickle have been replaced by something even more sinister – organised crime, with Russia at the centre of a new European mafia whose tentacles spread across the world. Against this backcloth, Bond is assigned to retrieve a hijacked secret NATO helicopter which is now a tug-of-peace prize between the great powers and a vicious criminal mind, code-named Janus, who takes control of *GoldenEye*, a Russian Star Wars-type satellite system with immense destructive power. The breathtaking title sequence was the first of many chases, stunts and punch-ups that peppered *GoldenEye*, helping to make it the most thrilling Bond film for years.

After the opening credits, the action shifts forward nine years – though 007 doesn't look as if he's aged a day. Bond is at the wheel of his famous Aston Martin DB5. Sitting beside him is Caroline (Serena Gordon), a Sloane Rangerish young woman sent to evaluate him. Suddenly a blood-red Ferrari 355 pulls up with a beautiful woman, Xenia Onatopp (Famke Janssen), at the wheel. The two proceed to conduct a high-speed game of cat and mouse down a treacherous mountain road – with near perilous results for a party of cyclists.

The most destructive chase takes place in St Petersburg after Bond has once again escaped an appointment with death, courtesy of the odious General Ourumov. Swinging from a ceiling like Errol Flynn, he crashes through a circular window and lands on a lorry's tarpaulin canopy. Clambering on to a tank, he takes the controls and chases Ourumov through the city's streets, destroying a bridge, road island and alley-way, and slicing a Perrier lorry in half. As if that's not enough, the tank ploughs into a statue of Tsar Nicholas sitting astride a winged horse, smashing the plinth and leaving the statue perched on the tank's turret. It was fantastic stuff – and virtually guaranteed to have cinema audiences across America cheering out loud.

Originally, Pierce was to fly out to St Petersburg to film the complex action sequence, which involved the use of three 36-ton tanks and the destruction of a dozen Lada cars. But worries over red tape, the likely damage to city streets, not to mention gas pipes and water mains, and ironically the Russian mafia, led to a last-minute change of plan. Instead – thanks to a vast set, 750 feet long and 50 feet wide, made up of 62 miles of scaffolding – St Petersburg was brought to Leavesden. While somewhat bizarrely, the Queen's stand at Epsom race track doubled up as St Petersburg Airport.

Having somehow evaded Bond and got to the train station, Ourumov boarded a train with a huge armour-plated battering ram and made a dash for the open country – only to be confronted by Bond's tank emerging from the mouth of a tunnel. Everyone knows that a Bond movie is pure fantasy, but having the metal monster outpace the train was perhaps pushing things a little too far.

True to form, *GoldenEye* finished with an epic fight to the finish between 007 and the traitorous, blood-thirsty Trevelyan, who is bent on destroying the world in a bid to make himself fabulously rich. The two men, both trained by British Intelligence, battle it out on a satellite communications tower high above a giant radio dish. 'Pierce was up and down the ladder like a hod carrier,' says one insider. But, of course, there could be only one outcome – despite the young Brosnan's inclination to turn the other cheek when confronted by a bully in the playground.

For all the talk of toning down certain aspects of the Bond films, there were still girls, glamour and gadgets aplenty. In Xenia Onatopp, (played by the five-foot-eleven Dutch ex-model Janssen), the movie-makers had stumbled upon the sexiest, most gloriously over-the-top Bond villainess since Barbara Carrera starred opposite Connery in 1983's unofficial Bond film, *Never Say Never Again*. 'How do you take it?' says 007, offering to buy her a drink. 'Straight up with a twist,' responds the cigar-smoking beauty.

A deadly Russian assassin, Xenia Onatopp kills her victims by crushing them between her thighs during lovemaking – giving new meaning to the expression 'killing with kindness'. Poor Pierce gets to experience her version of rough sex first hand when, as 007, he visits a steam room to relax. Pretending to be attracted to him, Xenia circles her arms around him, but within seconds has wrapped her legs around him in a bid to squeeze the life from his lungs.

One American tabloid reported that Pierce had 'flipped' for the 29-year-old beauty fluent in four languages. 'My God, if this woman is half as nice as she looks, I'm in deep trouble,' he allegedly told friends. 'I'm absolutely crazy about her. She has that European way of being sexy without even trying; I've always been a sucker for European women.' The only trouble was that Janssen was married to film director Tod Williams, and Pierce was going out with Keely Shaye-Smith. The magazine claimed the star was 'torn between the two women' but he laughed off the report, saying: 'It's rubbish.'

The *GoldenEye* girl, Natalya Simonova, played by Swedish ex-model, Izabella Scorupco, was as beautiful as any 'Bond bird' from the past. 'She's got luscious lips,' Brosnan joked in one interview. But this time she also had brains and worked as a computer programmer. Sadly for the guys, she favoured sexy but stylish modern outfits over the skimpy bikinis worn by former Bond girls like Ursula Andress and Barbara Bach. However, despite this being the politically correct nineties, few can have been surprised when 007 eventually had his wicked way with the 'luscious-lipped' lovely. 'Everywhere I go, women ask me, "What was it like kissing Pierce Brosnan?" ' says Scorupco.

Indeed, Pierce showed beyond doubt that 007 hadn't lost his touch with the ladies. He wooed the upper-crust woman sent to evaluate him by secret service chiefs with the help of a chilled bottle of Bollinger champagne hidden inside his Aston Martin. 'Let's toast your evaluation,' he tells her before planting a kiss on her lips within minutes of the film opening. 'A very thorough evaluation . . .' He also continued his 33-year-old flirtation with M's secretary, Miss Moneypenny, played for the first time by the wholesome Samantha Bond, wearing a slinky black silk dress. However, this time she gave as good as she got. On learning that she's been on a date, 007 feigns jealousy and teasingly says: 'What would I do without you, Moneypenny?' She coolly replies: 'As far as I can remember, James, you've never had me.' Not to be outdone, he cheekily adds: 'Hope springs eternal.'

One of the highlights of making *GoldenEye* for Pierce was working with an altogether different type of 'Bond girl', in fact more of a woman – Dame Judi Dench, one of Britain's foremost stage and screen actresses. At 60, she was at the peak of her profession and her casting as 007's domineering boss, M, lent an air of gravitas to the picture. It was the first time a female had got to play the part in a Bond movie, in recognition of the fact that Britain's real-life secret service chief was now a woman (Stella Rimmington). She also got to say one of the most widely quoted lines of the film, bluntly telling Bond: 'I think you're a sexist, misogynist dinosaur . . . a relic of the cold war.' The scene – which Dench says she enjoyed 'enormously' – theoretically took place at MI6's striking, highly visible new headquarters on the bank of the River Thames at Vauxhall, just a few hundred yards from the Oval House, although it was actually shot at Leavesden.

Beforehand, Pierce had admitted he was terrified of Dame Judi – hardly the sort of confession one would expect from Bond – and said her superb track record left him feeling vulnerable. To his surprise, though, he discovered that she was even more nervous about shooting the scene than him, and not for the first time 'found himself in the role of comforter', according to one insider. Both initially botched their lines, but the scene was soon in the bag. (Incidentally, the 'whisky' in their glasses was nothing more lethal than apple juice.)

The movie also had its share of glamorous settings – including Russia, the Caribbean and that old favourite, Monte Carlo. Once Pierce arrived in the millionaire's paradise, he visibly relaxed. It was as if the sunshine, sparkling sea, yachts, stunning women and sleek sports cars – the sheer glamour of the place – rekindled childhood memories of old 007 films and reminded him of just how big a part he'd landed, truly the 'most famous film role in the world'.

However, despite drawing inspiration from his presence there, he was unable to live up to the supercool Bond myth all the time. 'We had to shoot a scene outside the casino,' says the actor, who was joined in the principality by his mother, May, and son, Sean. 'All of Monaco had turned out to see Bond and the car. I'm driving up to the building for about the sixth time when I'm overpowered by this smell of burning rubber, and suddenly realise I've been driving with the handbrake on the whole time!' The following day, he blundered again – with his Walther PPK falling from its holster and plopping into the sea. A diver had to retrieve it from several feet of water between takes.

While in Monte Carlo, Pierce couldn't help recalling a trip there with Cassie in 1986, when he thought he was about to succeed Roger Moore as 007. 'I saw a beautiful gold watch in Cartier and went to try it on at some point every day of our three-day stay. It cost £4,000 and I thought, "I'm going to buy this watch when I sign the Bond contract".' But to his delight, his wife bought it as a present for him anyway. 'Her attitude was "If you like to spend money, then spend money – worry about it later on",' he says. 'I'm glad she thought like that because you never know what's around the corner, as we both found out.'

At the casino, Pierce first uttered the immortal lines: 'the name's Bond, James Bond' and 'vodka martini, shaken not stirred'. He wasn't worried about asking for the drink. 'I genuinely order them,' he says. 'One of them sets you up for the night – four and you're anyone's!' But saying the other line was a different matter. 'I was cleaning my teeth that morning saying it over and over again, and felt really foolish when the toothpaste started running all over my chin,' he says. Fortunately, an extra's mother had been at a gambling table opposite Sean Connery when he first said the lines in *Dr. No*, and told Pierce how it took him 32 takes to get the words right. 'That makes me feel a lot better,' he said.

The film also had its fair share of gadgets, demonstrated as usual by Q, played by Desmond Llewelyn, 81, making his fifteenth appearance in a 007 film. Among the deadly toys he came up with for Pierce's first outing as Bond were a BMW Roadster, fitted with radar, a self-destruct system and Stinger missiles behind the headlights. Sadly, no such traffic-jam-defeating extras grace the real car. In addition, 007 took possession of an exploding pen, a £5.95 Parker modified at a cost of £4,000 ('They always said the pen was mightier than the sword,' laughs Bond); a 'detonator' Omega Seamaster watch, usually costing £895, but adapted at a cost of £12,000; and a £4,000 customised leather belt, concealing a wire and piton in the buckle.

It was a long shoot, and with Brosnan working up to twelve hours a day, six days a week – even though he was picking up a cool £1.5 million, compared to the extras who earned just £80 a day – it was essential to conserve his strength, and focus on the task in hand. 'It's a real ballbreaker,' he said. 'If you're working six days a week on a low-budget picture being filmed in seven weeks, then it's more acceptable. I fought hard against it and had my say.' But, a true professional, he buckled under and got on with the job when movie executives refused to relax the filming schedule.

With this in mind, he stuck to a rigid diet and routine. 'I had to stay disciplined and not get involved with late nights or drinking,' he says. Pierce would eat nothing but a bowl of fruit and a glass of orange juice until lunch. He would then retreat to his trailer where he would paint, practise yoga for twenty or so minutes 'to clear the mind' or play the clarinet which he'd bought at Christmas. His stand-in and personal assistant, Adrian Bell, reports: 'It was a bloody awful racket – but it was a good way for Pierce to let off steam.'

Over the years he had developed his own particular way of coping with the strains and stresses of shooting a TV series or film. For instance, he would move his jaw from side to side and bend his legs before every scene to make himself feel more relaxed. As for learning his lines, he would read a script a few times from cover to cover, then concentrate on the sections he was doing day to day. 'I stand in the kitchen, drinking a can of lager with the telly on and the kids around. Otherwise it can get too intense.'

However, even with all his experience, he still confessed: 'Some days are rough and I lose confidence, lose power, lose everything and feel as if I'm standing there naked. It's very important to stay relaxed – that's the hardest part of acting. I keep replaying certain scenes in my mind, looking for imperfections. I don't think it's a part I can leave behind, like other films.' But as shooting on the film drew to a close, Pierce eased up a little. He popped out to a local pub, The King's Head, for lunch one day, eating a cheeseburger and chips and downing two pints of lager. 'It was as if after all the careful eating, cautious drinking and self-discipline, he couldn't resist letting go for an hour,' says an insider. He also played snooker with his chauffeur in the Rolls-Royce social club during a break in filming.

Two events brightened up those last, long days of work on *GoldenEye*. First, a surprise appearance by Roger Moore, who was going to visit his son, Christian, who was working as a third assistant on the film. Limping from a knee operation, he greeted Pierce by telling him: 'I've been called up. The chiefs said: "We've seen the results on poor old Brosnan, so once the knee's right, the job's yours!" ' It was a typical Moore wind-up. Then on 16 May Pierce celebrated his 42nd birthday. 'I don't feel a day over 90,' he joked. Later that day, the film crew wheeled in a cake – shaped like a Walther PPK.

* * *

The movie-makers were so pleased with the picture that immediately afterwards they signed Pierce up for a further two adventures. Pierce celebrated by paying £52,500 at Christie's the auctioneers for the gold-plated typewriter that Ian Fleming had splashed out on after completing the first draft of *Casino Royale* back in 1952. It was a lot of money to pay for a typewriter, but Brosnan wasn't exactly short of money following his *GoldenEye* payday.

Soon afterwards, a new round of promotional interviews would begin. Even though some pundits saw 007 films as a licence to print money, *GoldenEye*'s success was by no means assured. A lot was riding on the film, as can be seen from the size of the MGM/United Artists advertising budget. The film company spent a staggering $21.5 million (£14 million) – 15 per cent of its entire 1995 advertising budget – plugging *GoldenEye*. That was more than the combined budget of most of Brosnan's other movies.

As for Pierce, he faced the prospect of dozens of press and TV interviews with resignation – but knew they could make the difference between box office success or failure. 'My gut feeling is no, Bond isn't dated,' he told journalists. 'He's the ultimate fantasy character and there's a big audience out there waiting for the picture. I want this to be a big fat success. I want to be kicking ass against Arnold Schwarzenegger and all the other guys out there.'

How had he played Bond? 'Very much the Pierce Brosnan way – fast and exciting! Although Sean Connery was a great inspiration. When you read the books, they're quite dark. It was Connery who brought the humour; and you can't just play him for real. You have to have a wink at the audience. Whether you're playing Chekhov at Stratford or James Bond, being an actor is about turning the punters on, making them feel good.'

He was cheered by the news that the poster for the film would declare: 'Pierce Brosnan is James Bond.' The promotional campaign in the sixties involving Connery had also stressed the 'is' angle. While both Moore and Dalton had been billed 'as' playing James Bond. However, Pierce drew the line at certain promotional gimmicks. For instance, he declined to be photographed in a pyramid shot with the usual cluster of Bond beauties, wanting to get away from what he perceived as the old-fashioned 'glamour picture' image. Similarly, he would not repeat 007's two most famous catchphrases for the camera. By the end of 1995, asked by a US entertainment magazine to single out the year's low spot, he unhesitatingly replied: 'People asking me, "Can you say you're 'Bond, James Bond'?" '

The success of the movie in America was crucial to its success in the rest of the world. A bad opening there would jeopardise its success elsewhere. All the stops were therefore pulled out to make sure it was a hit. Firstly, *GoldenEye* was sold to the American public as an action film – in the tradition of *Die Hard* and *Cliffhanger* – even though Martin Campbell is on record as saying that 007 is the 'cinema's last great romantic hero' in contrast to 'blue collar heroes like Willis and Stallone'.

A host of celebrities, including Liam Neeson, Jeff Bridges, supermodel Elle Macpherson and, of course, Pierce himself, (joined by his mother, May, and Keely), attended the movie's world première in New York. 'Evenings like this come but once in a lifetime,' said the star.

The film opened to generally favourable reviews in the United States. The country's showbusiness bible, *Variety*, said: 'James Bond is definitely back in business. This is among the best of the seventeen Bond films and breathes fresh life into the series. Brosnan makes a solid gold début.' While the *Hollywood Reporter* called the film 'dynamite' and went on to say: 'Bond is back in top form.' And *Entertainment Weekly* raved: 'This is the spy who came back from the cold.' Its critical and commercial success in the USA boded well for its release in the rest of the world, where it was felt the Bond brand was stronger. The advertising campaign therefore emphasised all those things people had come to expect from a 007 movie – girls, guns and glamour.

The British press responded as one – a rare thing – in giving *GoldenEye* a resounding thumbs up. The general tone was reflected in the *Daily Mirror*'s review which proclaimed: 'Glorious *GoldenEye* will prove wrong all those doubters who argued there was no place for 007 in today's movie world – and while Brosnan has yet to displace Sean Connery in people's affections, other Bonds will soon be forgotten.' Other papers were equally positive. The *Daily Mail* called it 'one of the finest action adventures of recent years'. The *Evening Standard* waxed: 'Bond is back at his best.' While *Today* raved: 'Brosnan has come up trumps with the best 007 since Connery – Ian Fleming would have been proud of the lad.'

Predictably, most Irish papers were equally supportive. The *Irish Independent* said: 'He's a natural. He strides through the movie with an assured but mocking sense of self, making Bond a kind of modern-day buccaneer.' Even diehard fans thought Brosnan was great in the part. 'Pierce is superb,' enthused Graham Rye, president of the James Bond Fan Club. 'He's got the physical attributes, the charm and is right for the times.'

Not everyone was so complimentary. Actor George Lazenby, who played 007 in the 1969 film, *On Her Majesty's Secret Service*, described

Brosnan's Bond as 'sad'. The 55-year-old Australian, who ironically now lives just a few miles away from Pierce in Los Angeles, said: 'Brosnan is too nice for the part. Bond is supposed to walk into a room and fight three guys at once. If Brosnan walked into a room I doubt if anyone would look up. But I suppose this is the nineties and women want a man who shows his feminine side, and Pierce definitely has that.' Finally, Lazenby, who was fired by Broccoli after making just one 007 film, boastfully added: 'I was a more fitting Bond than Brosnan.' A case of sour grapes, perhaps?

A majority of today's students at the Drama Centre, where Pierce had trained, gave it the thumbs down in a straw poll. The most damning verdict of all, though, came from Christopher Fettes, who says: 'It was quite dreadful. I find the entire concept of James Bond just so baroque, and all the sabre-rattling deeply disturbing. The message seems to be that as long as we have secret agents going around the world blowing things up, we still rule the waves. It's absolutely potty. But the fact that Pierce could bring some reality to the role in the nineties is a major achievement. Without him, *GoldenEye* would have been a thoroughly tedious experience.'

However, Pierce could take consolation from an unexpected accolade. A panel of Tinseltown health experts hailed him as the fittest 007 ever. 'The change in fitness thinking is apparent when you compare the Bonds,' claimed *Longevity* magazine. 'Sean Connery looked like he'd had his share of shaken and stirred martinis, Roger Moore was slim but not particularly well-muscled. But Pierce has a brilliantly chiselled form – making him one of Hollywood's ten best bodies.'

As it happened, the detractors did little to dent *GoldenEye*'s box office appeal. To date, it's taken nearly $350 million at the box office. Besides making it the most successful Bond movie ever, this also puts it among the all-time box office winners. 'The whole world waited to see Brosnan as Bond and I didn't disappoint,' he says proudly. 'Now I can stand back and say, "Goddammit, I did it!" '

13. SUPERSTAR

After finishing work on *GoldenEye*, Pierce took off to Ireland with Keely Shaye-Smith. The long-limbed ex-model with the high cheekbones had become Pierce's constant companion. And so special a place did she have in his heart that she had now become the first woman since Cassie that he'd taken to his homeland.

For weeks she had been telling him that swimming with the dolphins off Ireland was the perfect way to relax after the punishing movie-making schedule. The couple travelled to the Dingle peninsula, County Kerry, on Ireland's west coast, which had become popular with Hollywood stars such as Tom Cruise and Julia Roberts, who were in search of the 'real' Ireland. 'I hate to admit it but I have not been to County Kerry before,' admitted Brosnan. 'But all my American friends have raved about the place.'

The dolphin, called Fungi, had lived in the waters off Dingle Bay for eleven years, and one morning Pierce turned up at the house of boatman Jimmy Flannery, asking if he would take him and Keely out to see the animal. 'When I saw 007 standing at the door I couldn't believe my eyes,' says Flannery's daughter-in-law, Bridget. The Flannery family had been arranging boat trips for the rich and famous to see Fungi for the last eight years. But Jimmy says: 'Most of them send their minions – and some can be pretty demanding. But not Pierce and Keely. She was totally unaffected, there wasn't a trace of make-up on her face. They weren't all over each other but they were very affectionate. They were a joy to watch.'

About twenty minutes after they'd set sail, the twelve-foot-long bottle-nosed dolphin leaped from the waters in a great silver arc. Zipping up his wet suit and donning his flippers and snorkel, Pierce slipped into the chilly waters, followed by Keely. 'My God,' he said, as Fungi suddenly appeared within arm's reach. 'He's majestic, truly majestic.' Playfully, Fungi slipped away, arched his back and dived deep into the bay. For nearly an hour, Pierce and Keely swam with the dolphin, who repeatedly circled the couple, then leapt into the air, showering them with spray, as Brosnan made clicking noises, trying to communicate with him. Afterwards the actor said: 'It was a truly spiritual experience; an absolute slice of poetry. It makes you realise that when it comes down to it there's far more to life than just being James Bond.'

*   *   *

As Pierce had predicted, landing the 007 role instantly transformed his life. As one Los Angeles-based showbusiness writer says: 'Before *GoldenEye*, everyone here was aware of him but he was in limbo – his sex appeal never wavered but he just wasn't cover star material.' Suddenly, though, he was catapulted on to Hollywood's A-list. Whatever he did, wherever he went, he was now news. Cameras clicked as soon as he got out of his car or left a restaurant. He was a superstar.

Autographed Pierce Brosnan photographs shot up in price to $50 – putting him on a par with stars like John Travolta, Sandra Bullock and Johnny Depp. He was voted the most romantic man in America – capturing more than one in five votes – ahead of Harrison Ford, Brad Pitt, John Travolta, John F. Kennedy Jr and ER hunk George Clooney. And he scooped a Best Action Hero award.

He presented an award at the 1996 Oscars ceremony, and was joined on the podium by supermodels Claudia Schiffer and Naomi Campbell. He had agents in London (Jonathan Altaras) and LA (Fred Spector), not to mention his very own publicist (Dick Guttman). He was invited to Madame Tussaud's to pose for 30 minutes for a new 007 waxwork. He was photographed and measured from every angle, jacket on and off. At the end of the session, he was asked to sign the waxworks' book of fame. 'You missed one very important measurement,' he wrote, smiling broadly. And, like Tom Hanks, Kevin Costner and Michael Douglas, he had to put up with cheeky TV interviewers, like the BBC's bespectacled Dennis Pennis, asking impertinent questions. 'Is it true you've got a short fuse,' he was asked at the première of one film, casting doubt on the size of Pierce's 'very important measurement'. Unlike all too many celebrities, who suffer a severe sense of humour failure in such situations, Pierce replied with a smile: 'You've heard wrong – I've got a very healthy fuse.'

He also inspired a heroic degree of devotion in his ever-growing army of, mostly female, fans. Take Rebecca Edson, 51, of Bradford – arguably his number one fan. She first got the Brosnan bug back in the eighties when she saw him in *Remington Steele*. 'It was love at first sight,' she says. 'He's got everything.' She saw *GoldenEye* at the cinema six Saturdays on the trot. The shelves at the bungalow she shares with her mother groan under the weight of her 50-odd collection of video tapes devoted to her idol. Two photograph albums are crammed with glossy pictures, several scrapbooks are bulging with cuttings. Then there's the calendar, the T-shirts, the clock . . . the list is endless.

However, perhaps the ultimate tribute to Pierce's new A-list star status was that he even got his own celebrity lookalike, Douglas James. The Surrey-based double dons 007's trademark black bow-tie and tuxedo on average a couple of times a week. He's worked for everyone from Aston Martin to BMW, and travelled to Europe and America, raking in up to £500 an assignment. Needless to say, he's a happy man and says: 'Pierce's casting as Bond has changed my life and it seems pointless appearing on stage as myself when I'd earn a fraction of what I earn appearing as Pierce. I'm very grateful to Pierce's mother for having him!'

Newspapers and magazines around the world jumped at any chance to carry a story about the star. One day he'd be pictured attending a movie première, the next a charity dinner, and then rubbing suntan lotion on to Keely's back as the couple relaxed on a beach. You name it – the *Legends of the Fall* première, the Queen's Cup Polo Final at Windsor – he'd be there. It wasn't long before he was a regular feature of the glossy celebrity magazine, *Hello!*, rubbing shoulders with the royals, superstars and tycoons who graced its pages.

When Keely objected to staying at the £1,000-a-night Royal suite at the five-star Eden Hotel in Rome, which had played host to King Constantine of Greece, Ingrid Bergman and Nicole Kidman, the papers leapt upon the news – giving the story a suitably cheesy headline: 'No No 7.' The couple subsequently booked into a £2,000-a-night suite at The Hassler, reportedly one of the ten best hotels in the world.

Then there was the bizarre, widely reported tale of the marriage that never was. In the dying days of 1995, Pierce and Keely were seen browsing in an upmarket jeweller's in Sydney, Australia, and the world's media were suddenly awash with stories that the lovebirds had secretly tied the knot. It was a nice story except for one thing – it wasn't true.

Even more prominence was given to a story that was the ultimate storm in a teacup – but amazingly made the splash (front page lead) in one British tabloid. It seems that Brosnan accidentally bumped into Radio 1 DJ Chris Evans's girlfriend, Suzi Aplin, at a showbusiness bash. After apologising, he cheekily added: 'How can I make it up to you – dinner, perhaps?' She declined on the grounds that she was 'with someone', whereupon Pierce retreated, commenting that 'he must be very special'. The following morning, Evans heaped abuse on the actor and told his ten million listeners: 'What a tosser!'

However, while Miss Aplin proved impervious to his charms, more famous women were falling over themselves in a bid to win the heart of Tinseltown's latest superstar. One such admirer was stunning 41-year-old model Christine Brinkley, one-time wife of singer Billy Joel, now involved in a messy divorce from second husband Ricky Taubman.

'He's the most attractive man I've ever met,' she reportedly told a friend. And when he visited New York, she saw her chance – even though he was dating Keely at the time. She allegedly called Pierce at his hotel and the two arranged to meet. Over dinner Brinkley told the actor how happy she was to be available again, and – hint, hint – was ready for a new romance. 'Pierce was flattered and surprised,' says a friend. 'But he gently told her that while she'd always be one of his best friends, he was still deeply involved with Keely.' Such were the perils of fame.

Nevertheless, the actor still found time to raise money to fight the disease which had so cruelly snatched Cassandra from him in her prime. Invited to open a Harrods sale, he donated £50,000 of his appearance fee – the other £10,000 going to the Drama Centre – to the ovarian cancer research centre at Addenbrooke's Hospital. He made clear that he would continue to raise money for research. 'It's not a crusade but it's part of my life,' he said. 'I have a voice which I didn't know I had. It's vital that women should be screened. We have lost too many to this disease. This is to make up for the times I wasn't able to help.' He also donated the Brioni tuxedo that he wore in the opening 'gunbarrel' sequence of *GoldenEye* to an American Heart Association charity auction. It went under the hammer for $12,007. (Someone obviously had a sense of humour.) In addition, he was honoured at a special gala evening by Irish premier Albert Reynolds for his work in the fight against breast cancer. And he announced an ambitious plan to raise further money for charity by auctioning off his paintings.

Ironically, one of the few places that hasn't gone 'Brosnan barmy' is the the quiet backwater where he spent his early years. After being cast as 007, excitable newspaper reports claimed: 'From now on the little town of Navan will be known as the birthplace of James Bond – or James O'Bond, as locals have been quick to dub him.' It was a nice angle, as they say in the business, but wasn't strictly true. No doubt, if Navan had been in America, the roads for miles around would have been dotted with signs proudly proclaiming: 'You're entering Pierce Brosnan country' above a cheesy portrait of the star. Enterprising bars would be selling bottles of Pierce Brosnan beer and there would be a Pierce Brosnan tour ending at a tacky souvenir shop, selling everything from Pierce Brosnan cups to keyrings. But Navan is not in America, and even today you'll be hard-pressed to find a single reference to the fact that 'James O'Bond' spent the first eleven years of his life there. 'I think if he'd come back more often and established a link more could have been made of the connection,' says Ken Davis, editor of the *Meath Chronicle*. 'But should he ever want to return to Navan we'd obviously welcome him back with open arms.'

* * *

His casting as 007 also transformed his career prospects. Before landing the part, his big project of 1994 was to be the making of yet another TV mini-series, this time a version of Daniel Defoe's *Robinson Crusoe*. However, as soon as the New York-based production company, RHI Entertainment, heard its star was to be the new Bond, Brosnan became hot property. Suddenly, the mini-series became a full-length feature film and Pierce's salary soared to a reputed £1 million.

He flew out to Papua New Guinea less than 24 hours after the press conference announcing his casting in the 007 role – but even in this remote part of the world he discovered he could not escape Bond's long shadow. One morning he awoke to find a group of native children excitedly pointing at him and saying: 'James Bond, James Bond.' He stopped and asked: 'What did you say?' They shouted: 'James Bond, James Bond!'

'I was dumbstruck,' says Pierce. 'Here I was in the middle of nowhere, being recognised as Bond. At that moment, any lingering doubts I had that *GoldenEye* was just another film left me completely.'

The *Robinson Crusoe* project was another period drama – but a period drama with a difference. This time Pierce swapped the fancy uniforms he had donned in *The Deceivers* for a startling disguise – a coating of mud, tattered rags and animal skins, shoulder-length hair and a filthy, matted beard which led to islanders dubbing him 'Mouth Grass'. It couldn't have been further from his forthcoming Bond role. As one insider jokily observed: 'In place of 007's trusty Walther PPK was a flintlock rifle; instead of the usual megalomaniac millionaire bent on world destruction, he was taking on a band of cannibal "Mud Men".'

He spent two months in the jungle – shooting scenes where he fought with a python, became entangled in a sticky spider's web and came face to face with the fearsome Mud Men, who hid their faces behind spooky grey masks of clay meant to feign death. As in Defoe's story, Crusoe teams up with the native Man Friday, played by 42-year-old William Takaku, from Bougainville Island in the neighbouring Solomons. However, the producers took 'some artistic licence', as Brosnan admitted, giving the seaman a fiancée, played by *Restoration* star Polly Walker, who says: 'Pierce went out of his way to put me at ease.'

During filming, production was held up by a change of director and then another day was lost when Brosnan hurt his back. But he retained his humour through it all. 'Pierce is number one,' said the 19-year-old son of the chief at the village where much of *Robinson Crusoe* was being shot. 'He always has a nice smile for us and even gives us food paid for out of his own pocket.'

The movie was originally set for a May 1996 North American release. Then an August 1996 release – with a probable British release a couple of months later. However, in late August it was decided to delay *Robinson Crusoe*'s cinema release 'indefinitely'. The very fact that its May release had been put back indicated that the distributors weren't happy with the finished product.

Ironically, it now looks likely that the drama could, after all, become a television mini-series, as originally intended, and subsequently get a video release. This would seem the most sensible option. In truth, a new big screen *Robinson Crusoe* always had questionable cinematic appeal. It's one of those stories that everyone is so familiar with that you can't help wondering who would want to pay good money to see yet another version of the classic. Its shelving as a movie release shouldn't be seen as a reflection of Pierce's appeal – it is simply that whoever decided to turn the project into a big screen project in the first place hadn't thought the matter through. And its likely consignment to the small screen is probably a blessing in disguise, as far as Pierce is concerned.

Thankfully, he enjoyed better luck with his next three projects – *The Mirror Has Two Faces*, *Mars Attacks!* and *Dante's Peak* – although none proved to be runaway box-office winners.

The first film, *The Mirror Has Two Faces*, was a romantic comedy – also starring Barbra Streisand and Jeff Bridges – that supposedly explored modern myths of beauty and sex and how they complicate relationships. Based on the 1958 French movie, *Le Miroir à Deux Faces*, it cast Streisand as a frumpy, bespectacled, unmarried Columbia University professor – Rose Morgan – teaching romantic literature. She tells her students the concept of courtly love involved a union of souls untouched by physical intimacy. 'Consummation,' she says, 'led only to despair and ruin.' In reality, she herself is desperate for physical intimacy.

In contrast, Bridges plays handsome mathematics lecturer Greg Larkin, who after a string of soulless affairs with beautiful women (one of whom is played by Australian supermodel Elle Macpherson), has concluded that sex is the main stumbling block to a perfect relationship. He longs to bond with a woman spiritually and intellectually, but wants to avoid any of that messy sexual business. Brosnan plays Alex, the handsome, suave charmer married to Rose's younger and infinitely more glamorous sister Claire (Mimi Rogers). Rose secretly adores her brother-in-law while knowing the chances of him ever falling for a plain Jane like her are remote. As for Alex (who Brosnan admitted is 'a bit of a shit'), he's happy to flirt with Rose, as he is with all women, but has no desire to take things further.

In the hope of fulfilling his dream, Larkin takes out a lonely hearts advertisement. Claire replies to it on Rose's behalf and helps the two professors hook up. Friendship blossoms and a whirlwind wedding ensues. But the relationship is doomed: while Rose hopes a combination of sexy lingerie, classical music and fine wine will help her achieve her goal – consummating the marriage – she discovers that however much cleavage she displays, her partner seeks nothing but companionship.

Despairing of her husband, Rose sets about transforming herself – with the help of a tough workout regime, a bottle of blonde hair dye, slinky dresses, black stockings and high heels – into a sexbomb who soon has the attention of both Greg and Alex . . .

The movie was shot on location in New York during the exceptionally cold winter of 1995/6 and featured city landmarks such as Bloomingdale's department store, Columbia University and Central Park. From the start, though, it was dogged by reports of directorial tantrums and firings: Dudley Moore was replaced by George Segal and cinematographer Dante Spinotti walked out, citing 'creative differences' with Streisand, who also directed the film. However, Pierce defended her, saying: 'I encountered a woman who was pretty damn sure of what she wanted and doesn't like to be bullshitted. But I also saw a woman who is very vulnerable.'

Admittedly, the film had a top-drawer cast. Streisand first shot to fame nearly 30 years ago in *Funny Girl* and went on to star in a string of hits such as *A Star Is Born*. Bridges is one of the most respected actors in the business, having appeared in acclaimed films such as *Jagged Edge*, one of the top-grossing pictures of 1985. Hollywood legend Lauren Bacall – who played Rose's embittered mother, never missing an opportunity to put her daughter down – starred in *The Big Sleep* and *Key Largo* and was married to Humphrey Bogart. In addition, the film boasted Segal, Rogers and, of course, Brosnan.

Yet *The Mirror Has Two Faces* failed to live up to its billing as a modern screwball romantic comedy – and the critics showed it no mercy. The American magazine, *Time*, thought Bridges was miscast and said: ' "Second Hand Roses" have been part of Streisand's act for decades . . . but the fine feathers of a star we all know to be strong, smart and sexy keep peeking through her ugly duckling get-up, spoiling whatever suspense the story might hold.'

The British press was even more hostile. 'The movie is well and truly defeated by Streisand from the first round,' commented the *Sunday Times*. 'Look in the mirror, Barbra, if you want to see who's responsible for this ugly mess.' The *Independent on Sunday* said acidly: 'The film should bear the credit "An Exercise in Screaming Vanity by Barbra Streisand".' Its sister paper, the *Independent*, was no more complimentary, denouncing Streisand's movie as 'a little hymn to herself'. *Midweek* thought the trouble with *The Mirror Has Two Faces* was that 'both belong to Barbra Streisand', while London's *Evening Standard* called the film 'a total mess', concluding its review with the putdown, 'Vanity, thy name is Barbra.'

Such reviews did little for *The Mirror Has Two Faces*' box-office appeal. Released in late 1996 in America, its sentimental storyline was expected to appeal to audiences in the run-up to Christmas. However, it grossed a disappointing $40 million. It did even worse in Britain, where it was released early in 1997, grossing a pitiful £1 million.

Streisand blamed the film's limited success on sexist critics. 'A woman is called demanding; a man commanding,' she said in response to accusations that she was a control freak diva. But she was in for another shock when the film picked up just a couple of 1997 Oscar nominations. (Bacall was nominated in the Best Supporting Actress category but the gong went to Juliette Binoche for her role in *The English Patient*, which scooped nine awards.) So upset was Streisand that she reportedly turned down an invitation to sing the film's Oscar-nominated song, 'I've Finally Found Someone', at the awards ceremony.

In truth, the film wasn't as bad as some critics claimed, but while it found favour with Streisand's core audience, there was little in it to appeal to other cinemagoers. What's more, at 54, Barbra was getting a little long in the tooth to play the traditional glamorous leading lady.

Working alongside the likes of Streisand and Segal certainly did Pierce no harm, though, and fitted in well with his declared aim of wanting to work with good people. His appearance – which was in some ways more of a cameo than a starring role – could not be held responsible for the film's lack of success.

His next movie, *Mars Attacks!*, was more important from a career point of view. An affectionate big-budget paean to science fiction films of the fifties, it was inspired by a bubblegum card series of the same name created at the height of the Cold War, depicting a *War of the Worlds*-style invasion of earth by Martians.

It's unlikely the $80 million (£53 million) sci-fi spectacular would have ever got off the ground had it not been the pet project of Tim Burton, the 38-year-old *wunderkind* director responsible for some of the greatest box-office triumphs of the previous decade including *Beetlejuice* and the first two *Batman* films. After securing the rights to the cards from Topps, Burton turned to British-born screenwriter Jonathan Gems for help in developing the script, and together they conceived a storyline inspired by images from the original Mars Attacks! cards and classic post-war alien invasion films.

The film opens with a herd of cows, their backs on fire, stampeding in a collective blaze past a lonely Midwestern farmstead. Suddenly, a spaceship – looking for all the world like an old car hubcap – shoots off into the distance. Next we see legions of Martian spaceships departing the red planet for earth. The film proper then starts, the action shifting back and forth between the stately grandeur of the American capital, Washington, D.C., New York City, a desolate Kansas doughnut shop, the Arizona desert and the bulbs and buzz of Las Vegas.

Casting posed the first problem. Many Hollywood agents didn't want their stars playing 'losers' zapped by invading Martians. But once Jack Nicholson – a Burton fan since playing the Joker in *Batman* – had signed up to play two parts (bungling US president James Dale and slick Las Vegas real estate hustler Art Land), the director was able to assemble his so-called 'dream team' of Hollywood talent.

The story followed the fortunes of a dozen-odd characters across the United States, many of whom never met up. The Washington D.C. cast included Glenn Close, who played the imperious First Lady; Brosnan, as Donald Kessler, an urbane, pipe-smoking English professor and aide to the president; Rod Steiger, who played General Decker, the White House's military adviser; and Martin Short, as a philandering presidential press secretary.

The Las Vegas cast featured Annette Bening as an ex-stripper turned UFO-obsessed, New Age philosopher; Danny DeVito as a leering, loudmouth Las Vegas lowlife known simply as the Rude Gambler; and Tom Jones camping it up as himself at a Las Vegas cabaret show performing 'It's Not Unusual'.

Other players included fashion correspondent Nathalie Lake (Sarah Jessica Parker) and her television news reporter boyfriend Jason Stone (Michael J. Fox); Nathalie's beloved four-legged friend, Poppy, portrayed by Burton's own pet chihuahua; and a Kansas redneck (Joe Don Baker who, of course, played 007's Russian CIA contact, Jack Wade, in *GoldenEye*).

Asked by Lake to explain the significance of the alien 'invasion', Kessler explains that 'it's the most important thing to happen since Jesus walked in Galilee'. But he reassures the president that the genderless, nitrogen-breathing little green men pose no threat to the human race. 'The indications are that they are peaceful and enlightened,' he says authoritatively. 'I suspect they have more to fear from us than we from them.'

His prediction proves disastrously wrong: the bug-eyed visitors unleash their deadly firepower on the curious crowds who gather to greet them in the Arizona desert, killing thousands.

The pipe-smoking Kessler is among those in the Oval Office who witness the tragedy unfold live on television. Afterwards, the hawkish General Decker is all for nuking the invaders while the First Lady wants to 'kick the crap out of them'. But Kessler's pacifist, liberal views prevail. 'Mr President, I know this seems terrible but let's not be too rash,' he says, scratching his head. 'It could just be a cultural misunderstanding.'

The president transmits a message announcing that he believes human and alien can still live in peace, and invites the Martian ambassador to address Congress. This proves to be another fatal miscalculation for the aliens turn their rayguns on the massed ranks of politicians and blast them into oblivion. Kessler rushes forward and begs: 'Mr Ambassador, it doesn't make sense!' But a Martian trooper hits him over the head and takes him hostage.

Incarcerated in a Martian spaceship, Pierce falls victim to the invaders' fondness for Nazi-style human experimentation. His character, Kessler, is beheaded – but remains alive from the neck upward thanks to their fiendish alien gadgetry. 'I'm not feeling myself,' he understandably comments. Poor Nathalie Lake (Parker) suffers an even greater indignity – her head is attached to her pet chihuahua's body (a move not entirely without justice for she did seem to prefer the pooch to her now-dead reporter boyfriend).

Meanwhile, the Martians launch a full-scale invasion of Earth, blowing up Big Ben and the Houses of Parliament, the Eiffel Tower and the Washington Monument. All looks lost until a grandmother in the American Midwest accidentally stumbles upon the only way to kill the aliens – play them Slim Whitman yodelling tunes, an aural outrage that bursts their brains. The tide miraculously turns, alien craft plunge into the sea and the human race lives to fight another day.

Sadly, poor Pierce never gets the chance to smoke his beloved pipe again, let alone live to fight another day, but his character does get to kiss Lake seconds before their Martian spaceship crashes into the sea, freeing them from their living hell.

The part gave Brosnan a unique opportunity to play against type and show the flipside to his supercool Bond persona. Hamming it up for all he was worth, he obviously enjoyed himself enormously. He made no secret of his delight at being in what he called this 'silly, goofball romp', yet again getting to work with a high-calibre cast. When he first arrived at the film's Oval Office set he could barely contain himself. There was his name on the call sheet alongside some of Hollywood's biggest stars. 'I looked around,' he recalls, 'and there was Jack – the man – Glenn Close, Rod Steiger, Martin Short and yours truly. It knocked my socks off. I don't think I've ever been so nervous on a set as I was that day.'

The movie was largely shot in LA. However, despite work starting on *Mars Attacks!* before *Independence Day*, it didn't reach the screens until six months later. And when it was finally released in America in December 1996, it performed indifferently at the box office. Whereas *Independence Day* grossed $50 million (£33 million) in its opening weekend, *Mars Attacks!* took just over $9 million (£6 million). All Bob Daly, the president of Warners, could say when he attended a preview was, 'It's weird, really weird.'

That pretty much summed up America's reaction to the film: audiences just didn't get the joke. Gems, among others, blamed the film's disappointing US box-office gross – it recouped less than half its costs – on America's 'problem with satire', claiming, 'They think irony is an attack on them.' But that's too glib an answer. In truth, the film was perhaps too clever for its own good.

The movie opened to decidedly mixed notices in the UK too. The quality press, hitherto Burton's biggest fans, were by and large unimpressed. 'It's never quite funny or sharp enough,' thought the *Guardian*. The *Mail on Sunday* said the film failed 'thanks to a lame script and Burton's misguided belief in cheesiness as an end in itself.' In a review headlined 'Attack of the Giant Turkey', the *Sunday Times* declared: 'Tim Burton has made a terrible movie – a real stinker.'

In contrast, the tabloids – so often the villain of the piece in Hollywood's eyes – loved the movie. 'It's cracking stuff,' commented the *Daily Mirror*'s film critic. 'I roared with laughter throughout – and look forward to seeing *Mars Attacks!* again and again.' The *Sun* was equally enthusiastic, raving, '*Mars Attacks!* is black, sick, infantile humour at its best – kitsch, crazy, brash and brilliant.'

Such positive reviews – along with a new advertising strategy built around a wacky family portrait-style campaign – helped the movie power to No. 1 in the UK box-office chart, grossing more than £2 million in its first week. It went on to gross nearly £7 million in Britain, and performed comparatively well in a number of European countries, pushing *Mars Attacks!* closer to its break-even point. And despite its relatively disappointing performance following the phenomenal success of *Independence Day*, Pierce emerged from the picture with his stature enhanced.

* * *

His next movie, *Dante's Peak*, was an entirely different proposition. First, he was playing the lead. Second, it was an even bigger budget film, initially costed at $100 million. Third, should it fail, it could have a damaging effect on his career. In short, *Dante's Peak* was his most important movie to date, excluding *GoldenEye*.

Directed by Australian-born Roger Donaldson – the man behind *The Bounty* and *Species* – from a screenplay by *Daylight* writer Leslie Bohem, the lead role had originally been offered to Michael Douglas. But when he turned it down, Pierce signed on for a cool $5 million (£3 million). 'I jumped at the chance of starring in it,' he says. 'I've always had a soft spot for disaster films, growing up on pictures like *The Poseidon Adventure* and *The Towering Inferno*. And much as I love playing Bond, I hoped the role would help me avoid being typecast as 007.'

Donaldson reveals: 'I was enthusiastic about Pierce for a number of reasons. He comes across as a very sensitive character in real life, essential for the character in the film. I also felt he was on an upward curve in terms of his acting career. I was looking for someone with a truly international appeal because *Dante's Peak* was, in effect, a universal story – a volcano, after all, can go off anywhere in the world at any time.'

Pierce plays volcanologist Harry Dalton (presumably no relation to former 007 star Timothy Dalton?) who is sent to the idyllic Pacific north-west town of Dante's Peak – whose 8,000 people live at the foot of a towering mountain of the same name – to investigate recent seismic activity. Locals scoff at suggestions that the long-dormant peak could erupt and he expects to find little more than the routine rumblings common to the region.

However, Dalton finds evidence of the increasing geological activity, such as ground deformation and sulphur dioxide and carbon dioxide emissions, that precede a catastrophic eruption. He appeals to the town's mayor, Rachel Wando, a single mum and businesswoman (played by *Terminator* star Linda Hamilton), and she calls a town council meeting. Enter Harry's boss, who dissuades the council from declaring a state of alert, questioning the scientific accuracy of Dalton's findings.

Yet mounting evidence suggests something is seriously wrong. The town is rocked by a series of earthquakes, a cloud of ash appears over the volcano and terrified townsfolk jump into their cars, jamming the only route out of town.

Once again Brosnan plays a widower. (His fiancée was killed by a lump of molten rock smashing through the cab of their truck as they tried to outrun a Colombian volcano eruption several years earlier, a tragedy that unfolds during the film's opening sequence.) It's almost as if Pierce, himself a widower, is drawn to playing such parts.

Somewhat predictably, though, romance blossoms between him and Wando. Following the initial tremors, Harry and Rachel dash back to her house to fetch her children, Graham and Lauren, only to discover they have gone up the mountain to get their grandmother Ruth, stubbornly refusing to leave her home. With the clock racing against them, the couple must rescue Ruth and the kids before the volcano blows.

The fireworks don't really get going until the last half-hour of the picture, when hot ash rains down like snow, molten lava forms a torrential river of liquefied rock, sweeping all before it, lakes turn acidic, oozing sulphur and bursting dams, and 800-degree, paint-searing, pyroclastic clouds scream towards the earth.

Former geology student Donaldson – who visited recent hotspots such as Mount Kilauea in Hawaii and Mount St Helen's in Washington State to experience volcanic activity at first hand – left nothing to chance while shooting the movie in Wallace, Idaho, and in and around Los Angeles, between June and October 1996. He constructed a 100ft × 30ft wood and steel model of the mountain, digitally composited its image against live-action footage and photo-realistic paintings, and used computer-generated smoke and lava, in conjunction with bio-degradable ash, to create a volcanic eruption that buckled bridges, toppled buildings and buried homes, cars and hundreds of innocent people under a sea of ash. (Shocked locals in Wallace – which doubled up for the doomed town of Dante's Peak – witnessed a fake church, motel and freeway, not to mention four-foot high drifts of fake volcanic ash, suddenly appear as if by magic in the town, only to see them disappear again equally quickly once the fictional mountain erupted.)

Indeed the ground-breaking special effects created by Digital Domain stole the show, as Brosnan himself modestly admitted, although he claimed, 'The relationships between the characters have not been compromised as a result.'

Ironically, just weeks after Dante's Peak got the go-ahead, Fox green-lighted the less than imaginatively titled Volcano, a disaster picture to be directed by Britain's Mick Jackson (who made LA Story) about a volcano that erupts in Los Angeles, sending lava flowing through the streets of Beverly Hills. Pitting two such similar films head to head virtually guaranteed one of the movies would be a box-office flop, placing still more pressure on Dante's Peak's cast and crew.

So great was the stress that it reportedly led to bitter clashes between Brosnan and his leading lady. 'Pierce is getting his biggest-ever pay packet to star in Dante's Peak but no amount of money could reward him for the nightmare he's been going through,' said an insider. After one bust-up he and Hamilton refused to speak for several days. However, Pierce later sought to play down their differences, saying, 'I love Linda. We got along really well and I wish this woman the greatest success in life. She has become a really good friend.'

The 40-year-old actress had troubles of her own, being accused of having a lesbian relationship with her 32-year-old stand-in, Cindy Deerheim. 'Linda has stolen my wife,' claimed her husband. I'm devastated.' Crane operator Deerheim said an anonymous caller told him: 'I think you should know that your wife is a lesbian.' Then Cindy allegedly called to say she wasn't coming back and asked her husband to send on her things to Hamilton's $1.5 million Malibu, California, mansion. Hamilton denied the reports.

Meanwhile, Brosnan – who rented a £6,000 a month chateau during the Idaho shoot – was caught speeding four times in his BMW 850i, travelling at speeds of up to 125 mph. 'It just begs to be driven,' explained the actor. (His other car, a £75,000 black Porsche turbo, with an ICY CALM registration plate, went even faster.) But each time his famous charm won over the state traffic police and he was just given a ticking off.

As 1996 drew to a close, Universal Pictures pulled out all the stops. 'We were up against the clock,' says Pierce. 'I felt the pressure every day.' They had to ensure that *Dante's Peak* reached cinemas before its big-screen rival, *Volcano*, sparking a game of cat and mouse with Fox.

Shooting on *Volcano* ended a fortnight before that on *Dante's Peak*, so millions more were spent on a speeded-up post-production schedule, pushing up the final cost of the film to nearly $120 million. But when Universal announced that *Dante's Peak* would be released in America on 7 March 1997, Fox brought forward *Volcano*'s release date to 28 February. Then Universal trumped Fox by bringing forward *Dante's Peak*'s release a full month to 7 February. Fox was committed to re-releasing the *Star Wars* trilogy in late January/early February, and risked harming their box-office takings if it brought *Volcano* forward again. It was checkmate – and Fox quietly shelved *Volcano*'s release until later in the year.

As *Dante's Peak*'s release date dawned, Brosnan displayed a quiet confidence. The US reviews were mixed but he said: 'Some people might think the movie's a bit schmaltzy but I'm pleased with it. When you say yes to a film, you're always a bit nervous about the end result, because you're at the mercy of the director and – particularly in a movie like *Dante's Peak* – the special effects people. But I have to tip my hat to Roger Donaldson – he's made a very tight movie.

'The human story was pretty thin at the start of filming, but Roger, Linda Hamilton and I fleshed it out so that audiences would care about Harry, the children, their mother and the townsfolk. We ad-libbed a lot. The scene with the children – where I perform a trick with the handkerchief – was all mine. I remembered my grandfather doing that trick. I also brought in the song "Row, row, row your boat" on the water.'

Pierce was only too aware of how important the picture was at this point in his career. If the film was a whopping great success he would take the credit. On the other hand, if it bombed he would take much of the blame – even if it was a special effects-driven picture. 'I'm sure *Dante's Peak* will get the adrenalin pumping,' predicted Brosnan. 'It has the potential to be a real humdinger of a movie.'

As it happened, *Dante's Peak* was neither a runaway box-office hit nor a flop. It grossed an impressive $18 million in its opening week in the States, spurred on by a big-budget promotion. Usually that would have been enough to make it America's No. 1 movie, but it was denied the top spot by the 1977 sci-fi epic, *Star Wars*, which had been re-released the previous week and took a further $22 million in its second week, pushing its total earnings to $400 million and making it America's biggest grossing film ever.

In all, *Dante's Peak* grossed about $65 million in North America – no mean achievement, although it failed to match the success of the previous year's disaster blockbuster, *Twister*.

The following month, *Dante's Peak* was released in the UK after a promotional blitz that included, among other things, the offer of hundreds of survival-style mini-rucksacks containing goodies such as a baseball cap, CD soundtrack, poster and tie-in novel – none of which would have been much use in the event of a real-life volcanic eruption.

British critics were much less impressed than their American cousins. The *Sun* called it 'good Saturday night nonsense', but the *Daily Mirror* felt the film was 'a disappointment', criticising 'its limp ending' and describing some of the effects as 'ridiculously naff'. And while *The Times* was impressed by the special effects, it hit out at 'the silly script and bland characterisations'. The *Evening Standard* commented that 'The clichés fall on the town as thickly as volcanic ash.'

The movie magazine *Empire* criticised 'the appalling dialogue', singling out the scene where Dalton tells Wando that 'making love is like riding a bicycle – you never forget'. 'Brosnan says the words with all the seductive charm of a rutting rhino,' it commented. *Film Guide* thought it 'watchable' but added: 'It never fully erupts.' But the most damning criticism came from the *News of the World* which usually gets caught up in the hype surrounding big-budget movies. 'Dante's Peak is a different type of disaster film,' it said icily. 'The film itself is a disaster.'

This mauling at the hands of the critics may have harmed the picture for it grossed a little under £1 million in its opening week and never made the top three. As in America, *Star Wars* reigned supreme. The No. 2 film, *Space Jam*, appealed to youngsters, while the Oscar-winning *The English Patient* held on to the No. 3 slot. However, *Dante's Peak* did go on to take a total of £4.5 million at the UK box office and its worldwide box-office gross exceeded $150 million. That's certainly no disaster, and was ample proof that Pierce didn't need to strap on 007's Walther PPK to make it big at the box office.

Recognition of his new superstar status was also reflected in *Empire* magazine's inclusion of him in its list of the biggest movers and shakers in the British film industry. He shot straight into the chart at No. 20 – placing him above Oscar-winning actors Jeremy Irons and Daniel Day-Lewis, *Schindler's List* star Ralph Fiennes, producer David Puttnam and directors Ken Loach and Mike Figgis. The movie magazine predicted his future would be 'off the scale'.

Everything finally seemed to be coming together in his personal life, too. He took Keely to see the memorial plaque erected to Cassie at the whale-viewing station at Bluff Park, with its brass plaque that reads:

> In Loving Memory of
> Cassie Brosnan
> For the children and families
> of Malibu and the dolphins
> and whales of the world
> October 16, 1994

He'd also taken her to see his father's simple grave in Tralee, County Kerry. Just as importantly, a year after the couple began dating, she became his first girlfriend since the death of Cassie to join him on a family holiday. Within a month of their trip to Ireland, Pierce and Keely jetted off to the Pacific Island of Bora Bora – together with Charlotte, Christopher and Sean – for a holiday in the sun. The five spent the best part of a month lazing on the island's deserted stretches of white sand, splashing around in its blue lagoon and cruising a custom-designed catamaran, *Tara Vana*, while living in a palm-thatched Tahitian cabin.

The invitation implied that Keely had been accepted by the children – indeed, accepted as a part of the family. 'It has been difficult for her, very difficult,' granted Brosnan. 'It takes a lot of accepting for a young woman to enter into this. You have to have a big heart to make way for the other person who's been there before you.'

Unlike so many Tinseltown stars, Pierce could be proud of his children. They'd survived a childhood in the public eye pretty much unscathed – and both Charlotte and Christopher seemed exceptionally level-headed for their age. Schoolmates of Charlotte say that she was always a sweet, down-to-earth girl, despite a glamorous group of friends and home life. Equally unusually, he and the kids have remained close, as Charlotte says: 'Dad really is central to my life and my brothers' lives. But as Dad, not some glossy 007 figure.'

Both have opted to pursue a career in showbusiness, like their parents. After passing seven O-levels, Charlotte enrolled on a course at London's prestigious Actors' Institute, but determined not to trade on the Brosnan family name, she decided to use her mother's maiden name, Gleeson. 'Dad was a bit taken aback when I first told him I wanted to act,' she says. 'But once he got used to the idea he was really thrilled.' And she was mature enough to be able to draw on the pain and trauma of her mother's death for a role in an end-of-term production, *Chamber Music*.

She was equally settled in her private life, sharing a flat in central London with her actor boyfriend, Alex, whom she'd known since her days at Millfield. But despite having a millionaire dad, she enjoyed anything but a millionaire lifestyle. A typical night out for the two of them would be dinner at £5.95 a head. As for the future, she planned to take any roles that came her way, like any budding young actress. 'I'm certainly not about to turn anything down at this stage,' said Charlotte, who had already appeared in an episode of *NYPD Blue*. 'Although ultimately I'd like to go into the movies.'

The love felt by Pierce for his children is reciprocated by Christopher too, who reveals: 'There is a lot of love in our family. We don't feel any awkwardness in declaring our feelings.' Having worked on *GoldenEye* and *Robinson Crusoe*, he's currently studying at a New York film school and has already written his first screenplay.

Son Sean had set his sights on being a policeman. But, much to his dad's relief, he changed his mind after watching some of the gory cop shows on American television. A good-looking, well-built boy in his early teens with a crew cut and eyes like his father's, he played guitar with a rock band called Joined At The Head in his spare time.

Unlike his elder brother and sister, he's grown up a Hollywood 'child'. He's only lived in the Malibu mansion or stayed at luxury hotels. He's also been 'indulged', as they say, by his father. On one occasion Sean sprayed the garden with water to make mud for his and his friends' dirt bikes, then rushed from the mud back to the swimming pool and back. 'The dogs soon joined in,' reveals Pierce. 'Soon the pool was brown and there was mud all over the house.'

But what parent wouldn't indulge a child whose mother had died when they were such a tender age? Striking the right balance in such a situation is not easy. Especially with Pierce being so aware of the sense of loss the absence of a parent, particularly a mother can place on a child.

Photographs have appeared showing Sean and Keely holding hands and larking about, but rumours persist that he is the main stumbling block to her and Pierce walking down the aisle. It is hard for any child to accept another woman in his mother's place – and Sean may see in Keely a rival for his father's affections. 'Sean's my biggest critic,' Brosnan tellingly once said. 'He always approves or disapproves of my dates.'

He also doesn't want him to grow up in LA. 'At the moment I have a certain amount of control and guidance in his young life,' said Brosnan, shortly before the boy's thirteenth birthday. 'But he may go to boarding school later. LA means nothing to us. The only thing keeping me here is my work.'

However, Pierce does at last seem to have come to terms with the break-up of his parents' marriage. And he remains close to his mother May and stepfather Bill – who now both live quietly in his old Merton Park home.

As for his real father, Pierce finally appears to accept that the split wasn't all Tom's fault. And when *The Kerryman* interviewed Brosnan at the Sheen Falls Hotel during his short Irish trip in the summer of 1995, he seemed to have made his own private peace with his late father. 'His attitude towards him had mellowed,' says the newspaper's Conor Keane. 'He referred to him, almost affectionately, as "Old Tom" – I think a certain amount of remorse may have set in.'

After finishing *Dante's Peak*, Pierce started work on *The Nephew* – a low-budget Irish film produced by Irish Dreamtime, the company Brosnan had set up with business partner Beau St Clair.

Shot in six weeks on location in County Wicklow, the picture – directed by Dubliner Eugene Brady – tells how an unknown American relative's arrival in a small Irish community rekindles an old grudge between respected farmer Tony Egan (Donal McCann) and his arch-rival, publican Joe Brady (Brosnan), and brings to light secrets the locals have kept to themselves for decades.

The film was slated for a late 1997 release, though it finally premièred a year later – *The Nephew* was proof of Pierce's seriousness about giving something back to the Emerald Isle, a place he felt would always be his spiritual homeland.

14. TOMORROW NEVER DIES

After the success of *GoldenEye*, it was assumed the next 007 flick, *Tomorrow Never Dies*, would be a smooth ride for all concerned. In fact it was anything but. Tight deadlines, a constantly rewritten script and casting dictates from above all caused friction.

Everything seemed to conspire against the film-makers – the effect being that *Tomorrow Never Dies* was soon regarded as a jinxed movie by many of the cast and crew. So much so that it's a miracle the finished film is as good as it is.

Almost from the word go things went wrong. Pierce turned up for the first day of filming in the suffocating heat of Bangkok – April Fool's Day, 1997, with a temperature of 102 degrees Fahrenheit, although that would prove the least of the filmmakers' problems.

Cast and crew had been looking forward to returning to Leavesden, Hertfordshire – a former airfield where the highly successful *GoldenEye* had been shot. But communication with the new Malaysian owners, who had renamed the site Millennium Studios, had broken down. During one frantic week in August 1996, Eon was convinced it would get the go-ahead to shoot there. Then it discovered another film – *The Phantom Menace* – was to be made there. Wilson was livid. 'I feel badly let down,' he said. 'Particularly as we put the place on the map.'

The race was on to find another site big enough to house the Bond movie-making juggernaut – or else Eon would have to look abroad. This was something no one wanted to do since the last Bond film shot overseas, *Licence To Kill*, had been a comparative flop. At the eleventh hour, a former Kwik Save warehouse on an industrial site in Hertfordshire was found. It looked as if it might fit the bill – even if it had 'about as much glamour as a night out in Cleethorpes', as one cynic observed. But time was of the essence so £2 million was spent converting it into a bona-fide film studio with three sound stages, dressing facilities, toilets, showers, kitchen, canteen, plus a viewing theatre and small gymnasium.

The time-scale was thrown into further confusion by the baffling behaviour of the Vietnamese authorities. After much deliberation they decided to ban Bond, an icon of the Western world, from filming in the country despite long preparations by the film crew. The news arrived only two days after a container ship had left for Vietnam, loaded with equipment. At the last minute it had to be diverted to Singapore to await instructions. After frantic negotiations, officials in Bangkok luckily agreed that the Thai capital could 'double' for an unnamed Vietnamese city.

Then there were the personality clashes – most notably between the film's British director, Roger Spottiswoode, and its American screen-writer, Bruce Feirstein, over the script. As with every Bond film, the search for a story which would carry drama and meaning is the first step towards screen success. 'The big question was how to make the eighteenth Bond film an event,' observed Jeff Kleeman, senior vice-president for United Artists at the time. 'GoldenEye was an event because there had not been a Bond movie for six years. But you need to give people a reason to come back again and leave the cinema looking forward to the next one. This is the problem the Batman series is having after just four films.'

With the Ian Fleming novels having long dried up as source material, the writer had to come up with a script as well as an original story. The first plan was to create a plot around the handover of Hong Kong from the British to the Chinese during the summer of 1997. This was rejected because the handover would already have taken place in reality. Feirstein, who worked on GoldenEye, was commissioned to come up with a story and delivered the idea of a megalomaniac media mogul who tries to trigger a third world war in a bid to boost TV ratings. Feirstein's first draft was given the green light.

Then British director Spottiswoode (who was behind hit films such as Air America, Turner & Hooch and Shoot To Kill as well as the flop Stop! Or My Mom Will Shoot) agreed to helm the picture, and things turned nasty. Spottiswoode sidelined, then sacked Feirstein, and replaced him with another writer. Yet the rewritten script was clearly not good enough either. And two weeks before the cameras were due to roll, Brosnan himself expressed his dissatisfaction at a meeting with the producers, Barbara Broccoli and Michael Wilson.

'It was not articulate or cohesive enough,' he says. 'We should have had that script up and ready the moment the cash register started ringing after GoldenEye. I let my feelings be known.' Having triumphed in his first outing as Bond, the producers listened to Pierce and insisted on reinstating Feirstein who rewrote the script day by day from his hotel room.

The chilly atmosphere between Feirstein – who insisted 'the film is my baby no matter what' – and Spottiswoode quickly froze to a standoff. At one point the two were no longer speaking and there was talk of mass resignations among the film crew. And while Feirstein was frantically rewriting virtually every word of the script, the producer Michael G.

Wilson was having to act as a go-between between him and Spottis-woode.

Others were offended by Spottiswoode's working style and acerbic manner. One executive, who had worked on ten previous Bond films, quit in fury. Only a case of champagne and a letter of apology saved the resignation of Chris Corbould, the special effects supervisor.

The constant last-minute script revisions – of the original 113-page script, only three pages would remain unchanged – caused further convulsions. 'What we are getting is an awful mishmash with changes virtually every other day,' said one senior member of the film crew. 'The actors don't know if they are coming or going. Pierce, to his credit, has remained calm about the whole thing. But other senior actors are horrified at the change. When Judi Dench, who turned up word-perfect to play M, was told that there were new lines to learn, she was mightily upset. They had to learn whole new sections only to find they had to relearn lines the night before filming.'

Key casting decisions were also overruled. The respected casting director Debbie McWilliams had lined up the beautiful Italian actress Monica Ramichi to play Paris Carver, the villain's wife. Brosnan was also keen for her to play the part. But MGM/UA insisted on casting Teri Hatcher (best known for playing Lois Lane in the hit television series *The New Adventures of Superman*) in the role – presumably with a view to boosting the flick's appeal in the States. However, the primadonna-like Hatcher did not hit it off with Pierce, widely regarded as one of the most professional and down to earth stars in Hollywood. She was annoyed that her part was smaller than expected, unhappy with her hairstyle and complained that his stubble burnt her face in a love scene. When the time came for her to slap Bond's face in a scene, she appeared intent on getting her own back by hitting him so hard that an ice-pack had to be applied to his red cheek.

After the movie had wrapped, Pierce, usually the model of discretion, did not mince his words when asked in the *Sunday Times* if he had enjoyed working with Hatcher. He said acidly: 'She acquitted herself grandly in many ways. I am sure she will learn, as she goes on, a bit of humanity and a bit of grace and a bit of charm go a long way.'

Furthermore, despite Albert Finney having been proposed as the prospective villain, Spottiswoode went for Jonathan Pryce. As it happened he, in turn, was alarmed as the script took the screenplay further and further away from the Feirstein original. 'I have never encountered anything that has changed so radically,' he said afterwards. 'Thankfully, by the time I started shooting everything was back on course.'

Then in July Pierce suffered a bad gash on his mouth while filming at Frogmore. 'I honestly thought filming would have to be halted for a couple of weeks,' says his make-up man on the film, Bron Roylance. 'There was blood pouring from the right side of his face after he was accidentally hit by a stuntman's protective helmet in a fight scene.' Even Spottiswoode, a notoriously hard taskmaster, took one look at the star's face and gasped: 'Oh my God, this is bad.' Adds Roylance: 'We went straight from the studio to hospital at Northwood in Middlesex. He needed eight stitches, but because it would show on camera, they stitched him on the inside of his mouth. It must have hurt like hell.' Typically Pierce made light of the episode, joking: 'I have always wanted a scar – look what it did for Harrison Ford.' A true professional, he was back on set that afternoon.

Midway through the shoot, one worried movie executive working on the project confided to a newspaper: 'We're nowhere near ready and we all fear for the future. If we miss the deadline and the film doesn't come out until January or February 1998, it's going to be a disaster. It could even be the end of Bond.'

How on earth had things been allowed to descend into such chaos? Some suggested it was down to the fact that it was the first Bond flick to be made without the legendary Cubby Broccoli, who died the previous year. For the first time, his daughter Barbara and son-in-law Michael G. Wilson had complete control. The real problem, though, lay with a decision that had been taken to go ahead with Bond 18 (the film that would become known as *Tomorrow Never Dies*) before shooting had even finished on *GoldenEye*, locking Eon into a ridiculously tight time frame.

Producers Barbara Broccoli and Michael G. Wilson were under intense pressure from Los Angeles-based studio giants MGM/UA to have the film ready for worldwide release by Christmas 1997 to assist a new share launch by the company. They were locked into a deal; they could not back out. Speaking with unusual frankness during the shoot, Wilson admitted things hadn't altogether gone to plan. 'I feel trepidation. Getting it all planned out and the script right has been a big problem. Usually, if the script is not right, you postpone the picture. But we can't do that. We have a deadline, which is the tightest ever, to be on screen in December. To be frank, we have never been under so much pressure.'

On the plus side, with *GoldenEye* under his belt, Brosnan slipped into the role he was born to play with consummate ease. 'Doing Bond a second time is a big advantage,' he said at the time. 'It cuts out having to figure out how it should be done.' While Wilson observed: 'In Pierce we have a Bond who is now confident and comfortable in the role.'

Furthermore Brosnan now admitted: 'I'm glad I didn't get the part back in 1986. As painful as it was then, I wasn't ready.'

However, while virtually everyone agreed he was the best Bond since Connery, and had laid to rest the immediate question mark over 007's future, there was still the big question: would Brosnan's Bond prove to be a one-hit wonder?

It's worth bearing in mind that Dalton's first Bond film, *The Living Daylights*, was considered a success, grossing $191 million – about $10 million more than Roger Moore's last outing in *A View To A Kill*. Everyone rushed to see *The Living Daylights* just to see what he was like as Bond. But by the time of 1989's *Licence To Kill*, the novelty of a new Bond had worn off. People had seen him once. Why see him again? The pressure was now on for the movie-makers to prove themselves all over again. It was the movie equivalent of 'the difficult second album syndrome'.

For all intents and purposes, *GoldenEye* represented a new era in the Bond saga. Nothing could be taken for granted. 'Logistically, this movie is much more difficult than *GoldenEye*,' said Wilson at the time. 'We have to top it and that means more impressive locations and an even more dramatic script.' Brosnan agreed, saying: 'I wanted a bigger story all round – with more gadgets, more girls, more sex appeal and more action.'

Topping *GoldenEye*'s spectacular opening sequence was always going to be a challenge. This time around the traditionally explosive opening sequence found James Bond on a routine assignment in mountains near the Khyber Pass, Afghanistan – a fitting location in view of recent events. (In actual fact the pre-title sequence was shot in the snowfields of the French Pyrenees, at one of the few high-altitude operational airfields in Europe, at the start of 1997 . . . without Pierce. His lookalike, Douglas James, doubled up for him during the three-week shoot. Close-up shots of Brosnan were added later.) Arms barons are staging a car boot-style sale of some of the world's deadliest weapons including a MIG fighter, a Chinese Scud missile, French A-17 attack helicopters, Chilean mines and German explosives.

Cut to the Ministry of Defence (MOD) Situation Room in London where M (Dench), her Chief of Staff Charles Robinson (Colin Salmon) and a handful of military brass including Admiral Roebuck (Geoffrey Palmer) are watching satellite pictures of this international conference of killers and terrorists. Roebuck decides to launch a cruise missile from HMS *Chester*. Only after firing do they see that the terrorists have SB-5 nuclear torpedoes on the wing of a MiG plane. If the missile strikes home 'there will be enough plutonium to make Chernobyl look like a picnic,' observes one onlooker in the MOD nerve centre.

But Bond is already on the case. He commandeers an L39 combat fighter armed with torpedoes. He causes predictable havoc, blowing up and gunning down the motley collection of terrorists before taking off. Once he is airborne, the plane's reluctant co-pilot tries to garrrotte him from the rear seat while the Royal Navy's cruise missile is fast closing on the arms bazaar. In desperation Bond hits the eject button, sending his attacker blasting upwards into the underbelly of a MiG in pursuit. 'Back seat driver,' remarks Bond laconically as he peels away. Seconds later what's left of the arms bazaar is hit by the cruise missile – and the sky becomes a wall of fire and smoke. ('In the course of the rocket attack we blew up in a missile launcher, a helicopter and a truck – while a jeep went up in a big bowl of flame,' according to special effects supervisor Chris Corbould. 'It all culminated in the cruise missile explosion which involved around 400 tons of petrol and 30 pounds of dynamite.')

Back in London, M and her colleagues fear that it really is curtains for 007. There is silence. Then, suddenly, Bond's voice booms over loud and clear: 'I've evacuated the area. Ask the Admiral where he'd like the bombs delivered.'

By now Brosnan had established something of a routine during the making of a Bond film. As before, he rented a house in Hampstead, London and, being very much the family man, did his best to make it a family affair. His step-son Chris worked as a third assistant director on the film, while his fourteen-year-old son Sean was based with his father in London for most of the shoot. 'Family life feels good and it helps to have everyone around me,' said Brosnan at the time. 'If we can't enjoy the good times together, then I can see little point to the hard work. On film I have to strive to be better. I want the film to be really good, so I want to stay relaxed and at ease and make it flow.'

He would start the day by going for a run across Hampstead Heath or reading the papers in his chauffeur-driven car on the journey to Frogmore. 'To be blunt, the days vary,' said Brosnan in between shooting scenes. 'I'm usually on set by 7.30 a.m. When it's a dialogue day I have to be more focused so I don't read anything. If I have done my preparation, it's easy. Then the morning just slides by.

'Hopefully we have lunch at 1 p.m. but it can be as late as 3 p.m. Wherever we are, things wrap at 7 p.m. Then I'm fast away, straight to my driver Colin's car. He keeps a couple of beers in an ice box and I have a drink which is a great way to unwind after a hard day's work. 'In the evening I eat or go out with Sean and my secretary Laura, or have a few friends over. If I'm feeling disciplined I'll do half an hour on the weights in the gym at the house. But I'm not perfect – sometimes I have one beer too many and can't face the weights!'

Having already made a Bond film, getting the look right was relatively easy this time around – although there was a subtle shift in emphasis. As before, Brosnan's Bond wore the best clothes money could buy. His suits came from Brioni, his shirts and ties from Turnbull and Asser, London, and his shoes from Church's, London. 'There was no doubt in our minds that we should turn again to Brioni for James Bond's tailored clothing,' says Lindy Hemming, costume designer on *GoldenEye* and *Tomorrow Never Dies*. 'The suits he wore in *GoldenEye* went a long way to re-establishing the character in the public eye. 'But Roger (Spottiswoode) gave us a different brief this time around. He wanted this Bond to be a bit more contemporary. In fashion terms, this meant a little looser styling and less formal – hence the decision to get rid of the pocket handkerchief.'

Physically, Pierce was a stone and a half (20 pounds) heavier than he had been in *GoldenEye*. 'Pierce wanted a strong look,' says his trainer on the film, Richard Smedley. 'So we'd run five or six miles across the Heath, ride bikes for 45 minutes or, if the weather wasn't good, work out in the gym.'

The star's dietician, Peter Titterrell, also put him on a low-fat diet to make sure that he didn't put on too much weight. 'On set he ate mostly chicken or fish cooked in their own juices with plenty of broccoli and asparagus.' But sticking to the diet wasn't always easy. 'It's a pretty boring diet,' admitted Titterell. 'And Pierce can't resist Kit Kats and the occasional blowout breakfast of bacon and eggs if he's had a few drinks the night before. I remember one day he couldn't stand the discipline any longer. He joined the crew for a huge plate of roast lamb and all the trimmings. Afterwards I'd never seen him happier and he told us "It would suit me to live like this every day." '

The plot of *Tomorrow Never Dies* centred on a power-hungry media mogul, played by Evita star Jonathan Pryce, ready to trigger off World War III in a bid to boost profits and TV ratings. Not surprisingly, Eon was coy about the model for its mogul. 'Have they – as David Hare did in the play *Pravda* – taken Rupert Murdoch as their original?' asked the *Daily Telegraph*. But an Eon spokesman slapped down the suggestion, diplomatically stating: 'We don't have anyone in particular in mind.'

The film proper opens in the South China Sea with a Royal Navy frigate, HMS *Devonshire*, being buzzed by Chinese interceptors. China threatens to bomb the ship which it says is too close to its shore. The ship threatens to shoot down the plane. A sinister-looking, all-black stealth ship (complete with twin hulls, huge pontoons and strange smooth outlines) moves into position nearby. It releases a Sea-Vac (a jet-sized drilling machine) which penetrates the ship's hull with massive loss of life. The stealth ship then fires missiles to bring down the Chinese jets. The surviving British sailors swim towards the stealth ship in the hope of being rescued. But instead they are confronted by a man in black, Stamper (Gotz Otto), with spiky blond hair and hooded eyes (one blue, one black). There is a burst of machine-gun fire and the men die in a hail of bullets. The order to massacre the men comes from mysterious media mogul Elliot Carver (Pryce).

Cut to Oxford, England. Underwear lies strewn across the floor. Bond is making love to a beautiful Danish linguistics professor when he is summoned to a meeting with M. She tells him that the Secret Service's Singapore station has picked up a mysterious signal which could have sent the *Devonshire* off course. It came from a commercial communications satellite owned by Carver – owner of a flagship newspaper, *Tomorrow*, with a global circulation of 100 million and satellite systems able to access every television on earth. M wants him investigated.

Bond flies to Hamburg (the nerve centre of Carver's worldwide media empire) where he picks up his new gadget-laden BMW from Q (played yet again by Desmond Llewelyn, making his sixteenth appearance in a Bond film). Posing as a banker at one of Carver's parties, 007 meets Carver's wife Paris (Hatcher), one of his legion of former lovers.

While investigating Carver he clashes with the dreaded Stamper – but also meets the stunning Wai Lin (played by kick-boxing Hong Kong actress Michelle Yeoh – best known for her starring role in *Supercop*). She has assumed the identity of a journalist but in reality is a spy working for the Chinese Secret Service. Her mission – like Bond's – is to dig up enough evidence on Carver to prevent the *Devonshire* incident escalating into a world war.

Suspecting Paris of renewing her relationship with Bond, Carver has his wife killed – and in due course both Bond and Wai Lin (who have formed an uneasy alliance) are captured by Carver's private army and taken to his Asian HQ in Saigon, Vietnam. The duo spring a remarkable escape, leaping down a giant banner of Carver's face hanging 100 feet from the side of the skyscraper where they are being held hostage. Handcuffed together, Bond and Wai Lin commandeer a powerful motorbike – and a thrilling chase ensues. Eventually they discover Carver's stealth ship and his madcap plan to start World War III. But when Wai Lin is captured once again, 007 is locked in a race against time to save the beauty from Carver's wrath – and, even more importantly, the world from oblivion.

The plot might have been preposterous. Because let's face it, the idea of Britain (with its 60 million people) squaring up to China (with its billion people) in the late twentieth century was stretching the imagination to breaking point. Especially when Britain had so meekly handed over Hong Kong to the Chinese in the year of the film's release. There again, it wouldn't be the first Bond film, and it probably won't be the last, to have such a far-fetched plot.

Some Bond fans (the author included) felt that the larger-than-life Finney might have made for an appropriately larger-than-life villain, but Brosnan was happy with the casting. 'I hadn't worked with Jonathan before though I had watched him rise through the ranks,' said Pierce at the time. 'I saw him in a play called *The Comedians* years ago at the Nottingham Playhouse, which really put him on the map. I was thrilled when I heard he was going to be playing Carver which he does with great panache.'

He was equally pleased to be working with Michelle Yeoh. 'I did not know anything about her beforehand,' he said. 'I had not seen any of her movies but I've become a big admirer. Her kick-boxing is incredible. From what I've been told, we have a good chemistry on screen. And off screen she's been a joy to work with.'

As Pierce would be the first to admit, one of the reasons the 007 films have been such a joy to watch over the years is the relationship Bond has forged with the supporting cast of characters. For instance, Q (Llewelyn) is not particularly enamoured by MI6's leading agent because 007 is insufficiently in awe of his gadgets. The relationship is therefore somewhat frosty – as shown by their exchange in *Tomorrow Never Dies*. The first thing Q says to Bond – in schoolmaster fashion – is: 'Now, pay attention 007.' While his last words are: 'Oh, grow up, 007.'

A similar frostiness characterises the relationship between Dench's M and Bond. She views the legendary secret agent – as famous for his between the sheets conquests as his overseas exploits on behalf of Queen and Country – with understandable ambivalence. This is reflected in the forthright approach in her dealings with Bond – although one can't help feeling she has a secret soft spot for him.

Perhaps the most enjoyable interchanges – certainly the most laden with sexual innuendo – are those with the long-suffering Miss Moneypenny (Samantha Bond). The Canadian actress Lois Maxwell is always likely to be most associated to the part, having played Moneypenny in the first fourteen films. But the Samantha Bond–Pierce

Brosnan exchanges are certainly saucier than anything that Connery or Moore could have got away with in the Maxwell era. Take the scene where Moneypenny calls him on his mobile while he's making love to his linguistics teacher. 'James, where are you?' she says, a note of concern in her voice.

'I'm just up at Oxford, brushing up on a little Danish,' replies Bond with his usual cool.

Explaining that they've got a situation at the Ministry of Defence, Moneypenny then says, 'You'll have to kiss off your lesson.'

Or a little later, when Bond is in a limousine with M and Moneypenny. Intrigued by the mysterious Carver, M tells Bond to talk to his wife, Paris (who she knows is a former 007 flame). 'Pump her for information,' orders M.

'You'll have to decide how much pumping is needed, James,' interjects Moneypenny.

'If only that were true of you and I, Moneypenny,' replies Bond with a grin.

Indeed, after the attempt to make Bond marginally more politically correct in *GoldenEye*, in *Tomorrow Never Dies* it's business as usual for Bond – with more girls than ever. This was fine with Pierce who said: 'I think audiences know Bond for what he is and realise that the man likes women. So we are a bit less politically correct in this film than we were in the late eighties.'

Not only did Brosnan's Bond have two leading ladies – in the shape of Yeoh and Hatcher (who admittedly bowed out of the film early but is memorable for appearing in little more than stockings and suspenders in one scene), but he gets to bed his blonde linguistics teacher Professor Inga Bergstrom (played by Cecilia Thomsen, the only character in the film who did not have a costume) and flirt with various other beauties. But of course, this is all in a day's work for our hero.

Predictably enough, the film has its fair share of glamorous settings too – with scenes shot in Thailand and Bangkok among other places.

A decision had also been taken to up the ante when it came to the number of gadgets – following Pierce's disappointment that a number of *GoldenEye*'s gadgets didn't actually appear in the finished movie. This time around 007 was equipped with a Dunhill cigarette lighter which became a grenade at the flick of a switch and an Omega watch which concealed a detonator, while his latest car, the BMW 750, was a veritable box of tricks. It had a voice-assisted navigation system, GPS tracking, a bullet-proof body, self-inflating tyres, a rack of rockets in the sunroof, metal spikes behind the rear bumper and a metal cutter hidden under the BMW badge. As if that was not enough, the car was programmed to give electric shocks to unauthorised personnel trying to gain entry. In addition, Bond had a new gun: a Walther P99, an updated version of his favoured 7.65mm Walther PPK.

The gadget-packed BMW 750iL (17 identical cars were actually used in the film) may not have been the sexiest car Bond had driven in his long career, but it is certainly put to good use – notably in a thrilling sequence in the multi-storey car park of the Hotel Parkhaus in Hamburg (in reality, Brent Cross, London), when 007 discovers that Carver's goons are waiting by his car. Using his Ericsson mobile phone (which doubles as a remote control handset), Bond presses a button and the car roars to life. With lights blazing, it skids from its parking space, scattering the guards. A chase ensues which culminates with the car shooting off the hotel roof and crashing into the window of an Avis car rental showroom on the other side of the street. This was one of a string of all-action scenes set up by Vic Armstrong, the 2nd unit director responsible for shooting all the action sequences. Says Pierce: 'I could only stand back in amazement as I saw the car fall, inch-perfect, through the window.'

There was another spectacular chase, this time involving a 1700cc BMW motorbike which Bond commandeers in Saigon. Handcuffed to Wai Lin, 007 operates the throttle while she manipulates the clutch. Together they race across the city's rooftops, a gunship helicopter in hot pursuit – which climaxes with the bike crashing through a balcony 45 foot up and clearing a 44-foot-wide gap to land on top of a building on the other side of the street. 'To make sure this bike chase was different we got the biggest bike BMW could supply and the world's best stuntman – Jean-Pierre Goy,' says Armstrong. 'Pierce did some of the riding himself but there was no way I was letting him do that jump. It was just too dangerous.'

The entire cast, not least Pierce, were relieved when shooting on the troubled film finally wrapped. The budget had escalated from the original $70 million (£46 million) to around $90 million (£60 million) – thanks in part to the number of major stunts such as the BMW hotel jump sequence which cost £400,000 alone. But what would the press and the public think?

True to form, the film's première at the Odeon, Leicester Square, London, was a star-studded affair. Thousands of fans braved the cold December night to see some of Britain's biggest showbiz stars celebrate the movie's release. Pierce and Keely were among the first to arrive. And for all the actor's outward confidence he admitted: 'There's just as much trepidation for me as with my first Bond première. I desperately want this to be as successful as *GoldenEye* but I'm really nervous.'

Other guests included Pierce's co-stars Jonathan Pryce, Judi Dench and Michelle Yeoh. Also present were Shirley Bassey, Bob Geldof, Chris Evans, Hugh Laurie and Sheryl Crow (who sang the film's title song). However, Cecilia Thomsen, who arrived with rock star boyfriend Bryan Adams, made the most memorable entrance in a figure-hugging Versace dress that left little to the imagination. Afterwards the celebrities moved on to a £250,000 party at Bedford Square where champagne corks popped until the early hours.

The British media could usually be relied upon to rally to the support of Bond – one of the few icons of British cinema with worldwide pulling power. So it proved this time, albeit it with a few notable exceptions. The film opened to largely positive reviews such as the *News of the World*'s which said: 'It is two hours of non-stop edge of the seat excitement'. Most other tabloid and mid-market papers also gave it the thumbs-up though the broadsheets were not quite as enthusiastic. However, on one thing the press was agreed: Pierce was better than ever. He was more confident than in his first outing as 007 – and it showed. He displayed echoes of the depressed secret agent of Fleming's novels, drinking alone in his hotel room. He delivered his lines with a coldness that befitted a man of his profession. And he showed no hesitation about killing at point-blank range.

The release of the film was accompanied by an unprecedented marketing blitz, largely paid for by its sponsors. Product placement was increasingly popular in Hollywood as studios sought to offset the ever-greater cost of making a movie. It was a trend that really began in its present form in *GoldenEye* when Pierce is seen fleetingly in a BMW sports car. That helped bring the company orders worth £190 million. But this time around it was felt by some that the brand placement was becoming so blatant that it was in danger of turning the film into a glorified commercial. 'To publicise *Tomorrow Never Dies*, 007 has lent his name to more gadgets than Tiger Woods,' complained *The Times*. 'In so doing he has lost a good deal of his Englishness. His suits are now from Milan, not Savile Row. His cars and motorcycles are from Germany, not Aston Martin. Worst of all, his most useful gadget is now a Swedish cellphone.'

Critics had a point. But the fact was *Tomorrow Never Dies* would need all the help it could get at the box office – for it was released Stateside in the same week as *Titanic*. Not altogether surprisingly for a film with such an epic budget, *Titanic* took the No. 1 spot, grossing around $28.6 million in its opening weekend. Still, the 007 flick ran it a close second, grossing a respectable $25.1 million in its opening weekend. In all *Tomorrow Never Dies* grossed around $32 million in the UK and around $123 million in North America. And the final worldwide tally would be around $350 million – virtually the same as *GoldenEye*. It was a desperately needed success for MGM/UA, which had bankrolled the picture, as the studio had only had one major hit in the two years since *GoldenEye*, 1996's *The Birdcage*. Some Eon and MGM executives had privately hoped it would gross even more money. But the film's success at least proved that Brosnan's Bond was no one-hit wonder. In fact, after all the trials and tribulations suffered during the shooting, the fact that it had grossed $350 million was a tribute to Pierce's success in the role.

Still, not everyone in the Eon camp was happy. One executive privately admitted at the time: 'Things could so easily have ended in disaster. The Bond business is very much a family affair. We just cannot afford to let personality clashes so sour a shoot again. Next time things will be different.' In other words, Spottiswoode would not be directing the follow-up.

15. ESCAPING BOND'S SHADOW

In June 1996 came the bombshell news that Pierce and Keely were expecting their first child. 'We weren't planning but sometimes life gives you wonderful surprises,' said Brosnan at the time. 'We're both in a state of shock.' The development naturally heightened speculation that the actor would 'make an honest woman' of her and escort her down the aisle.

He was caught in a gut-wrenching dilemma. After cancer stole away his beloved Cassie, the actor had vowed to himself that he'd never wed again. 'But now with a baby on the way, I don't know what to do,' he told a friend. 'I feel guilty about breaking my vow. But I'm also a devout Catholic, and having a child out of wedlock is against all I believe in. I'm in a terrible quandary.'

Stories emerged claiming Brosnan had made a bizarre contract with Keely requiring her to get DNA testing when the child was born to prove he was the father. It allegedly included a clause requiring 'lifetime fidelity' on her part. Should she ever stray, claimed one magazine, her monthly baby allowance would drop from $13,000 to $3,000 a month. This contractual agreement between Pierce and Keely was called a 'non-nuptial civil contract'.

The reports so angered Keely, an environmental reporter on American television, that she felt compelled to speak out. 'The stories are obnoxious and untrue, and I think it's important for me to say something,' she stormed. 'I would usually ignore something like this because it's so unfounded, but this was such a malicious attack on Pierce's character. He is such a wonderful man and a good father.'

On 13 January 1997, Keely gave birth to a healthy nine-pound baby boy by Caesarean section after an eight-hour labour. Pierce had driven her the 34 miles from his Malibu home to the Cedars-Sinai Hospital in Los Angeles after she started contractions. The baby was born a week early but Pierce pronounced it 'a magical moment'.

The child was christened Dylan Thomas, but contrary to what many people thought, not after the lyrical Welsh poet. 'If anything, Bob Dylan was the inspiration,' revealed Brosnan. 'Then, the day we found out it was a boy, we started considering middle names. Keely's father is Thomas, and my father's name was Thomas, and we thought, well, we'll call him Dylan Thomas.'

Ever since, the star has been sharing nappy duties with Keely. 'As a father, I have more patience now,' he said, speaking of his joy at becoming a father again. 'I'm more in awe of the spectacle of life and I have a greater appreciation of the preciousness of a baby. I'll be in my late sixties by the time Dylan reaches Charlotte's age and that's sobering but something to look forward to.' Furthermore, his other three children welcomed the new arrival with open arms. 'Sean's thrilled to have a kid brother,' Pierce revealed with evident delight.

However, despite vowing to support his girlfriend and baby boy 'in every possible way', marriage still didn't seem to be on the agenda, at least on Brosnan's agenda. 'The sacramental vows of marriage are wonderful and I cherish them,' he said. 'I did it once and I did it brilliantly – and there's no reason why I can't do it again. But I'm not going to be bullied or cajoled. I'll find the altar in my own good time. Keely and I aren't ready yet. Just because you get married, it doesn't mean you're going to end up with a wonderful relationship. It's the relationship that counts, not the piece of paper.'

Ironically, having just become a father again, in January 1998, Pierce discovered he was going to be a grandfather, triggering a rash of tongue-in-cheek tabloid headlines such as: 'The name's Bond, Granddad Bond.' His step-daughter Charlotte, who had called him 'dad' since she was a toddler, revealed that she was expecting in August. When she broke the news to him, he joked: 'Oh no! You've gone and made me a granddad and I'm only 44!' Joking aside though, he confessed to being 'delighted at the news'.

The beautiful 26-year-old, who inherited her mother's good looks, and her fiancé Alex Smith, whom she met at Millfield School, had been dating for nine years. However, she had been advised to have children early as a result of fears that she might too develop the ovarian cancer that had killed Cassie in her prime. (Doctors had told her that she must have surgery to remove her ovaries by the age of 35.) Seven months later, Charlotte duly gave birth to a daughter, Isabella Sophia. Family man Pierce was naturally over the moon and admitted: 'It gives me great contentment to see my daughter so happy; to see her do something she's really wanted to do. It's nice, the whole continuity of life.'

Meanwhile the actor was himself relishing the joys of fatherhood again – as was apparent when he was pictured frolicking in the sea with Keely and thirteen-month-old Dylan during a holiday in Jamaica. Appropriately enough, they were staying at Ian Fleming's one-time home, GoldenEye – now owned by Island Records tycoon Chris Blackwell who rented it out for £13,000 a week. The trio had been joined by Pierce's stepson Chris and fourteen-year-old Sean, making it a family affair.

The doting dad admitted: 'I love waking up next to him on the pillow. I get up in the night with him and I can change a nappy in nine seconds. I can even get around in the dark without falling over.' And despite his initially mixed feelings at hearing that Keely was expecting, he had obviously consigned any doubts to the past. 'Being a father again is a wonderful warm feeling,' he said, adding wistfully: 'It's given me a new sense of contentment.'

Later that year, insurers finally agreed to pay the Bond star £1 million to compensate him for the damage caused by storms and floods to the beautiful house that he had shared with Cassie. Taking it as a sign that it was time to make a fresh start with Keely, he finally decided to sell up and move on for good.

'I felt sad about it but I should have left the house years ago,' he says. 'The only reason I stayed were the memories. But there are too many other great things happening to let it become a worry. I have a new life and I'm looking forward to the future.

'I'm a great believer in taking notice of signs – and you can't have a greater sign than your house falling down. I've taken out all my furniture and paintings and they're now in storage. In the meantime, Keely and I have a lovely little place on Malibu Beach which we bought to do up. But it's not permanent. We'll get away at the end of next year and move up to Northern California.'

For the first time since Cassie's death he hinted that he may be ready to tie the knot again, saying: 'Keely and I have been on a remarkable journey so far and we will probably get married – we'll just steal away. But these decisions are for later.'

However, the bigger a star he became the more he was discovering that fame was a double-edged sword. 'There were some dreadful stories about my splitting with Keely,' he says. 'I supposedly bought her a house so we could live apart. Absolute rubbish, of course. There was even someone snooping around my California home.

'I also found that, despite putting out a statement denying it, the story was then published again and again as if it were true. It makes me angry but I have to balance it with how my career has taken off in the last couple of years and try to stay calm.'

Unfortunately at the same time his stepson Chris was beginning to get something of a reputation as a hellraiser. The previous year the 24-year-old had been given a three-month jail sentence for being three times over the drink-drive limit. In actual fact, he only served six weeks, at the high security Wormwood Scrubs Prison in London.

The press, all too predictably, had a field day. And on Chris's release, the *Sun* carried a story headlined: I'M 0-0-OUT. But for all the embarrassment the episode caused him, Pierce stood by Chris, even arranging for a chauffeur-driven Mercedes to meet him at the gates when he was let out a couple of weeks before Christmas.

Afterwards he said: 'I was so scared for Chris because the Scrubs is such a tough place. As far as I'm concerned Chris is my son so it was hard to see him jailed. But I'm proud of the way he handled prison. He took it on the chin like a man.' Pierce was aware that Chris's pampered lifestyle might be partly to blame for the boy's irresponsibility – but having lost his mother so young, wasn't it only natural that a father would want to spoil his son? Still, one friend says: 'Pierce hopes that something good might come out of the ordeal. He hopes that, at the very least, Chris will develop a new maturity.'

But in late 1998 Chris again hit the headlines – for the wrong reason – when he was banned from the leading London club Browns after getting involved in a brawl. Trouble flared while 6ft 3in tall Chris and two friends were partying in the VIP room. After a furious fight in one of the club's toilets, they were asked to leave. Chris was escorted out of the club with married Radio 1 DJ Lisa l'Anson who tried to hide her face. It increasingly looked as if Chris was another poor little rich kid who was going to seed. But Pierce's friend points out: 'It's easy to criticise Chris but he's not a bad kid. He's just a young bloke doing what young blokes do – but because he's Pierce's son as soon as he puts a foot wrong, it's in all the papers.'

All might be quiet on the Bond front but that did not mean Pierce was turning into a slacker when it came to his career. On the contrary he used the break between Bond films to make two big budget movies: *Grey Owl* and a remake of the 1968 flick, *The Thomas Crown Affair* (in addition to having the briefest of cameos in *The Match*, a romantic comedy set in the Scottish Highlands). The first film, sadly, would turn out to be a critical and box office flop; the second among the finest films in his long career.

On paper the remarkable story of Grey Owl, the world's most famous 'Red Indian' in the 1930s, perhaps sounded the more promising project. Standing six feet tall and resplendent in a headdress of eagle feathers, Grey Owl found fame as a chronicler of a wilderness lifestyle that was disappearing. A 'rock star' of his age, he filled huge theatres and concert halls during two lecture tours of England in 1936 and 1937.

As boys, Lord Richard Attenborough and his brother David, the wildlife programme presenter, queued for hours to witness Grey Owl in action. 'He was a magnificent, noble Indian,' Richard Attenborough recalls. 'We came away, transfixed.' On the same tour, King George VI and Queen Elizabeth (the Queen Mother), plus Princesses Elizabeth and Margaret, requested a private audience. And Grey Owl duly went to Buckingham Palace to deliver a lecture.

But the truth, when it emerged following Grey Owl's death, put all his wilderness stories in the shade. In reality, Grey Owl was plain Archie Belaney from Hastings, Sussex. He had left his home, aged 17, in 1906 and reinvented himself as a North American Indian, living in a log cabin in Canada, hunting for his food and living by his wits.

He had flown the flag for conservation long before it became fashionable, campaigning for the preservation of forests and wildlife. The Canadian beaver, in particular, would have been hunted to extinction had it not been for his efforts. Yet, throughout, he fooled governments and people in Canada, Britain and the wider world into believing that he was the real thing: an Indian with a Scottish father and an Apache mother. For all his missionary-like zeal, though, Grey Owl was no saint. He liked women and drink, finally marrying a beautiful Indian girl called Anahareo, 25 years his junior.

The only man to discover his secret was a journalist called Britt Jessup working on a little Canadian newspaper, the *North Bay Nugget*, who sat on the story for three years on the orders of his editor until Grey Owl's sudden death from pneumonia. It was considered that he was doing too much good work to ruin his reputation while he was alive.

The movie was the brainchild of Lord Attenborough, one of the most influential figures in the British film industry, best known for making 1982's award-winning *Gandhi*. The septuagenarian filmmaker commissioned writer William Nicholson, who delivered *Shadowlands* to screen success, to craft a moving script based on the love story between Grey Owl and his young wife. He first approached Pierce about starring in *Grey Owl* before he landed the part of Bond, insisting that he should be the star of the film.

But even after Pierce's success in *GoldenEye* and *Tomorrow Never Dies*, Hollywood's moneymen could not see him cutting it as Grey Owl, and refused to bankroll the film. To the actor's anger, even the giant American company MGM/UA, which had made vast profits from 007 films, flatly refused to back him in the role.

'I knew that studio financial backing was not forthcoming,' says Pierce. 'It is not the first time there has been doubt about me; I had to treat it as another battle.'

Having waited 18 years to see his Oscar triumph *Gandhi* reach the screen, Attenborough was not about to give up that easily, and showed a touching loyalty to his leading man as he struggled to raise the film's $30 million (£20 million) budget. Meanwhile Brosnan, who had been sent a number of potential blockbuster scripts since starring in *GoldenEye*, held out to play Grey Owl. 'I always knew that things were against us,' he says. 'There's no violence, no sex and no action. It is just a simple, beautifully told story.'

Eventually their prayers were answered when Jake Eberts, the man behind Goldcrest, the British production company responsible for *Chariots Of Fire*, came to the rescue, risking millions of his own money to bypass Hollywood and cover the budget.

The importance of the movie's conservation message had a special appeal for Pierce who had met girlfriend Keely Shaye-Smith through their mutual interest in the environment. 'When I read the script, I said to her, "This is like our story,"' he says.

Other facets of Grey Owl's story also attracted the actor to the project. 'Archie was the consummate actor,' says Brosnan admiringly. 'There is a great line in this script, from an Indian chief, when he tells Grey Owl, "Men become what they dream. You have dreamt well." That line stood out to me, probably more than any other. I have dreamt about movies, making them and being in them. I started off as an actor and wanted to be a movie star. There were so many things I wanted to do with my life and this story parallels some of those dreams and ambitions. This is why, when I was being turned down, I kept on thinking, "You don't get rid of me that easily." '

There were further parallels between Brosnan and Belaney. Archie Belaney was deserted by his father, George, when still a baby; Brosnan was 'abandoned' – at least in his eyes – by his father Tom when he was two. Belaney was brought up by two maiden aunts, Ada and Carrie; Brosnan was also cared for, in his home town of Navan, County Meath, by aunts Rosie and Eileen when his mother May left for England.

What's more, Belaney was a dreamer: while others wanted to be cowboys, he always begged to play the Indian. When he was thirteen, he had those dreams fired by witnessing Buffalo Bill's Wild West show in Hastings. For Brosnan, it was his first visit to the cinema in Putney, London, to see *Goldfinger* that stirred his own imagination.

Finally, both men looked across the Atlantic to realise their dreams. Belaney took a boat across the ocean before World War I and headed for Canada. Brosnan left Britain in 1980 with his wife Cassie and adopted young children, Charlotte and Christopher, to seek fame in Hollywood.

'I don't think Archie meant his deceit and storytelling to take on such huge importance,' says Pierce. 'He took risks and campaigned for what he believed in and it probably all just ran away with him. He was a great speaker and people were overawed by him. He found that he had a gift for talking and writing and huge audiences listened because they believed he was an Indian. If he'd said his name was Archie and he came from Hastings, then they wouldn't.'

The spring of 1998 duly found Pierce donning shoulder-length hair extensions and a buckskin tunic as he prepared for the cameras to eventually roll. His face was made up to give an appearance of having spent the past year camping out-of-doors.

Newcomer Annie Galipeau, a 20-year-old Algonquin Indian who was as beautiful as any Bond girl, was cast as his wife in the movie, most of which was shot in the Massawippi Lake region, 100 miles from Montreal (the Hastings scenes would later be shot in Britain).

Pierce was all too aware that such a choice of film left him open to ridicule. How many Bond fans wanted to see their hero appear on screen in braids and feathers, eating berries and carrying nothing more dangerous than a hunting knife? As a test, he had his long hair extensions glued in a 10-hour process back in Los Angeles and walked into a bar to gauge the result. 'It was full of Saturday-night revellers and there was a bunch of guys drinking at the bar who had a lot to say,' he says. 'You just have to stay calm. Archie would have had the p*** taken out of him, too.'

The film itself focuses on the relationship between Grey Owl and 'Pony' (Annie Galipeau) who follows him North where their friendship blossoms into romance. But horrified by the cruelty involved in trapping beavers, she begs him to turn his back on hunting. At first he is sceptical, explaining: 'Everything dies. The fly is killed by the fish, the fish by the otter and the otter by the wolf.' But eventually he comes round to her point of view and turns to writing about his love for the endangered Northern wilderness.

Filming went smoothly enough. But after the movie had wrapped and post-production work was completed it soon became apparent that finding the film distribution was going to be a problem. In fact, *Grey Owl* ended up going straight to video in the USA, did not get released in the UK until the tail-end of 2000 and is unlikely to ever recoup its costs.

The usually diplomatic Pierce attacked Hollywood bosses after they decided not to release *Grey Owl* in US cinemas, telling BBC radio that Hollywood executives were 'lazy and lacking in imagination' for not releasing the film. Echoing Pierce's words, Attenborough said: 'As far as Hollywood is concerned, it (*Grey Owl*) does not have sufficient scale, does not have sufficient special effects and does not demonstrate or illustrate either the pornography of violence or sex.'

So were Brosnan and Attenborough right and the rest of Hollywood wrong? Yes and no. The scenery might have been stunning but *Grey Owl* was no *Gandhi*. However, nor was it an unmitigated disaster. Its biggest failing was that it never quite seemed to make up its mind whether it was an old-fashioned love story, a clarion call on the need to save the environment, or a story about Archie's intriguing metamorphosis from white man to red man.

In contrast *The Thomas Crown Affair* was not only a box-office smash but would help Pierce to escape 007's long shadow in the eyes of both Hollywood and the general public. The film was a remake of the 1968 classic starring Steve McQueen. Several recent remakes, such as Gus Van Sant's superfluous rehash of Hitchcock's *Psycho* not to mention a lavish makeover of *The King And I* starring Jodie Foster, had met with a critical and commercial drubbing. And with the 1968 original being an exercise in sixties style and glamour – almost a period piece – remaking it was especially risky.

Directed by Norman Jewison, the McQueen film had pioneered the split-screen effect and been accompanied by a spatial jazz score. It starred McQueen when he was being hailed as the new James Dean, playing against type as a bored millionaire turned bank robber in silk suits with penthouses, gliders and a Rolls-Royce. Faye Dunaway had played an insurance investigator who tried to regain the loot but ends up losing her heart.

Yet Pierce immediately realised the potential of the remake which he would co-produce through his Irish DreamTime company. 'I knew that if I didn't do it they'd give it to Tom Cruise or some other fella out there,' he says. 'I'd already had a pretty exhausting year but I knew such an opportunity wouldn't come twice so I cleared the decks.'

Intriguingly though, even now, Pierce seemed to shadow Sean Connery. For in 1968 when *The Thomas Crown Affair* was picked up, Jewison wanted Connery, then nearing the end of his Bond career, to play the lead role. But McQueen pitched hard and fast, and got the part.

What the original did have was a tantalising core about a hunter falling for the hunted. And it was this that Pierce sought to update for a modern cinema audience – the result being one of the most enjoyable romantic capers ever.

'The film is kind of a tribute to Steve McQueen,' said Pierce, speaking on the eve of the shoot. 'He was a real hero of mine. I remember queuing up to see the film in London in my teens. I came out of the cinema wanting to be him. I want his family to see the film and be proud.'

The casting of Rene Russo in the Dunaway role was a master stroke, and the beautiful 45-year-old model-turned-actress obviously revelled in the fact that she was not playing Mel Gibson's wife in a *Lethal Weapon* film yet again.

But following in the footsteps of McQueen gave Pierce more than a few sleepless nights. 'I practically had a nervous breakdown two weeks before filming,' he says half-jokingly.

In a nod to the original, the film opens with a wry cameo from Faye Dunaway as a shrink analysing Pierce's character. Then we cut to the action. For a thrill, Crown (Brosnan) steals a priceless Monet from New York's Metropolitan Museum – in front of security guards, cops and unsuspecting museum-goers. He masterminds the heist with the help of a hollowed-out sculpture concealing three men – a modern real-life Trojan horse. But Russo's character (Catherine Banning, the insurance company investigator) is determined to get the picture back at any cost.

A conflict of interest quickly emerges between the smart, sassy Banning and the streetwise, down-to-earth NYPD cop on the case, Detective Michael McCann (comic Denis Leary). He thinks the thief will want to sell the painting. But proving somewhat faster at getting the measure of the man behind the crime, she observes: 'This is an elegant crime done by an elegant person. It's not about the money.'

However, Crown always seems to be one step ahead of his pursuers. For instance, when the police arrive to search his multimillion-dollar townhouse early on in the movie he calmly emerges from the kitchen to ask: 'Why are you in my house?' When told, he calls out a man's name and is promptly joined by another smartly dressed man. 'This happens to be my lawyer,' Crown calmly informs the police.

The more Banning learns about Crown – she sees him sink a $100,000 yacht for no other reason than 'because he likes a splash' – the more convinced she becomes of his guilt. She starts to pursue her own individual investigation independent of the NYPD, cornering Crown at an art world function.

'Do we know each other?' asks the millionaire thief.

'Not yet,' she replies, as quick-witted as he.

They talk. She says she's in insurance. 'I'm covered,' he replies.

'Not for this,' she snaps back.

Later, Crown, as ice-cool as always, nonchalantly asks: 'Do you always get your man?' She replies that she does.

'Are you going to get me?' he asks teasingly.

'Oh, I hope so,' she replies.

But while she is out to nail him, she is as fascinated by him as he is by her – a woman with a charm, intelligence, sense of humour and single-mindedness that are the match of his own.

On their very first date Crown takes her to, of all places, the museum where he committed this most audacious of crimes. In passing, we learn a little of his backstory. He's gone from Glasgow to Oxford on a boxing scholarship (a nod to Connery perhaps?) – and he even does a creditable Scottish accent.

For all the flirtation Banning pointedly asks him: 'Do you really think I'm going to flirt with the man I'm investigating?' Soon afterwards she breaks into his house and finds a painting she triumphantly says is the missing Monet. Unfortunately it turns out to be 'a ghost' – that is, a fake. Now Banning knows the only way she is going to outwit Crown is indeed by sleeping with him – and she begins to spiral out of control as she falls under the spell of the enigmatic mystery man.

Cue one of the movie's most memorable scenes: a smouldering dance sequence in which Russo's character brazenly flaunts her curves in a see-through dress. After a spin on the dancefloor, a sweating Pierce's character asks her: 'Do you wanna dance – or do you wanna dance?'

It's no surprise when they head back to his place for a passionate romp that is raunchy – by Hollywood standards – but tasteful. Even now, though, Russo's character tells him that she has no intention of backing off from her investigation. 'I'd be hugely disappointed if you did,' replies Crown with calculated cool.

The action moves from caper to cover-up and back with dizzying speed. All the while, the audience are kept guessing about the motivations of the two leads. Will Banning discover the location of the Monet? Will she rat on Thomas Crown? Or is Crown manipulating her affections like a grandmaster manipulating the pieces on a chess board?

It was a film that appealed to men and women alike – but for different reasons. Men enjoyed the thrill of the chase, Crown's ability to win over the smart, sassy woman on his tail and his attempt to get away with the ultimate heist. Women marvelled at the suave Brosnan and his life of wealth, and all the while wondered if he would betray her, or she him . . .

Making a smart sexy romantic thriller had always been Pierce's intention. 'I wanted it to be a turn on – a film that you would come out of afterwards with your date and say, "Right, darlin', your place or mine?"' he says, adopting a cockney accent. 'I wanted it to have a touch of cinematic Viagra.'

Knee pads and a huge 'pizza platter' were used to slide the couple in and out of shot while filming the movie's love scenes and Pierce admitted: 'Filming love scenes can sometimes be very unerotic. It's difficult to know where to put your hands a lot of the time and it can be quite odd standing there in nothing but a G-string.' Still, he later confessed that it had been difficult to stay emotionally detached while lying on a king-sized bed, naked except for a tiny G-string, with Russo straddling him. 'I don't normally get aroused but I must say that lying on my back feeling that warm body of hers . . .' said Pierce, a twinkle in his eye. 'I did take a minute to turn over and tell the crew, "Yes, you can move now but I'll just sit here for a while and have a nice cold glass of water." Maybe I should have put some bromide in my tea beforehand.' Luckily for him, his girlfriend was broadminded as he revealed: 'Keely doesn't get jealous. She and Rene are friends.'

But while keeping the film's two central characters, the new film did not just recycle the original film's plot, it made almost as many changes. Some were trivial: Brosnan's Crown, for example, steals a priceless Monet, rather than bags of cash, and he takes a more hands-on role in the actual theft. Others were more substantial: the erotic chess game enjoyed by McQueen and Dunaway, for instance – which now comes across as an embarrassing piece of sixties kitsch – was also discarded. Nonetheless the basic premise of the film was the same: it's all about games and risks and an attraction that undermines both protagonists. It's about a man who has everything materially but needs to do something riskier than sit on his millions.

What helped make *The Thomas Crown Affair* stand out was the fact that it was that rare thing: a romance involving two older people of the same age group. Even if the main function of the love affair was to power the plot, the chemistry between the two stars was enough to make their attachment a credible narrative motor.

The film delivered on all levels. Its setpiece heists struck the right balance between credibility, glamour and complexity. Moreoever they were deftly handled by John McTiernan, a veteran of action movies such as *Die Hard*. Glossy and ingenious, this was a film that didn't overreach itself. Compared with its closest relative among 1999's summer's crowd-pleasers, the disappointing *Entrapment*, *The Thomas Crown Affair* was a treat.

When filming wrapped, art lover Pierce – who had long relaxed in his spare time by painting – kept a Van Gogh copy from the shoot, one of a string of fake masterpieces knocked out for the movie by a team of expert forgers. It now hangs above the fireplace of his Malibu mansion, alongside the real works of art in his multi-million pound collection.

In the UK the film premièred at the Edinburgh Film Festival. Pierce and Rene Russo flew in to attend. They were joined at the première by Scotland's First Minister, Donald Dewar, and the actor Robbie Coltrane.

The film won unexpected plaudits from the critics. Furthermore it was generally agreed that Pierce's film was superior to the Steve McQueen original. 'Unlike Connery's *Entrapment*, Brosnan's *Thomas Crown* is clever, succinct and as bone-dry as a martini on a New York roof terrace,' gushed the *Guardian*. 'Without one gunshot or explosion, it is a lustrous holiday from real life but with a hard edge. It is a remake that nods politely to the original without tripping over into pastiche, and it is all wrapped up in a louche jazz score.'

Empire magazine dubbed it: 'Smart, stylish, sophisticated and sexy.' While the *Sunday Times*'s Edward Porter went on to observe: 'It is appealingly glossy and ingenious, and it doesn't overreach itself. The stunts are much better in the remake; the romance more alluring.' However, he went on to take some swipes at Pierce. He asserted that most of the film's weaker scenes came from the Brosnan–Russo relationship, 'largely because no couple that is 50 per cent Pierce Brosnan will ever burn up the big screen.'

In fact, the new film departed so substantially from the original that some questioned whether it should even rightly be billed as a remake of the 1968 film. Bob Flynn in the *Guardian* argued: 'It makes you wonder just how far a remake can depart from the film it remakes before it ceases to be one and becomes something different: a reworking, perhaps, or a reinterpretation.'

But despite this, the film proved an instant box office hit, especially in America where it grossed more than $75 million (£50 million), and revealed a serious intent by the actor to take control of his career after a long, hard climb to stardom.

Not everyone was happy about its success though. Some Eon executives felt Brosnan was trading on his Bond persona in the film. Moreover they feared that its release so soon before the next Bond film might harm the latter's box office chances. In fact their fears were misplaced as the success of *The World Is Not Enough* would show.

For all his success, though, Pierce remained resolutely down to earth – as can be seen by an interview he gave with the British 'lad mag' *FHM* around this time. As the actor observes: 'I am perceived as this rather suave sophisticate but that ain't me. I make a living being something I am not.'

The interview, in which Pierce was quizzed about everything from whether he uses a 'butt double' or had ever tied a rubber band around his 'willy' to make it look bigger, only emphasises the point. Unlike so many actors who make it to the top, Pierce made it abundantly clear that he was no precious thesp, never losing his cool, no matter how personal (or downright rude) the question.

Perhaps it was something to do with growing up in the British Isles, but it's impossible to imagine just about any other Hollywood heartthrob, be it Tom Cruise or Brad Pitt, getting into the spirit of such an interview in quite the same way.

16. THE WORLD IS NOT ENOUGH

Within weeks of *Tomorrow Never Dies'* release, work was starting on the nineteenth Bond film. This time producers Michael G. Wilson and Barbara Broccoli were determined to avoid the problems that had dogged its predecessor. At the same time they were preparing to take a gamble with Bond's future.

The *Die Hard*-style action hero that 007's cinematic alter ego, Pierce Brosnan, had seemed in danger of becoming in *Tomorrow Never Dies* was about to get a makeover. The die was to be recast. A new Bond was set to replace 1997's virtual superhero.

The first challenge was to come up with a suitably gripping story for the last Bond film of the century. With this is mind, Wilson and Broccoli invited the young British screenwriting team of Neal Purvis and Robert Wade to write the screenplay in early 1998.

'We thought the success of *Tomorrow Never Dies* would put pressure on Barbara and Michael to repeat its formula,' says Wade. 'But they encouraged us to take Bond in a very different direction.'

The screenwriting duo behind the acclaimed Britflick *Let Him Have It* were flown out to LA and installed in the penthouse suite of the Shangri-La Hotel. Over the course of the next three months, in a series of brainstorming sessions with Wilson and Broccoli, they hammered out a new celluloid future for the ageing secret agent.

Wilson, who had co-written all the 007 movies from *For Your Eyes Only* to *Licence To Kill*, and had produced or co-produced all the films since *A View To A Kill*, had a keen sense of the need to see the big picture when it came to carving out Bond's big screen future. 'I think of Bond as a pretty consistent character,' he explained at the time. 'But the world has changed around him, so now it's about how this character interacts with the present world.'

What emerged was a blueprint that should see Britain's best-known screen icon continue to make a splash at the box office, repulsing foes on and off screen alike, long into the future.

'We thought some of the core Fleming elements in the story had been lost,' says Purvis. 'Rather than blasting at people with a machine gun as 007 did in *Tomorrow Never Dies*, it was felt he should make his mark by picking up his Walther PPK and firing one shot. We also decided to delve deeper into Bond's character and to make the new film a little bit Hitchcockian. After all, the screen Bond of the sixties owed a lot to Hitchcock pictures like *Foreign Correspondent* and *North by Northwest.*'

If it hadn't been for the phenomenal success of the last two Bond films, Wilson and Broccoli could never have contemplated revamping their celluloid secret agent. But with *GoldenEye* and *Tomorrow Never Dies* between them grossing a staggering $700 million (nearly £500 million) at the box office, it was obvious that the beast called Bond was in no danger of extinction. But the biggest danger, all agreed, was to simply go on churning out a formulaic product – something the 007 series could be accused of doing in the 1980s – until the films became a joyless Batman and Robin-style parody of themselves.

Cue the new, vulnerable 007 of *The World Is Not Enough* (*TWINE*): a movie that would show a more flesh-and-blood Bond, a Bond with an Achilles heel. In short, a Bond who was not impervious to bullets and bombs.

Crucially, Pierce himself concurred with the new blueprint. 'I don't want to just run around with a machine gun from start to finish,' the 45-year-old actor admits. 'Having big, punchy set-pieces is a hallmark of the Bond films. But I also want to be tested as an actor and make my character more of a flesh-and-blood man.'

With every new Bond film, the baggage of the past also became that much greater. Where do you go for glamorous locations when 007 already lays claim to being the world's best-travelled secret agent? How do you top stunts such as *GoldenEye*'s vertigo-inducing bungee jump? Is it possible to dream up as chilling a villain as Ernst Stavros Blofeld?

'We watched the films on video night after night and eventually we realised we had to ask "not where he'd not been" but where Bond had "not been recently" because he's been just about everywhere,' says Wade. As for creating a villain, Purvis and Wade admitted that 'a Bond film is only as good as its villain' but reckoned that in Elektra and Renard – the film's villains – they had delivered.

Another worry faced by Wilson and Broccoli, as well as Brosnan and the scriptwriting team, was whether Sony would succeed in its long battle, being fought out in the US courts, to win the right to make a rival Bond series. A year earlier, it seemed a distinct possibility and there were rumours that Liam Neeson might be cast as a rival 007 and Sean Connery might even play the villain. But following a pre-trial victory by MGM (which bankrolled the official Bond films) this threat had receded, much to Eon's relief.

The cameras were ready to roll at Pinewood Studios, Bond's traditional home, in January 1999, by which time the speculation in the press about who would appear alongside Pierce in the new flick had reached fever pitch.

One week it was claimed that Spice Girl Victoria Adams was in the running to be a Bond girl. The next it was said that soccer hardman turned actor Vinnie Jones was to play a Bond baddie. Then New Zealand rugby star Jonah Lomu was linked to the flick. But perhaps the most preposterous story to emerge from Fleet Street was a claim that legendary Bond girls Ursula Andress, Honor Blackman and Shirley Eaton were to have parts in the picture. (As it happened, none appeared in the film – which just goes to show that you can't believe all you read in the papers.)

Nonetheless, with Pierce having re-established 007 as a screen icon, it had become possible once again to attract the sort of top-drawer talent that was harder to come by in the series' dog days in the mid-to-late 1980s. Thus the gorgeous French actress Sophie Marceau agreed to play the villainess, Elektra; *Full Monty* star Robert Carlyle signed on to play her equally malevolent accomplice, Renard; Denise Richards was lined up to play Bond's sidekick Dr Christmas Jones; and John Cleese debuted as Q's assistant, R.

The director this time around was Britain's Michael Apted. Best known in his homeland for the *7 Up* documentary series he had also made big Hollywood movies such as *Gorillas In The Mist* and *Blink*. Meanwhile Judi Dench returned as M; Robbie Coltrane returned as former KGB agent Valentin Zukovsky; and 84-year-old Desmond Llewelyn returned for his final Bond film (he was later tragically killed in a car crash).

The producers also showed a flair for publicity in the casting of minor roles. For instance, British drum and bass star Goldie, who was almost as famous for his gold teeth as his music, was cast as a baddie. While Ray Brown, the traffic warden star of British TV docusoap *The Clampers* who had become a hate figure after boasting of clamping 12,000 vehicles, was given a cameo.

On the eve of the film shoot, Apted announced that in stark contrast to *Tomorrow Never Dies*, the new film would be notable for a more feminist slant. 'The women will be a lot more than objects, they will be centre-stage,' he said. Although in case anyone got the wrong idea he quickly added: 'That's not to say they won't be sexy.'

The World Is Not Enough would feature one of the most memorable pre-title sequences ever in a Bond film – a spectacular boat chase along London's River Thames that would cost almost £4 million to shoot, making it possibly the cinema's most expensive boat chase ever. It took a crew of 170 around 6 weeks to film the chase that lasts just 15 minutes. But as Pierce comments: 'It was worth every penny.'

The movie actually opens in the offices of a private Swiss bank in Bilbao, Spain. For the first time in a Bond film, we see Pierce wearing glasses – and, damn it, he still looks as handsome as ever.

A shapely brunette, the Cigar Girl (Maria Grazia Cucinotta), hands the British secret agent a briefcase containing £5 million in stolen money. 'Would you like to see my figures?' asks the Cigar Girl. 'Oh, I'm sure they're perfectly rounded,' replies Bond. (So much for the film's feminist slant.)

The cash was taken from a murdered MI6 agent – and it's Bond's mission to retrieve the money and discover his fellow agent's killer. But when he presses the banker for information, the money man's henchmen round on him. Luckily 007 has a trick up his sleeve – his Q-designed glasses create a flash, temporarily blinding his attackers. A shoot-out ensues. Then, grabbing a length of cord, 007 jumps several storeys with the cash and flees.

Cut to MI6's headquarters on the Thames. Bond hands the £5 million back to its rightful owner, oil tycoon Sir Robert King. Moments later there is an explosion, killing King and blowing a hole in the side of the building. Through it we spy the Cigar Girl on a £140,000 Sunseeker motorboat which roars off. Bond takes the controls of a sleek black jetboat which shoots out of the side of the MI6 headquarters and gives chase.

The two vessels tear down the Thames with Bond's boat leap-frogging the Sunseeker and barrel-rolling in mid-air as they tear past the Houses of Parliament and through London's Docklands. Suddenly Bond presses the 'Dive' button – and the boat plunges under the surface, avoiding the low bridge that would otherwise destroy it. As the Thames rushes over him, Pierce reaches up his hand in a grooming reflex to check the knot of his tie.

Some 34 boats took to the Thames to ensure the safety of Pierce and his co-stars during the shooting of the thrilling sequence. Real footage of Pierce crashing around on the river was cut in with the special effects. It was probably the most dangerous stunt ever performed on the Thames although Pierce insisted on doing as much of his own stunt work as possible.

'The boat went like the clappers and being behind the wheel was so exhilarating,' says Pierce. 'It took six weeks to complete the sequence and I sometimes woke up in the middle of the night and thought, Oh my God! What on earth am I doing out there on the Thames, chasing a boat at 70 m.p.h. with the director's instructions coming over the radio: Fine, keep the Houses of Parliament in there, Pierce.'

Stuntmen were impressed at his skill in handling the jetboat which can operate in three inches of water and turn on a sixpence. Having said that, Pierce came worryingly close to 'braining himself' – as he puts it – one day. 'I had only one accident: a slight altercation with Lambeth Bridge,' he says. 'I had to make a split-second decision whether to go between the bridge and the Sunseeker, or go around. In the space of thinking, I lost some momentum and hit the bridge.'

The actor readily acknowledged his debt to stunt co-ordinator Simon Crane and his team: 'I have the greatest admiration for these guys. It's a brutal job no matter how simple or big the stunt – and all so the audience can go "Wow". But there's a life on the line. I've seen the blood spill and it ain't a pretty sight. I owe these guys – they make me look good.'

The chase climaxes with the Cigar Girl's speedboat crashing into a police launch at the Millennium Dome, and taking to the air in a hot air balloon. Moments later, with Bond hanging from the end of a rope, it explodes in a fireball . . .

Making a Bond movie increasingly bears the hallmarks of a military operation and this time around it would prove no exception. On taking delivery of the screenplay, online producer Tony Waye (who began his career in movies as a runner on the 1957 World War II classic, *Reach For The Sky*) despatched teams to 'recce' possible locations around the world, including Azerbaijan, the Bahamas, Bilbao, the French resort of Chamonix and Turkey.

By the spring of 1999, some 700 people were on the Bond payroll; a string of sets was being built by an army of 1,100 riggers, carpenters, plasterers, electricians and painters; and an additional 2,400 extras had been hired.

But despite the logistics there were advantages of being part of such a movie-making juggernaut. For instance, when MI6 obstructed efforts to film the chase outside its sandstone and glass headquarters on the River Thames, the producers simply picked up the phone and contacted Janet Anderson, the Arts Minister, who enlisted the help of Foreign Secretary Robin Cook to get the ban lifted.

A mile of the Thames had to be closed for up to two hours a day for three weeks during the filming. And a slipway was constructed by the side of MI6's headquarters to launch James Bond's jetboat. Meanwhile a 40-foot mock-up of the building was built at Pinewood to double up as the spy HQ for the scene when Bond's powerboat shoots out of the building. 'No one else in the British film business has Bond's clout,' notes Pierce wryly.

However, some things even the Bond team were powerless against: an avalanche in Chamonix, which swept away 17 chalets and claimed the lives of 18 people, delayed filming for a week.

Pierce was eased gently into his third Bond outing: his dialogue on the first day of shooting consisting of just two words: 'Stop! King!' But in truth, playing Bond was getting easier with each picture. 'I actually looked forward to making this film,' he revealed once the cameras had started rolling. 'The first movie was always going to be the test. A lot of the crew have worked on so many Bond movies that when I showed up for my first day's work on *GoldenEye* I felt I was being judged. But with time comes acceptance – and following the success of the first two films, I know what's expected of me. Above all, I feel more confident and relaxed.'

The World is Not Enough's storyline hinges on the importance of black gold – oil, not coal – to the modern world. The discovery of a huge deposit under the Caspian Sea has triggered a race between the multi-nationals intent on getting their hands on this fast-diminishing resource and pumping it back to their homelands. With the death of King, who had been planning to build an 800-mile pipeline to the West, Bond is despatched to protect King's beautiful daughter Elektra (Sophie Marceau). She has now taken control of the mammoth project.

Armed with an assortment of Q's latest gadgets, Bond sets off for the Caucasus and is soon smitten by Elektra. She is scornful of MI6 after they advised her father not to pay the £5 million ransom demanded by the terrorists who kidnapped her; she only escapes after seducing the psychotic Renard (Robert Carlyle). She also blames them for her father's death. 'My family have relied on MI6 twice, Mr Bond,' she says. 'We won't make the same mistake again.'

During a visit to the mountain pipeline they survive an avalanche and a surprise attack by gunmen on parahawks (a cross between a parachute and a snowmobile) descending from the sky like angels of death, then escape to her ornate villa on the shores of the Caspian.

That night they visit the nearby town of Baku where Bond encounters his old adversary, ex-KGB agent Valentin Zukovsky (Robbie Coltrane), a shadowy casino owner and entrepreneur with underworld connections. Bond suspects Zukovsky of being linked to Renard who, thanks to a bullet lodged in the brain, feels no pain. Meanwhile Elektra finally succumbs to the superspy's legendary charm.

Heading off to investigate a nuclear plant in Kazakhstan, 007 meets the hotpants-wearing scientist Dr Christmas Jones (Denise Richards).

'Don't make any jokes,' warns the brainy beauty. 'I've heard them all before.'

It soon becomes clear to Bond that Renard intends to steal the bomb and despite putting up a gallant fight, he fails to prevent the terrorist escaping with the potentially destructive weapon. The search for the missing weapon takes Bond, Jones and M to Turkey where it appears that Renard has secreted the atomic bomb on a rig inside the pipeline headed for the oil terminal. With Jones at his side, 007 enters the pipeline intent on defusing the bomb – but he rightly suspects the bomb is a diversion to conceal the theft of the plutonium. In the meantime, M has gone missing.

Now Bond has to discover why the notorious Renard wants plutonium – and what's more, who is bankrolling him?

After a detour to Baku, where Valentin's caviar fishery on the City of Walkways is destroyed by giant vertically suspended saws trailed by helicopters, Bond follows Renard to Istanbul. There he discovers the identity of his unscrupulous paymaster and they have a final showdown in the claustrophobic confines of a submerged nuclear submarine . . .

By now Pierce had established something of a routine when it came to making a Bond film. There was the hired house in Hampstead, where Keely and Dylan stayed during the shoot. 'Having them with me helps establish a pattern to the day because I'm thinking of others rather than just myself,' he said at the time. There were the runs on the Heath. And there was his regular driver Colin, by now part of his extended family.

'A few things I always bring with me on set: an alarm clock, some family photographs and one of those wonderful pillows you put on your face,' added Pierce. 'It's full of lavender and it helps me chill out. And I'll have a couple of books in case there's a long wait. I'm reading the letters of Samuel Beckett and looking at *Waiting for Godot* and his other plays. I like his spiritual leanings – he didn't particularly care about success or failure.'

At 1 p.m. Pierce would adjourn for lunch and tuck into a specially prepared meal. 'I sit in this great big trailer – it's bigger than the first house I owned – with some sounds on the CD player,' he continued. 'Back home I catch up on the day with Keely . . . She has a regime with the baby, running the house and a book she's writing on gardens, and we've got help in the house with a nanny.

'I keep in touch with all my children. If I can't see them, then there's a round of phone calls. And I try and have a massage. You're holding a lot of shit in your bones and body, and getting rid of it can be a tremendous renewal of the immune system. I'm in bed most nights by 10 o'clock, feeling on top of the world.'

Making the movie was also a much more pleasurable experience than filming the previous Bond flick, as Pierce was quick to admit. 'The last one was a bit like pulling teeth. This one's gone very smoothly and I've had a great time,' he said when the film had wrapped. 'I tip my hat to Michael (Apted) who's done a superb job and is a really great guy. I trust him and he listened to what I had to say about Bond having dialogue that was believable, and having an emotional base from which the character can work off. He's also surrounded me with wonderful actors like Robert (Carlyle) and Sophie (Marceau) – and that's made my job a lot easier.'

As usual, Pierce's Bond saw his fair share of between the sheets action. Not only does he woo Elektra (Marceau) and Dr Jones (Richards) in the film but he also has his wicked way with the cheekily named Dr Molly Warmflash (played by Serena Scott Thomas, the younger sister of *English Patient* star Kristin).

Still, shooting such scenes wasn't as easy as it sounded. Pierce's love scene with Marceau had to be re-shot 18 times after her breasts kept popping into view – threatening the movie's all important PG certificate. Most men might have happily gone twelve rounds with a Bond baddie to bed the French beauty but Pierce noted: 'It's difficult to make a love scene look spontaneous on Take 18. To be honest, it infuriated me. What's wrong with showing a little nipple if it's tastefully done?'

But in start contrast to the sixties, the Bond of *TWINE* seems genuinely interested in his partners as people. As one pundit commented: 'These days he will hardly look at a supermodel unless she's a nuclear physicist or an industrialist.' What's more, he is too much of a gentleman to monopolise the jokes. His women get to answer back.

If anything, *The World Is Not Enough* was even more of a gadget-fest than *Tomorrow Never Dies* although thankfully the product placement was not quite so blatant as in its predecessor. The opening sequence of course features 007's special glasses (with their blinding flash facility) and the hydro boat. When the action transfers to MI6's Scottish HQ, we glimpse another of Q's lethal little toys: a set of bagpipes that fires bullets and doubles as a flame-thrower.

Other new Bond toys include a watch with dual lasers and miniature grappling hook with 50 feet of high-tensile micro filament wire, able to support an 800-pound payload. And a ski jacket that inflates into a balloon – just in case he finds himself caught in an avalanche. Lastly, Bond's new car is as mean a machine as any of his previous motors –

his BMW (Z8) coming complete with the latest in intercept, surveillance and countermeasures. Translated into hardware, that boils down to this: titanium-plating and armour, missile-firing headlamps and a multi-tasking heads-up display including a thin beam able to pick up conversation at a distance and an infra-red tracking system. You had to hand it to Q.

The World Is Not Enough opened with the usual fanfare on both sides of the Atlantic. The US première of the film in Los Angeles saw Pierce 'surrounded by a bevy of busty beauties' as the *Sun* put it, squeezing every tabloid cliché out of the occasion.

As well as Keely, there was Maria Grazia Cucinotta ('sporting a daring low-cut dress that showed off her ample charms,' another tabloid excitedly told its readers), not to mention Denise Richards, and another Hollywood actress, Maria Conchita Alonso, in a see-through dress.

Shortly afterwards the Bond bandwagon descended on a wintry Leicester Square, London, for perhaps the year's most eagerly awaited screening of a new film. The latest batch of 007 lasses again turned out in force: Denise Richards (wearing a floor-length pink dress); Sophie Marceau (in a print dress slashed to the thigh), and Maria Grazia Cucinotta (in another figure-hugging number with a plunging neckline). Not surprisingly they were met by a chorus of whistles from the 2,000-strong crowd. Other guests included Judi Dench, Robert Carlyle, Robbie Coltrane, Vinnie Jones, Lee Majors, John Hurt and a heavily pregnant Emma Thompson.

But there was no question who the star of the night was: Pierce, who arrived in a long black jacket and blue waistcoat, elegant as ever. He was accompanied by Keely who was wearing a strapless claret silk gown with a dazzling £3.5 million necklace borrowed from the jewellers Asprey and Garrard. Superstar or not though, Pierce still found time to stop and sign a few autographs.

Getting the stars to turn out on the film's big night was one thing. Just as important was winning over the critics. As it happened, most of them gave the film the thumbs-up. The British tabloids were predictably gung-ho. 'At the heart of any great Bond movie are two essential ingredients – nuclear bombs and nuclear babes – and the new 007 adventure has shed loads of both,' said the *Sun*. It was just as enthusiastic about Pierce. 'Forget what anyone says about Sean Connery being the definitive 007, Pierce Brosnan has the twinkle, the class, the physique, the sex appeal, the sense of humour and the right taste in women. He is The Man. Brosnan is Bond.' Praise indeed.

Crucially, most of the broadsheets seemed in agreement – with *The Times*, for instance, in no doubt that the film-makers were giving the public what they wanted: 'The Bond series is formula film-making but at least it's Formula One – and increasingly fine-tuned since Pierce Brosnan replaced Timothy Dalton.'

Of course, there were the usual dissenting voices. The famously maverick Alexander Walker of the *Evening Standard* commented: 'This adventure will see Bond nicely into the Millennium; but it's not the one I'd want to place in my time capsule.' The film critic Angie Errigo told Britain's Radio 4 that 007 was losing his style, arguing that he was now 'more Austin Reed than Savile Row'.

This time round, though, Bond wasn't just fighting to win over the critics, he was up against a new challenge: Internet pirates. A string of websites sprang up in the weeks before the flick's official release, brazenly showing detailed footage from the blockbuster secretly video-recorded by computer geeks during filming. One site even showed the *The World Is Not Enough*'s breathtaking opening sequence. It looked as if netheads were going to make this the most leaked movie ever.

Executives at Eon and MGM feared that the massive collection of internet images could seriously undermine the film's commercial success at the box office. An Eon spokesman said: 'It's a losing battle. Using public locations means there's always a risk some pictures will leak. But this lot know exactly where we're going to film and what we're doing. There's little we can do – but it's obviously a worry.'

As it happened, their fears were misplaced and the film went on to do marginally better than the two previous Bond flicks starring Pierce. Taking $35.5 million in its opening weekend in the US, *TWINE* went on to gross a total of $127 million Stateside, making it one of the 15 biggest grossing films of the year.

It opened equally strongly in the UK where it delivered the fourth biggest opening weekend in British box office history with a mammoth £6.6 million ($10 million) in its first weekend. It would go on to play at the UK box office for three months, eventually grossing £30 million ($45 million) – 40 per cent up on *Tomorrow Never Dies*' takings.

The film launched powerfully in many other territories including Singapore, Malaysia, Australia, Israel and South Africa, and outperformed one of that year's biggest releases, *Mission: Impossible 2*, in Europe. In all its total worldwide gross would hit $355 million. With three 007 films under his belt, Pierce had truly become the billion dollar Bond.

17. FAIRYTALE WEDDING

The marriage between the James Bond star and his quiet, home-loving girlfriend, Keely Shaye-Smith, at Ashford Castle, County Mayo in the summer of 2001 was never meant to happen.

Those supposedly in the know insisted the movie star would not make the model turned TV presenter the second Mrs Brosnan. And when he did in due course signal his intention to make an honest woman of her, fate seemed to conspire to do everything in its power to prevent the nuptials from taking place.

The actor himself perhaps fuelled such stories with his assertion that he would never – could never – marry again following the death of his beloved Cassie. 'No one will replace Cassie,' he said 12 months after her funeral. 'I will always be married to her alone.' And he made it crystal clear that he did not expect to find the personal happiness he had found with his wife.

During their early years together, he might have spoken glowingly about Keely, saying: 'We have been on quite a journey together. She has been good for me and very supportive. You need a lot of understanding from partners in this business if you're going to enjoy anything like a real life away from the scripts and cameras,' but there was little indication that he saw in her a soulmate to rival Cassie.

However, while on the surface Keely Shaye-Smith, a glamorous former model with a career in television, might have seemed just like all the rest of the women Pierce had dated since Cassie's death, underneath beat the heart of an altogether different kind of girl. A committed environmentalist, she appealed to a softer side of Brosnan. Whereas his other girlfriends had largely ignored his parental commitments, Keely was keen to involve his ten-year-old son by Cassie on their dates.

'Sean hated a lot of his dad's girlfriends but Keely became a friend to him,' says one friend. 'He was just a kid, he was crying out for a mother figure. Keely gently filled that gap without anyone even noticing. She'd make sandwiches and cookies for him and watch *The Simpsons* with him and laugh. She'd tease him and she'd talk to him and most importantly she'd listen. She wouldn't just turn up in the evenings in full hair, make-up and drop-dead evening dress to go out with his dad. She'd hang out at the house in jeans.'

Right from the start Keely realised loving Brosnan involved embracing the sum total of his life – his family, his career, his spiritual and religious side (he is a Catholic) as well as his memories of his dead wife. She encouraged Brosnan to write poetry which often turned on his grief. Their favourite days were spent on the beaches during the day and in the home at night where Brosnan would play her the flute. She taught Brosnan about organic gardening (she has written a book on the subject) and began to interest him in cooking. 'The house started to smell good when Keely came on the scene,' says friend Dan Dresser. 'There were fresh flowers in vases and home-cooked food in the kitchen. It smelt like a real home.'

Remarkably Keely was unfazed by the presence of Cassie in the Malibu mansion. 'Most women would have found it impossible to compete with a dead wife but Keely found his devotion to Cassie very touching and very honourable,' says a friend. Indeed, to this day, Brosnan absentmindedly calls Keely 'Cassie' but she remains unperturbed. 'In many ways she takes it as a compliment,' adds the pal. 'Most women would find that very hard to accept.'

The birth of Dylan in early 1997 marked the start of a deeper, enduring, all-embracing love for Keely in Pierce. For him a child should be part of a proper family – something he felt particularly strongly given his own family problems as a child. He started thinking of the relationship as a permanent one and he began to appreciate that in Keely he had perhaps found a woman who could fill Cassie's shoes.

However, in 1998 floods in California, which left Keely and Dylan trapped, scuppered their first shot at a wedding. The following year he was busy with Bond. Then, after a date was fixed and the wedding booked, Sean was almost killed in April 2000, when a 4 × 4 truck he was in plunged 130 feet down a ravine in Malibu, puncturing his bladder and shattering his pelvis. A distraught Keely broke the shocking news at a charity event in LA, telling a shocked crowd at the Earth Fayre environmental conference: 'Pierce is not here because his son has been in a car crash.'

It turned out that the sixteen-year-old had been in the Chevrolet Blazer with five friends when the vehicle hurtled off a winding mountain road at 3.45 in the morning. It was being driven by a friend of Sean's, nineteen-year-old James Hall, who told police that he swerved to avoid a large rock. All but Sean and one other youngster, who suffered a broken collarbone, scrambled to safety. The boys had all been drinking and Hall was later charged with drink-driving.

Brosnan was first at the hospital and Keely joined him there as soon as possible. 'He rushed from his home to the crash site and held Sean's hand all the way to hospital,' reveals a friend.

News of the crash made headlines around the world and initial reports suggested that Sean's injuries were so serious that he might never walk again. So it was no surprise when Pierce immediately called off the May nuptials. 'I want my son to dance at my wedding,' he said by way of explanation.

Over the next few months, Pierce and Keely 'dedicated themselves to Sean's welfare' as Pierce's publicist, Dick Guttman, put it. And God was obviously on the 007 star's side, for Sean made a miraculous recovery. By the summer of that year he had put down his crutches and was walking up and down the stairs at the family's Malibu home – 'a momentous occasion' as Pierce put it.

The wedding plans were again reactivated. Then once again they were put on hold – this time for a happier reason. It was revealed that 36-year-old Keely was expecting their second child in March 2001. 'Babies come first,' observed Pierce with a chuckle. 'They need a lot more attention.'

A healthy baby boy was duly born in February 2001. It was a cause for great celebration. Pierce and Keely decided to call their second son Paris Beckett. But with Keely's pregnancy over, they vowed that this time nothing was going to stop their wedding.

The big day was set for Saturday 4 August 2001. The place? Ireland naturally. For even though Pierce had applied to become a US citizen (and seems unlikely to ever return to Ireland to live), he still has a deep romantic attachment to the land of his birth.

The venue was to be Ballintubber Abbey, a thirteenth-century Catholic Church in County Mayo, set on a knoll overlooking green fields, stone walls and grazing sheep. As for the reception, that was to be held at the magnificent Ashford Castle Hotel nearby.

This being Ireland, though, it rained in the morning although the sun did shine later. The flower girl, Pierce's three-year-old granddaughter Isabella, got a cold. And while Dylan finally agreed to don a tux (with his motorcycle boots) instead of the Hawaiian shirt he favoured, he lodged a last-minute protest against carrying the rings.

But it wasn't frustration that led Pierce to shed a few silent tears when, at 4.15 p.m., he momentarily sat in the 785-year-old church and scanned the pews, occupied by the 120 close friends and family who had flown in from London and Los Angeles to witness the exchange of vows.

According to best man Bron Roylance, a makeup artist and close friend who met Pierce while working on *Remington Steele* in the 1980s, it was down to the groom's emotional state: 'He was floating on a cloud of happiness.'

No expense was spared in making this a day to remember for Pierce, Keely and their families and friends. A six-tier carrot cake was specially flown in from England. London florist Rob Van Helden used 14,885 flowers to 'bring the garden indoors' and create elaborate dining table centrepieces, while Keely's friend Cynthia Wolff designed Pierce's platinum ring and the bride's three carat princess cut diamond band. Moreover, being one of Hollywood's biggest stars, Pierce naturally hired a wedding organiser, explaining: 'I'm hopeless at organising things!'

A £500,000 deal with Britain's glossy *Hello!* magazine – granting it exclusive access to the wedding – enabled Pierce, still conscious of his humble roots, to stage a wedding fit for a king.

However, denying other media outlets the opportunity to cover the nuptials lent the proceedings something of a cloak and dagger air – somewhat fittingly for an actor who had made his name playing a secret agent. Guests arrived under assumed names and were asked to sign confidentiality agreements to keep the details private. The windows of the black Mercedes which took Pierce to the church had had its windows blacked out to keep out prying eyes and, more to the point, camera lenses. Similarly, both he and Keely, who arrived in a white Rolls-Royce, shielded their faces as they entered a birch porch which had been specially built the day before to foil the paparazzi.

All too predictably, some newspapers claimed that such measures cheapened the proceedings. And the *Sunday Express* coined a clever headline reflecting this sentiment: 'The World is not invited'. On the other hand, how many people would turn down a six-figure sum to be allowed to take the photographs at their wedding if they were offered it, one could ask? The truth was that any sniping was inspired by sour grapes as much as anything else.

At the same time, it should be pointed out that Pierce donated around half the *Hello!* fee to building a school in Tibet where young people could be taught skills like metalwork. 'That money was only forthcoming because Pierce did a deal with the magazine,' points out one close friend in his defence.

For all the glitz and glamour and the fact that guests came from as far away as Australia and America, in one respect this was an atypical Hollywood wedding. Unlike most Tinseltown nuptials, where you can't move for A, B or C list celebrities, this really was a wedding for the couple's family and friends. Figures from the showbusiness world were surprisingly thin on the ground. There was veteran Hollywood actor

Rod Steiger (who has appeared in dozens of films including the classic *On The Waterfront*); actress Peta Wilson (*La Femme Nikita*) and a couple of director friends: Britain's John Boorman (maker of the brilliant 1967 thriller *Point Blank*); and Roger Donaldson (*Dante's Peak*). And that was about it. Interestingly, no one from the Bond world was invited.

On the way to the church, Pierce declined a belt of Midleton Irish whiskey which best man Bron had thoughtfully brought along just in case the actor's nerves needed steadying. But at the wedding's 4.30 p.m. start time there was no sign of the bride. Pierce, walking up and down the aisle, reassured guests with a smile: 'She's coming. She is coming.'

Half an hour later Keely duly arrived, having catered to the needs of another man, Paris, who needed feeding. She looked stunning in a pearl-encrusted Richard Tyler gown. To the 'Allegro from Spring' of Vivaldi's *The Four Seasons*, Pierce's son Christopher walked Keely's mother down the aisle, followed by Pierce's ushers Sean Brosnan, son-in-law Alex Smith and best man Bron. Then Pierce appeared, dashing in the Gianni Campagna tuxedo he had helped design for the occasion. Finally, a radiant Keely, accompanied by her father Tom, walked down the aisle on a carpet of red petals.

The ceremony began with candle-lighting punctuated by the traditional Irish sounds of The Chieftans. Then Pierce and Keely sat facing the aisle while 76-year-old Steiger, a long-time friend, read from The First Letter of St Paul to the Corinthians.

Monsignor John Fleming, who was conducting the service, asked the couple to exchange vows. Standing in front of the altar, Pierce asked: 'Keely, do you consent to be my wife?'

She replied: 'I do. Pierce, do you consent to be my husband?'

Pierce: 'I do. I take you as my wife and I give myself to you as your husband.'

Keely: 'And I take you as my husband and give myself to you as your wife.' Throughout the prayer that followed the blessing of the rings, the two stood with fingers entwined.

After a final prayer and blessing and the signing of the register, the couple momentarily left one another's side to embrace their families. With applause and whistles speeding them on their way, Pierce punched the air victoriously, grinned and pulled the new Mrs Brosnan into the sunlight.

The wedding party then adjourned to the exclusive Ashford Castle Hotel, set in 300 forested acres, where a giant 150 by 45 foot marquee had been erected specially for the occasion.

Explaining the importance of the marriage to some of the guests, a clearly overjoyed Pierce gushed: 'We have been on a journey together and I want the world to know I love this woman. I don't know any better way than saying "Be my wife". To celebrate this wedding in the eyes of God, on Irish soil, in the oldest abbey in Ireland, and to have Keely as my bride, is the stuff of romance. It's old-fashioned but it's pretty wonderful.'

Guests dined on grilled Cleggan lobster, asparagus spears and Irish potatoes. When dinner ended Pierce read Keely a romantic poem by Chilean poet Pablo Neruda before Bron asked everyone to raise their glasses to the newly married couple.

Things moved into a higher gear still when the curtain at the back of the dining room fell away to reveal a sunken dance floor. Pierce swept Keely onto the dance floor for their first dance – to Bruce Springsteen's moving ballad 'If I Should Fall Behind (Wait For Me)'. The Chieftans later launched into 45 minutes of jigs, reels and ballads before the sky burst into colour with a vibrant fireworks display.

'It was a perfect enchanted evening,' said bridesmaid Cynthia Wolff afterwards. 'Weddings just don't come any more magical.'

In between fathering children, nursing Sean back to health and planning his much-delayed second wedding, Pierce had found the time to make another film, *The Tailor Of Panama*, also released that year.

Based on the John Le Carré novel of the same name, the story tells the tale of British spy, Andrew Osnard, who oversees proceedings leading up to the handover of the Panama Canal by the USA in December 1999. He recruits a tailor, Pendel, who is inexperienced in all matters of espionage, to act as a spy – with altogether unexpected results.

The novel might not have been up there with Le Carré's finest, such as *Tinker, Tailor, Soldier, Spy* or *A Perfect Spy*, but the film of the book was still a damn sight more thought-provoking and intelligent than most Hollywood products. What's more, in the ruthless, cynical, hard-drinking Osnard, Brosnan got to play a character who, in some respects at least, was closer to Ian Fleming's 007 template than the airbrushed figure of the Bond films.

The film, directed by John Boorman, boasted a stellar cast that included Brosnan, Geoffrey Rush (Pendel), and Jamie Lee Curtis (Pendel's wife). And Pierce did not hesitate when John Boorman offered him the role. Interestingly Le Carré was initially opposed to the idea of casting Pierce as Osnard, perhaps fearing the Bond baggage he would bring to the role. However, he quickly changed his mind after meeting the actor. 'When I walked with Pierce, I thought there was so much of a man there,' he says. 'With his classical training and background, he saw the part as a showcase for rage. It was daring for him to go against the Bond image. He makes a fool of Bond in the post-Cold War world with this role. He removes the hypocritical padding from Bond to reveal him in his nakedness.'

Like the big screen Bond, Osnard beds plenty of women. But he also behaves in a way that 007 is never likely to do on the big screen. In one scene the actor slaps Jamie Lee Curtis when she rebuffs his sexual advances. In another he takes Rush's character to a gay club and dances cheek to cheek with him. 'I liked doing that,' says Pierce with a chuckle.

After filming had wrapped, Pierce said: 'I enjoyed doing it enormously. It was a risky role. The guy's a swine, a shit, an immoral sleaze who's only out for himself. He's been in the game too long. He's disillusioned, bored and trying to keep his enthusiasm up.' But test screenings showed that audiences found it hard to separate the unscrupulous British agent Brosnan was playing from his usual Bond persona. 'The results showed that people wanted to see Pierce play a spy but hated the idea of him playing this nasty, ruthless, anti-Bond guy,' reveals Boorman.

Perhaps that's why the film failed to win the critical acclaim it deserved, even though Pierce gives a wholly convincing portrayal of the jaded, cynical MI6 man who is more interested in looking after himself than in serving Her Majesty's government. Having said that, the movie performed adequately at the box office even if it failed to reach out to the Bond audience.

The actor was also involved in a very different film released in 2001, the Oscar-nominated *Dolphins*, created by the same team, MacGillivray Freeman, behind the £66 million ($100 million) grossing IMAX smash, *Everest*.

The documentary follows a dedicated scientist, Kathleen Dudzinski, and her colleagues who have devoted their lives to studying wild dolphin behaviour and communication, investigating the mystery of these magnificent yet vulnerable creatures which have aroused curiosity for centuries.

Filmed in exotic locations in the Bahamas and Patagonia, it features some of the most amazing wide-angle views, aerial shots and close-ups of dolphins ever to grace the 20m × 26m IMAX screen.

With his long interest in dolphins, the environment and ocean conservation, Pierce jumped at the chance to narrate the documentary. 'I'm so proud to be involved with this project,' he said at the time. 'It can only help our understanding of this wonderful creature.'

However, if there is one other thing Pierce is likely to remember 2001 for, with the exception of his wedding to Keely and the birth of Paris, it is being voted the sexiest man alive by America's *People* magazine, an honour handed out every year by the popular women's weekly.

'What better fantasy man for these turbulent times than James Bond,' asked the magazine in the wake of the September 11 terrorist attack on New York. 'He's dashing, fearless, unshakable and, unfortunately, not real.

'Happily, the man who portrays him is cut from the same cloth. Suave and sophisticated, ruggedly handsome, caring and kind, he's also a total knockout – and a one-woman man. Who wouldn't bond with this breathtaking man?'

Flattered though he might be, Pierce took the accolade with a pinch of salt as one might expect. 'I am the sexiest man in the world!' he said with a twinkle in his eye. 'I know I am. I read it!'

18. BOND AND BEYOND

The cameras finally rolled on the twentieth Bond film in January 2002. It had been a long wait for fans awaiting the spy's return to the big screen. The new film, *Die Another Day*, wasn't due to hit cinemas until November 2002 – almost three years on from *The World Is Not Enough*'s release.

To help satisfy the hunger of Bond fans the world over for news of the secret agent in the meantime, dozens of 007 websites had sprung up on the Internet to help the press fill the information vacuum. Some stories were true. Some were not. Unfortunately the moviemakers, Eon, invariably denied everything whether or not it was true which simply fuelled the rumours and speculation.

Just about every good-looking starlet in the showbusiness world was tipped to be in the forthcoming film at one time or another. First, it was Catherine Zeta-Jones. Then it was Estelle Warren, the model-turned-actress best known for running around semi-naked in the 2001 remake of *The Planet Of The Apes*. Even Britney Spears was tipped to play a Bond girl at one point!

There were also reports that the movie was to be shot in all sorts of unlikely places, including Ireland and India; that the story was going to see Sean Connery returning as 007's father; and that it was going to have all sorts of names, among them *Beyond The Ice*. None of these stories, as it happened, turned out to be true.

However, some important developments did take place in the three-year gap between the making of *TWINE* and *Die Another Day*: perhaps most notably the reuniting of 007 and a British-built Aston Martin. Ford, the new owners of Aston Martin, had had to pay heavily, an estimated £100 million, to put Bond in the driving seat of the sports car. But the American parent company believed that seeing Pierce at an Aston Martin wheel would give a big boost to the V12 Vanquish.

After months of increasingly feverish speculation, some hard facts finally emerged at a high-profile press conference held at Pinewood Studios in January 2002, where the new movie would shoot. Taking to a stage in front of the world's media, a dapperly dressed Pierce told of his delight to be back as Bond for a fourth time. 'Time has gone by so quickly – it seems like only yesterday I was sitting here for *GoldenEye*,' he said.

It was also revealed that a former model for Ralph Lauren and Versace, Rick Yune, would play one of 007's adversaries, Zao. The

30-year-old Asian American actor and martial arts expert, who had appeared in *The Fast And The Furious*, told journalists: 'There have been many amazing characters before me but I promise, this time Bond will have his hands full.'

As usual, a couple of gorgeous actresses had been lined up to appear alongside Pierce. This time around Halle Berry, who starred in *The X-Men* and won a Best Actress Oscar for her role in *Monster's Ball*, was to play Bond's feisty new femme fatale. 'I'm proud to be here,' she said. 'I grew up watching Bond.'

Newcomer Rosamund Pike was the surprise choice to play the second Bond girl. The 22-year-old Oxford graduate was to star as a baddie scientist called Gala Brand who helps Bond out of a tight spot after falling for his smooth talk, like so many 007 girls before her. Regular cast members Judi Dench, Samantha Bond and John Cleese would be back as usual. The director this time around was to be Lee Tamahori (who had made *Once Were Warriors* and *The Edge*).

The film would open with a hovercraft chase in the demilitarised zone between the two Koreas and continue, via Hong Kong to Cuba, Iceland and London. The press conference also revealed that most of the filming was to take place in Britain, with as many as ten giant sets, including a futuristic ice palace dripping with stalactites and chandeliers, being constructed at Pinewood. In addition, the giant greenhouses of the Eden Project were to be used for a jungle scene.

True to form, Eon were doing their best to keep the script, written once again by Neal Purvis and Robert Wade, under wraps. But reports suggested that the villain would undergo a facial transformation to elude Bond. In fact, the rumours implied that the transformation would be so radical that Yune's character would re-emerge as the British actor Toby Stephens, son of the veteran, much-respected thesp Dame Maggie Smith.

With that, the cast and crew dispersed – and the media were left with as many questions as answers, only some of which have been resolved – for example, that Madonna would sing the title song.

So what of the future? There is no doubt Pierce loves the actor's life and enjoys the trappings – the fame, the perks, not to mention the money – that come with being a star. 'I'm very proud to be an actor and I can't think of anything else I want to do in my life,' he says. 'Having a few lines on my face has given me more character and led to me being taken more seriously as an actor.' But he's got a healthy scepticism for the industry as a whole, saying: 'It's a wonderful business but it's also a lot of nonsense.'

At the moment, he seems to be content juggling his Bond work with perhaps more stimulating, lower-profile projects like *The Tailor Of Panama* and *Evelyn*, a film made in late 2001 by his Irish DreamTime company, which he both stars in and co-produces.

Set in 1950s Ireland, the low-budget film, directed by Bruce Beresford and also starring former *ER* star Julianna Margulies and Stephen Rea, tells the true story of Desmond Doyle, an Irishman who battled against an outdated custody law to recover his four children after his wife ran off.

Pierce is all too aware that his Bond gig will not last for ever. He will turn 50 in 2003. And even though he wears his years well, and clearly looks after himself, eating healthily and exercising regularly, there is a limit to how long anyone can play 007. 'You only have so much longevity doing action films,' observers Pierce. 'In the Bond movies I'm in the thick of it and that becomes wearisome on the body. And being in action films can actually be like watching paint dry – you're just sitting around waiting for the special effects boys to set up their toys.'

If he really wanted to, he could conceivably carry on playing Bond until well into his fifties, like Roger Moore, who was 58 when he finally hung up his Walther PPK. But Pierce seems unlikely to follow his footsteps. 'I'm still enjoying playing 007 but I don't want people watching me get old and see my waist get bigger and my hair thinner,' says Brosnan. 'That would just be horrible. It takes stamina to play this role. I would like to get off the stage with grace. I am honouring my contract here but it would be wonderful to do another one.

'After that, I do not know. Much as I love Bond, there's more to life. You have to take risks, jump off cliffs and hope you'll fly.' As always when discussing his future as Bond, though, Brosnan wisely leaves the door open, never entirely saying 'never again'.

One of the most intriguing questions is whether he'll ever return to the stage. A lot of his old friends would love to see him make his mark in London's West End, having conquered Hollywood. His old Drama Centre tutor, Christopher Fettes, says: 'I'd say that Pierce had a potentially wider range as an actor than Sean Connery. But in effect, he chose not to develop it by going to America.

'I hope he won't get bogged down with James Bond for too long. He should be playing Shakespearean leads. I know he prefers making movies, but he's got what it takes to play the big stage roles at somewhere like the National Theatre. He's experienced great heartache in his life and that would be sure to give even greater depth to his performances.'

As recently as the late 1990s, Pierce seemed open to the idea of returning to the stage, saying: 'It's been too long since I've performed on stage. Part of me would like to get back to the theatre. It's more fulfilling because you get instant gratification. Filming is much slower and can be so frustrating.' But more recently he seems to have drawn a line under his theatrical career, saying: 'I don't think I have the bottle or desire to get back up there on stage. You have to need to go back, for artistic or personal reasons. Someone like Jonathan Pryce needs to go on stage and I am envious of that. What I do is what I do.' Then he adds with typical modesty: ' I am always amazed that I am here and have come this far.'

As with anything, being a superstar has its downside: chiefly the loss of privacy and the prospect of a pack-like press always digging for dirt on big-name celebrities, regardless of how clean a life they lead. In some respects, becoming a celebrity today involves entering into a Faustian-like pact with the Devil. Sure, there is an upside. But if you stumble – boy, is there a downside.

However, for all his success at playing the fame game and his obvious enjoyment of it, Pierce now seems able to contemplate a fame-free future – far ahead though it may be.

'I know what it's like to be famous,' he says. 'It's good money and it's great fun . . . Then, it's all a bit hollow because it doesn't really nourish you. Fame is like a big piece of meringue – it's beautiful and you keep eating it, but it doesn't really fill you up. It's a game, a great game, that's all.'

He's come to this realisation over the years. 'When I was younger, doing *Remington Steele*, it was wonderful watching it all grow and flourish. But then I watched it fade, too. I thought, Oh, it's going, it's going. I don't get recognised any more, people don't hassle me. There was a bit of regretfulness there, I could feel it. And it will happen again. As time goes on and I hang up the Bond mantle, it will pass. You know that, and you have to . . . deal with the ego and get back to the job in hand. Which is being an actor.

'I've had enough fame now. I'm restless. Where do I go in the next ten years? That's what drives me. Can I make more films? Can I build a company where I can own my own library? Would I be able to direct? Do I want to direct? I want control over my life, with the understanding also that I want to be hired.'

And if he is forced to quit acting through ill health, an accident or for some other reason, Pierce seems to possess the maturity and strength of character to turn his back on the movies and channel his creativity into other areas.

'I'd like to write,' he says. 'I've got a whole drawer full of stories I've started in a desk at home.' Of course, starting is the easy part; finishing a story is a lot tougher. There is also his love of painting and he says: 'If I hadn't been an actor, an artist would have been the next best thing. As it is, I can paint for pleasure without the worry of having to earn a living at it.'

There seems little doubt that he will continue to be the superb father and family man he's always been. 'He deserves a Best Dad in Hollywood Award,' quips a friend.

But superstar or not, some things don't change. He's still refused entry to London's Savoy Hotel for wearing jeans. And he succumbs to self-doubt like the rest of us do from time to time. 'Some days I feel great, I feel like a movie star,' he says. 'I feel strong, I'm going to grab the world by the lapels and shake it up. The next day I wake up and I feel a mess.'

Of course, nobody's perfect. And Pierce would readily admit that he, a mere mortal, has failings. Asked what embarrasses him, he once replied: 'Forgetting names.' He also seems to have forgotten about many of his old friends – genuine friends. People like Liam, from St Finian's Terrace. Or Stuart Turner, from Vera Road, Fulham. Indeed, he doesn't seem to be in touch with a single person from his Navan, Elliott School or Fulham days.

He may never have made a conscious decision to turn his back on his pals from outside the acting profession. But he has and some of them are genuinely hurt by the fact that he seems to have forgotten about them. 'I think he's changed completely,' says Liam. 'I think he's lost all interest in Ireland. He didn't even bring Keely to see Navan. I think he's too busy hobnobbing with the rich and famous at society events to have time for his old friends in Navan which saddens me.'

Jean Kirton, his old neighbour from Delamere Road, Wimbledon, says: 'We never hear from Pierce any more – though Charlotte's turned up on the doorstep a couple of times – which is a shame because we were quite close. You get the feeling that when people become rich and famous they don't want to know you any more. It would just be nice to be remembered – or get the occasional postcard. I'm sure I'd remember my old friends if I became rich and famous.'

On the other hand, it would be hard for him to stay in contact with everyone he had been friendly with down the years. Turner tries to be philosophical about the situation. 'It's funny,' he says. 'Even today, there are certain mannerisms, like the way Pierce puts his hand in his pocket or pouts, that haven't changed. But we haven't seen each other for twenty years. He's a busy man and people move on. I still love the guy and I'm glad he's done so well. But I'd be a bit hurt if he was in Wimbledon and didn't look me up.'

His father's side of the family would also like to welcome him back into the family bosom. 'He is the only Brosnan left to carry on the family name,' says cousin Pierce Wallace. 'We'd like to think we've patched things up with Pierce but there's still a few things that need to be settled. But he's family; he's one of us and we'd dearly like to see him again.' Having not been invited to Brosnan's recent wedding though, that seems a distant hope.

On the other hand, Pierce is renowned for little acts of kindness, as his regular Bond driver Colin Morris reveals: 'He's the kind of guy who would do anything for you. On his day off, he opened the fête at my daughter's school in Surrey. The kids almost dropped dead with shock at seeing James Bond striding across the playground.'

When I was writing the first edition of this book in the mid-nineties I closed it by asking: 'Perhaps the most tantalising question is whether the actor will ever really find the personal happiness he found with Cassie? 'For all his money, fame and success, there are those who feel that more than five years after Cassie's death "there is still an emptiness within him, a void at his core". One just hopes Pierce won't follow the path his fictional alter ego (Bond) pursued after the murder of his wife, allowing himself to become a "man adrift, seeking new pastures, going through women, woman after woman, looking for the woman who's gone." That would be too tragic for words.'

At the time it seemed open to debate whether Pierce would indeed ever really escape his first wife's shadow. She had been his soulmate, his wife and his best friend. How could anyone replace this wonderful woman, he constantly asked both in public and in private.

However, time is a great healer. The time for mourning is over. And Pierce has come to realise that in Keely he has a found a new soulmate. She is not a Cassie Mk 2. She looks different and is different. And that is surely a good thing. But nevertheless a soulmate is what she has become – a soulmate who has given him a new family and helped him embark on a new chapter in his life. For that, Pierce's family, friends and fans can only be thankful.

FILMOGRAPHY

The Long Good Friday (1980)
Starring: Bob Hoskins, Helen Mirren, Derek Thompson and Pierce Brosnan. Directed by John Mackenzie.

The Mirror Crack'd (1980)
Starring: Angela Lansbury, Edward Fox, Rock Hudson, Elizabeth Taylor, Kim Novak, Tony Curtis and Pierce Brosnan. Directed by Guy Hamilton.

Nomads (1986)
Starring: Pierce Brosnan, Lesley-Anne Down and Adam Ant. Directed by John McTiernan.

The Fourth Protocol (1987)
Starring: Michael Caine, Pierce Brosnan, Joanna Cassidy, Ray McAnally and Ian Richardson. Directed by John Mackenzie.

Taffin (1988)
Starring: Pierce Brosnan, Ray McAnally, Alison Doody, Jim Bartley and Jeremy Child. Directed by Francis Megahy.

The Deceivers (1988)
Starring: Pierce Brosnan, Saeed Jaffrey and Shashi Kapoor. Directed by Nicholas Meyer.

Mister Johnson (1991)
Starring: Pierce Brosnan, Edward Woodward and Maynard Eziashi. Directed by Bruce Beresford.

Live Wire (1992)
Starring: Pierce Brosnan, Ron Silver, Ben Cross and Lisa Eilbacher. Directed by Christian Duguay.

The Lawnmower Man (1992)
Starring: Jeff Fahey and Pierce Brosnan. Directed by Brett Leonard.

Entangled (1993)
Starring: Judd Nelson, Pierce Brosnan and Laurence Treil. Directed by Max Fischer.

Mrs Doubtfire (1993)
Starring: Robin Williams, Sally Field and Pierce Brosnan. Directed by Chris Columbus.

Love Affair (1994)
Starring: Warren Beatty, Annette Bening, Chloe Webb, Pierce Brosnan and Katharine Hepburn. Directed by Glenn Gordon Caron.

GoldenEye (1995)
Starring: Pierce Brosnan, Sean Bean, Robbie Coltrane, Judi Dench, Famke Janssen, Izabella Scorupco, Joe Don Baker and Desmond Llewelyn. Directed by Martin Campbell.

Robinson Crusoe (1996)
Starring: Pierce Brosnan, Lysette Anthony, Ian Hart, Damian Lewis and Polly Walker. Directed by Rod Hardy and George Miller.

The Mirror Has Two Faces (1997)
Starring: Barbra Streisand and Pierce Brosnan. Directed by Barbra Streisand.

Mars Attacks! (1997)
Starring: Jack Nicholson, Pierce Brosnan, Glenn Close, Rod Steiger, Martin Short, Annette Bening and Tom Jones. Directed by Tim Burton.

Dante's Peak (1997)
Starring: Pierce Brosnan and Linda Hamilton. Directed by Roger Donaldson.

Tomorrow Never Dies (1997)
Starring: Pierce Brosnan, Jonathan Pryce, Michelle Yeoh, Judi Dench, Teri Hatcher and Desmond Llewelyn. Directed by Roger Spottiswoode.

The Nephew (1998)
Starring: Donal McCann, Pierce Brosnan and Hill Harper. Directed by Eugene Brady.

The Thomas Crown Affair (1999)
Starring: Pierce Brosnan, Rene Russo and Denis Leary. Directed by John McTiernan.

The Match (1999)
Starring: Max Beesley, Laura Fraser, Richard E. Grant, Ian Holm and Pierce Brosnan. Directed by Mick Davis.

Grey Owl (1999)
Starring: Pierce Brosnan and Annie Galipeau. Directed by Richard Attenborough.

The World Is Not Enough (1999)
Starring: Pierce Brosnan, Sophie Marceau, Robert Carlyle, Denise Richards, Robbie Coltrane, Judi Dench, Desmond Llewelyn and John Cleese. Directed by Michael Apted.

Dolphins (2000)
Narrator: Pierce Brosnan. Directed by Greg MacGillivray.

The Tailor Of Panama (2001)
Starring: Pierce Brosnan, Geoffrey Rush and Jamie Lee Curtis. Directed by John Boorman.

Die Another Day (2002)
Starring: Pierce Brosnan, Halle Berry, Judi Dench, John Cleese, Toby Stephens and Rick Yune. Directed by Lee Tamahori.

Forthcoming releases:

Evelyn (2002)
Starring: Pierce Brosnan, Julianna Margulies, Aidan Quinn and Stephen Rea. Directed by Bruce Beresford.

TELEVISION

The Professionals: 'Blood Sports' (1980)
Starring: Lewis Collins, Martin Shaw, Gordon Jackson and Pierce Brosnan.

Hammer House of Horror: 'The Carpathian Eagle' (1980)
Starring: Anthony Valentine and Pierce Brosnan.

Murphy's Stroke (1980)
Starring: Niall Toibin and Pierce Brosnan.

The Manions of America [6-hour mini-series] (1981)
Starring: David Soul, Kathleen Beller, Simon MacCorkindale, Kate Mulgrew, Anthony Quayle and Pierce Brosnan.

Nancy Astor [6-hour mini-series] (1982)
Starring: Lisa Harrow, James Fox, Sylvia Sims, Nigel Havers and Pierce Brosnan.

Remington Steele [91 episodes] (1982–87)
Starring: Pierce Brosnan and Stephanie Zimbalist.

Noble House [8-hour TV mini-series] (1988)
Starring: Pierce Brosnan, Deborah Raffin, Ben Masters, John Rhys-Davies, Julia Nickson, Gordon Jackson, Tia Carrere.

Around the World in 80 Days [6-hour TV mini-series] (1989)
Starring: Pierce Brosnan, Eric Idle, Peter Ustinov, Julia Nickson, Christopher Lee, Robert Morley, Roddy McDowall, Patrick MacNee, Jack Klugman, Jill St John, Robert Wagner.

The Heist [TV movie] (1989)
Starring: Pierce Brosnan, Tom Skerritt and Wendy Hughes.

Murder 101 [TV movie] (1991)
Starring: Pierce Brosnan, Dey Young and Antoni Corone.

Victim of Love [TV movie] (1991)
Starring: Pierce Brosnan, Jobeth Williams and Virginia Madsen.

Great Golf Courses of the World: Ireland [narrator] (1992)

Death Train (aka *Detonator*) [TV movie] (1993)
Starring: Pierce Brosnan and Alexandra Paul.

The Broken Chain [TV movie] (1993)
Starring: Eric Schweig, Wes Studi, Buffy Saint-Marie and Pierce Brosnan.

Don't Talk to Strangers [TV movie] (1994)
Starring: Pierce Brosnan, Shanna Reed and Terry O'Quinn.

Night Watch (aka *Detonator II: Nightwatch*)
[TV movie] (1995)
Starring: Pierce Brosnan and Alexandra Paul.

APPENDIX

Bond film box office grosses (US dollars):

1962	*Dr No*	Sean Connery	$60m
1963	*From Russia With Love*	Sean Connery	$79m
1964	*Goldfinger*	Sean Connery	$125m
1965	*Thunderball*	Sean Connery	$141m
1967	*You Only Live Twice*	Sean Connery	$112m
1969	*On Her Majesty's Secret Service*	George Lazenby	$65m
1971	*Diamonds Are Forever*	Sean Connery	$116m
1973	*Live And Let Die*	Roger Moore	$126m
1974	*The Man With The Golden Gun*	Roger Moore	$98m
1977	*The Spy Who Loved Me*	Roger Moore	$185m
1979	*Moonraker*	Roger Moore	$203m
1981	*For Your Eyes Only*	Roger Moore	$195m
1983	*Octopussy*	Roger Moore	$184m
1985	*A View To A Kill*	Roger Moore	$182m
1987	*The Living Daylights*	Timothy Dalton	$191m
1989	*Licence To Kill*	Timothy Dalton	$156m
1995	*GoldenEye*	Pierce Brosnan	$350m
1997	*Tomorrow Never Dies*	Pierce Brosnan	$350m
1999	*The World Is Not Enough*	Pierce Brosnan	$355m

INDEX

PB, marries 229–34
PB, meets 150–1
PB, on location with 225
PB, rumours of secret marriage to 173
World Is Not Enough première, *The*,
    attends 227
Brosnan, May (PB's aunt) 4
Brosnan, May (PB's mother) *see*
    Carmichael, May
Brosnan, Paris Beckett (PB's son) 231,
    233, 236
Brosnan, Pierce Brendan
  accent 18, 42, 83, 84
  acting skills 49, 127–9
  adolescence in England 15–28
  ambition 27–8, 35, 46–7, 83
  appearance 6, 9, 20, 26, 35, 40–1, 46,
    86, 103
  becomes grandfather 206
  birth 4–5
  Cassie, life with 79, 83–4, 86, 103–10,
    171
  Cassie, meets and marries 69–70, 74–6
  Cassie's death, reaction to 134–5,
    137–8
  Cassie's illness, reaction to 110–14,
    131–5
  charitable donations 174
  childhood in Ireland 6–14
  Citz, work at 61–4
  commercial artist 29–30
  down to earth 216–17
  Drama Centre, attends 39–51, 54
  faith 107, 139
  films *see under* film titles
  future 238–42
  girlfriends 27–8, 44–5, 56, 147–8,
    173–4
    see also Beaumont, Denise; Beaumont,
    Lee; Bevans, Carole; Herley, Patti;
    Kinley, Kathryn; McKenzie, Rebecca;
    Orbison, Barbara; Patitz, Tatjana;
    Phillips, Julianne
  health 159–60, 196–7
  idiosyncrasies 46
  James Bond, cast as 153–8
  James Bond, misses out on 98–101,
    124, 154–5

Keely Shaye-Smith, life with 150–1,
    173, 186–8, 205–7, 210, 225, 227,
    229–34, 236, 241–2
Keely, marries 229–34
media, relationship with 112–13
Oval House, attends 30–8
production company *see* Irish
    DreamTime
sexuality 33, 64–5
superstar status 171–3, 175–6, 183–4
television appearances 78–81, 125–9,
    142–3, 154–5, 175–6, 177 *see also*
    Remington Steele
Theatre Royal, York, work at 53–8
Tom Brosnan, relationship with 24–5,
    26–7, 90–5, 110, 188, 210
voted sexiest man alive by *People* 2001
    234
wealth 107–8
Brosnan, Sean William (PBs son) 87
  birth 87
  car crash 230–1, 234
  Dylan Brosnan, reaction to birth of 206
  GoldenEye premières, attends xiii, 169
  mother's death, reaction to 138–9, 155,
    156, 186–8
  mother's illness, reaction to 111, 134
  PB on location, joins 93, 121, 162, 165,
    196–7
  PB's and Keely's wedding, at 233
  PB's girlfriends, attitude towards 229
Brosnan, Tom (PB's father) 2–6, 24–5,
    90–6, 99, 109–10, 186, 188, 210
Brown, Ray 221
Burnham, Len 29

Caine, Michael 117–18
Callow, Simon 39, 40
Campbell, Martin xii, 169
Carlyle, Robert 221
Carmichael, Bill (PB's stepfather) 4, 6, 8,
    15–16, 24–5, 46, 92, 188
Carmichael, May (*née* Smith, PB's mother)
  adult PB, relationship with 46–7, 92,
    138, 156, 166
  Bill Carmichael, marriage to 15–16,
    24–5, 188
  England, moves to 6, 8, 113, 210

Other P.B. Movies

Mamma Mia